Praise for

Robert Calderisi's

The Trouble with Africa:
Why Foreign Aid Isn't Working

"A fluent, deeply personal account of how aid has failed Africa, and how Africa, so often, has managed to fail itself. One of the best books of the year." (*The Economist*)

"Robert Calderisi and a few other authors are shaking up the aid establishment. That's painful, but also essential." (*The New York Review of Books*)

"A personal narrative of engagement with a beguiling but maddening continent, avoiding the familiar positions among old African hands of either expressing contempt or excusing failure." (*The Financial Times*)

"Mr. Calderisi clearly admires the drive and initiative of Africans freed of the disincentives he so well analyzes." (*The Wall Street Journal*)

"Excellent, original, refreshing." (*Times Literary Supplement*)

"A brilliant, striking book." (*The Irish Times*)

Earthly Mission:
The Catholic Church and World Development

"Few will approach this book with an open mind. The faithful will find his candid assessment of the Church's transgressions unsettling. Its critics will find his praise of its mission similarly discomforting. Both can learn, though, from his work." (*The Economist*)

"A balanced look at the contradictory and controversial stances of the Catholic Church. There are two sides to the Catholic coin." (*The New Statesman*)

"Calderisi's credentials are impeccable, and his decision to focus on individuals within the Catholic Church—nuns and missionaries as well as popes and cardinals—makes for lively reading." (*Literary Review*—UK)

"A comprehensive overview of the Church's charitable and development work, but also refreshingly honest and critical where [Calderisi] feels the Church has not been true to itself. Authoritative, impressive, moving." (*The Tablet*—UK)

CECIL RHODES AND OTHER STATUES

Dealing Plainly with the Past

ROBERT CALDERISI

Columbus, Ohio

Cecil Rhodes and Other Statues:
Dealing Plainly with the Past

Published by Gatekeeper Press
2167 Stringtown Rd, Suite 109
Columbus, OH 43123-2989
www.GatekeeperPress.com

This publication is designed to provide accurate and authoritative information in regard to the subject matter covered. It is sold with the understanding that the publisher is not engaged in rendering legal or accounting services. If legal advice or other expert assistance is required, the services of a competent professional person should be sought.

ISBN: 9781662916458

Printed in the United States of America

Also by Robert Calderisi

Faith and Development (2001)

The Trouble with Africa:
Why Foreign Aid Isn't Working (2006)

Open Letter to the Pope from a Gay Catholic (2007)

A Marriage of True Minds:
A Modern Love Story (2009)

Earthly Mission:
The Catholic Church and World Development (2013)

Quebec in a Global Light:
Reaching for the Common Ground (2019)

For Edwin Cameron,
The perfect Rhodes Scholar

Contents

Acknowledgements

T HIS BOOK DRAWS on fifty years of personal experience as a Rhodes Scholar, more than three decades of working and living in Africa, three years of research at the New York Public Library, and a January 2020 field visit to South Africa and Zimbabwe. It also reflects the contributions of the following people, to whom I am most grateful.

Allan Angerio, Nigel Biggar, Edwin Cameron, Joshua Chauvin, Duncan Clarke, Carol De Francis, Jacques Gérin, Solomon Gordon, Michael Holman, Ruth Lawson, Matt McTighe, Michael Paduano, Brian Petty, Kevin Phelps, Alexandre Poulin, Timothy Radcliffe, Andrew Sancton, Iain Sander, Ann Scott, Eric Southworth, and Susan Stenersen reviewed and commented on the manuscript.

Robert Baldock, Najwaa Francke, Anthony Gottlieb, R.W. (Bill) Johnson, the late Shaun Johnson, Elizabeth Kiss, Sandra Klopper, Heather McCallum, Edward Mortimer, Lucas Tse, and Michela Wrong introduced me to important individuals and information.

A talk by Professor Paul Maylam of Rhodes University at the first LGBTQ leadership forum at Rhodes House in February 2017 provided particular impetus for the project.

I am also indebted to Dr. Rayda Becker, curator of the Groote

Schuur estate in Cape Town, for allowing me to spend several days of discovery and reflection in Rhodes's home and offering valuable reflections on his personal life, and to Lila Komncik and Sadeck Kemal Casoojee of the South African Parliament Library for sharing documentation and artwork.

Finally, I want to thank the staff of the Schomburg Center for Research in Black Culture and the Center for Research in the Humanities at the New York Public Library (particularly Melanie Locay) and the Bodleian Library at Oxford for their highly professional support.

Explanation of Terms

"South Africa" did not exist as a country until 1910, but I will use the term for brevity's sake on occasion. During Rhodes's life, it consisted of two British colonies (the Cape Colony and Natal) and two independent Boer republics (the Zuid-Afrikaanse Republiek or Transvaal and the Orange Free State). I will refer to the 1899-1902 conflict as the "South African War" even if it is often called the "Anglo-Boer War" or "Second Anglo-Boer War" (as the British and Boers first fought over control of the Transvaal in 1880-1881). One predominant group in what was to become Rhodesia and later Zimbabwe were known as the Matabele, but are now referred to as the Ndebele; the latter term will be used in the book, except in direct quotations from the late 19th century and early 20th century. The same will apply to the Shona people, previously referred to as the Mashona. Sterling amounts will be in current values, except (again) where they appear in correspondence or memoirs of the time.

We have his corpse and you have his statue. We cannot tell you what to do with the statue but we and my people feel we need to leave him down there.

Robert Mugabe,
President of Zimbabwe,
on a State Visit to South Africa (April 2015)

Introduction

A S I EMERGED from Zimbabwe's Bulawayo airport into the dazzling sunlight, Simon was waiting for me. A receptionist at the 150-year-old Bulawayo Club, he perked up when he learned that I was to visit Cecil Rhodes's grave south of the city. "You know," he said, as we drove into town, "when his statue was taken down at Independence, not all of us agreed with it. Some worried that we would be cutting our ties with history and with other peoples in the world. Others pointed out that not every new US president feels obliged to change the name of JFK airport. And, if you start with statues, why not tear down buildings like the High Court that he built?" But when I saw who had replaced Rhodes in the city centre, I smiled at the appropriateness of it. Standing on the same plinth was a statue of Joshua Nkomo, Robert Mugabe's political rival at Independence, who later accepted the Vice-Presidency. Nkomo was a good-natured man with a girth worthy of his 19th century Ndebele predecessor King Lobengula; but, apparently for posterity's sake, the sculptor had settled for a mere suggestion of a paunch.

The next day, I visited the demoted Rhodes statue in the gardens of the National Archives. Next to it was a copy of George Watts's "Physical Energy" depicting a young man leaning back in the saddle of a horse that has started to gallop. The original is at the Rhodes Memorial in Cape Town and another copy stands in the middle of Kensington Gardens in London, largely neglected by passersby. This one had been erected in Northern Rhodesia (now Zambia) but given away at Independence by the country's new African leaders to the racist white government of Southern Rhodesia.

The reason was simple enough. In the mid-1950s, a colonial prime minister had heralded the statue as a symbol of racial partnership, with whites as the rider and Africans as the horse. "You see," he said, "they do not eat or sleep together, but there is a working relationship between them."[1] In the Zimbabweans' shoes, many of us would have blown the thing to smithereens. But, in their wisdom, they decided to consign it to History instead. When I was at the Archives, the late morning sun lit up the two neglected statues as if they were still important and dewdrops sparkled on a cobweb covering the right armpit of the young rider.

Writing About Rhodes

Even before Rhodes died, biographers had to justify writing about him. "Unfortunately," observed Howard Hensman in 1901," he acts with many people as the proverbial red rag to a bull . . . I have made it my constant effort to hold the scales of justice evenly and decline absolutely to regard Mr. Rhodes either as a heaven-sent statesman or the incarnation of all that is wicked."[2] Despite that effort, Hensman's assessment is among the most pious.

There have been more than thirty biographies of Rhodes since 1897. Even Winston Churchill considered writing one, but set it aside to focus on his life of the Duke of Marlborough. The most incisive and readable account was by the South

African poet William Plomer (1933). The most solid (*The Founder*, 1988) was by the distinguished American historian (and Rhodes Scholar) Robert Rotberg. It ran to 800 pages and took eighteen years to write. Collaborating with a psychiatrist, Rotberg analyzed key episodes in Rhodes's personal development in clinical terms. Setting out to debunk much of the lore about Rhodes—that he left England for South Africa for health reasons, that he operated from a very young age on the basis of a grand plan that he implemented methodically, that he was as successful in gold as he had been in diamonds, etc.—he was the first to broach the subject of Rhodes's homosexuality.

The South African historian Paul Maylam, author of *The Cult of Rhodes* (2005), has complained that most of the biographies have hewed to a common pattern, based on mainly secondary materials, including previous biographies. That is because Rhodes wrote very few personal letters and we depend mainly on the accounts of his contemporaries, particularly his close circle, and on his speeches in the Cape Colony parliament, to have a detailed sense of his beliefs and motives. Past writers have also tended to venerate or denounce Rhodes rather than strive for the middle ground.

Even fair-minded critics will admit that past accounts of Rhodes have been lopsided. In *#Rhodes Must Fall: Nibbling at Resilient Colonialism in South Africa* (2016), the Cameroonian scholar Francis B. Nyamnjoh suggests that "not enough has been written about him as a human being, consisting of flesh and blood, mind and body, emotion and reason, with everyday highs and lows, and the frailties of being human. Because Rhodes the individual human being is as scarce as a rare diamond, Rhodes the stereotype, the caricature and the figment of the imagination lends himself easily to prototyping and rationalizing and as an excuse or a scapegoat."[3]

This Book

This book will differ from previous ones by its brevity, its detailed look at the historical charges that have been made against Rhodes, and its attempt to be fair both to the historical record and to those who have criticized him. It will also examine Rhodes's story in the light of the broader debate about how to commemorate controversial historical figures.

Following a brief overview of the "Rhodes Must Fall" movement in Chapter 1, the book will summarize the man's personality (Chapters 2-3) and career (Chapters 4-7) with as little editorializing as possible, to allow readers to reach their own preliminary conclusions about him. Only then will Chapters 8-10 consider in detail the accusations that have been made against Rhodes and suggest a number of angles from which to assess them in a new light. Chapters 12 and 13 relate the history of the Rhodes Scholarships—generally seen as the man's greatest legacy—while Chapters 14 and 15 widen the lens to look at other contested figures as diverse as Robert E. Lee and Mahatma Gandhi and draw lessons from recent controversies about how to manage troublesome statues and memorials.

This book is not a defence of Rhodes—as some of his actions were simply indefensible. Rather, it attempts to fill in some of the blanks that have been left open in his story. If the book defends anything, it is the complexity of history and the human character and the need to examine controversial figures carefully before coming to firm conclusions about them.

Black Lives Matter

Cecil Rhodes is a sensitive subject at any time, let alone against the backdrop of the "Black Lives Matter" movement. That such a rallying cry is still necessary is hard to believe. That it should have spawned rebuttals—like "Blue Lives Matter" (referring to police) or "All Lives Matter"—is breathtaking. Yet the endurance of racism, especially towards people of African descent, is an ugly feature of our times, regardless of how enlightened we purport to be. I am no stranger to its effects.

Living and working in Africa over thirty years, I saw at first hand the devastating impact of racial and ethnic discrimination not just in South Africa, but right across the continent. Imagine my disbelief when my vice-president at the World Bank, himself an African, cancelled the appointment of a Malian to represent the institution in Mauritania because that country's government objected to his being black.

At Oxford in the late 1960s, I often wandered around town with a Grenadian political scientist, Jamaican lawyer, Sudanese forester, and Sri Lankan civil servant. Immigration and race were already sensitive subjects in British politics, with the Conservative politician Enoch Powell warning of "rivers of blood" if the country continued to welcome too many Africans and Asians. So, it was probably inevitable that we should attract attention. Once, in a quiet residential neighbourhood known as Jericho, a police car slowed down, spotting us on the sidewalk, apparently expecting trouble, then sped off as soon as I came into view.

One of the happiest days of my life was falling in love for the first time in New York City, with an African American. One of the saddest, four years later, was when a close Tanzanian friend was shot at random on the campus of Georgia State University by a white thug sitting in a parked car nearby. For eighteen years, I was a member of an African-American parish in Washington DC and sang in their Gospel Choir. When DC's mayor Marion Barry was caught in a drug "sting" and widely denounced, we prayed for him, proud of his historic contribution to the civil rights movement. Most of those who rejoiced in his downfall were not the descendants of slaves.

Facts Are Also Important

But, if racism is deep, pervasive, and abhorrent, disinformation can be just as divisive. Fanned by social media, information overload, and ideological echo chambers, faulty facts or exaggeration can derail debates on important subjects, including racism. Weighing information properly is as important as stamping out hatred—and sometimes a contribution to doing so, as well. This point may seem minor, compared with the deep social ills of our time, but it is not insignificant if we believe in pursuing solutions based on getting as close as possible to the truth, warts and all. Conspiracy theories feed on intellectual laziness and whip up hatred and violence unnecessarily.

Not all distortions of facts are intentional. Some are passed on quite innocently by good-hearted people too busy righting obvious wrongs to spend much time double-checking their information. Yet, they rightly object when their own intentions and arguments are misrepresented. It is better to face historical facts head-on than to surrender to hearsay or groupthink. And if we handle facts about the past too lightly, how can we come to reliable decisions about contemporary realities?

Above all, judgments must be based on solid information. However well-documented they may be, the lives of infamous men and women attract hearsay like barnacles on a ship too long in harbour. For example, on a visit to All Souls College, Oxford in 2008, the Attorney-General of England, a woman of Afro-Caribbean descent, was shocked to see a statue of Christopher Codrington (1668-1710) in the library named after him. Not only had he owned slaves, she told her host, but he *bred* them as livestock on the island of Barbuda, whose inhabitants to this day are unusually tall and strapping. Though often repeated and widely believed in the West Indies, this story was carefully investigated and soundly disproved in the 1970s.[4]

Even recent books on Rhodes have stumbled over the facts. Christopher Hope's *The Café de Move-On Blues: In Search of the New South Africa* (2018) suggests that, as a young man, Rhodes made a fortune as a fruit farmer. In fact, he grew cotton for just over a year and barely broke even. The same author refers to Rhodes's life-long "aversion" to the Boers (the descendants of the Dutch) and the Africans. That, too, is far from obvious as one of his deepest ambitions was to nurture good relations with the other European "race" as a way of promoting a South African federation. That led him to support legislation that, as a liberal, he might otherwise have opposed, in order to curry favour with rural whites, most of whom were Afrikaners. Nor is there any evidence of a deep animus towards the original inhabitants of the region. Rhodes used harsh words at times in the heat of war but otherwise prided himself—rightly or wrongly—on his relationships with Africans. Nor is it clear, as Hope claims, that Rhodes was "one of the chief manipulators" of the South African War (1899-1902). Up to the very last moment, he doubted it would happen.

What's New?

Certain moral standards evolve, while others are like granite. So, it is not obvious that the misdeeds of controversial figures can all be understood—and justified—in the light of the practices of their time. Even in his own day, though popular with the general public, Cecil Rhodes provoked controversy among sections of the British Establishment. He was refused membership in one of London's exclusive gentlemen's clubs (The Travellers) and saw his 1899 honorary doctoral degree at Oxford contested by ninety of its teaching staff.

"You worship Rhodes?" wrote the novelist George Meredith to a friend. "I would crown him and then scourge him with his crown still on him."[5] Shortly after his death, the French newspaper *Le Temps* concluded that he "lived only for his schemes and enjoyed life only as a cannon ball enjoys space, travelling to its aim blindly and spreading ruin on its way. He was a great man, no doubt—a man who rendered immense services to his country, but humanity is not much indebted to him."[6] The South African statesman Jan Christian Smuts was kinder: "Objectively [he was] like a natural phenomenon, where praise or blame is equally difficult."[7]

In 1968, when I won a Rhodes Scholarship for the Province of Quebec, my African history professor wrote to me from a sabbatical in Kenya to congratulate me but also to tease me for accepting the money of an "imperialist fink". The next year, behind closed doors, the Warden of Rhodes House—a character right out of an Evelyn Waugh novel or *Downton Abbey*— referred to Rhodes as a "scoundrel". My next-door neighbour in college (the British Caribbean Rhodes Scholar) insisted that he and an African American from Massachusetts that year were the only ones who really deserved the Scholarship as it was the product of black sweat and suffering. But he was being light-hearted. Almost fifty years later, the "Rhodes Must Fall" campaign raised the tone considerably, calling him a "mass murderer", denouncing his "crimes against humanity", and likening him to Hitler and Stalin. Some of the accusers were African Rhodes Scholars.

So, what was new about the "Rhodes Must Fall" movement and why did South African students wait almost a quarter-century after majority rule to campaign against the man? Of course, they hadn't waited. Most of them hadn't even been born in 1994. And each generation has the right—even duty— to question the past.

There are certainly grounds for confusion about Rhodes. We know where he was born and where he died, but much of the rest of his life is shrouded in debate. Even his last words are uncertain. For decades, he was believed to have said, "So much to do, so little done"—but a friend at his bedside later admitted to making this up.[8] It is more likely that his final phrase was addressed to his young companion: "Turn me over, Jack." At the time, it was said that the entire British Empire went into mourning. Now, except in southern Africa, where his name still casts a shadow, Cecil Rhodes is remembered only for the scholarships that he endowed and then only among those curious enough to wonder about their history. Ironically, it was the Rhodes Must Fall movement—first in 2015, then again in 2020—that resurrected him.

However else we judge Rhodes, his achievements were remarkable. Arriving in South Africa at the age of seventeen with a rather ordinary education and almost no capital, it took him only twenty years to create De Beers, a company that controlled 90% of the world's diamond production. At the age of 37, he was chairman of De Beers, head of another major mining firm (Consolidated Gold Fields), managing director of the British South Africa Company (which the British government had authorized to "settle" large areas of central and southern Africa), and prime minister of the Cape Colony, one of the four territories that would eventually make up the Union of South Africa. In the last twelve years of his life, Rhodes added 750,000 square miles to the British Empire, then died at the age of 48. One of the few people to have a country named after him (Rhodesia), he is still buried in what is now Zimbabwe, despite occasional suggestions that his body be exhumed and relocated.

Dedication

This book is dedicated to Edwin Cameron, one of the world's most distinguished judges, who sat on South Africa's Constitutional Court from 2009 to 2019. Rhodes would probably have admired his diamond-sharp intellect and deep sense of public service. He might also have envied Edwin's ability to live openly and proudly as a gay man. By announcing in 1999 that he was a person living with HIV—the first major public figure in all of Africa to do so—and by campaigning hard to promote testing and make anti-retroviral drugs widely available, he contributed to saving millions of lives in his own country and around the world. In that sense, his legacy is much clearer than that of Cecil Rhodes.

CHAPTER ONE

"Rhodes Must Fall"

O N 9 MARCH 2015, a politics student named Chumani Maxwele threw human excrement on Rhodes's large, brooding statue on the campus of the University of Cape Town (UCT) in South Africa. Given that his target was a diamond and gold millionaire, it was almost poetic that Maxwele should be the son of a poor miner from the Eastern Cape. That is because the purported purpose of what was to become the "Rhodes Must Fall" movement was not so much the statue as anger at how little had changed in South Africa since majority rule in 1994.

The UCT campus seemed a relic of yesteryear. Only five of its 174 professors were black; almost all the rest were white. A humanities student could complete a three-year course without meeting a single African woman lecturer or seeing any learning materials other than those steeped in Eurocentric views.[1] The protesters wanted Rhodes's statue removed, but—more than that—they wanted a transformation of UCT and the country as a whole.

The Vice-Chancellor of UCT, Max Price, was overseas when the storm broke, so his deputy, Sandra Klopper, had to step in. She never liked the statue, thinking it a pretentious copy of Auguste Rodin's "The Thinker", and she sympathized with the students' ultimate objective, which was to change the character and curriculum of UCT. But Klopper had to react in a way that most people would understand.[2] So, she described the soiling of the statue as "unacceptable" and "reprehensible", then added that "UCT endorses freedom of expression."

On his return, Professor Price—who had been a Rhodes Scholar himself—acknowledged that Rhodes was "a villain, the perpetrator of ruthless exploitation of indigenous people, land expropriation, illegal wars, and vicious conquest." Yet Price insisted that there be a proper discussion of next steps within the governing bodies of the University.

To the protesters, progress seemed painfully slow, but within a month the decision was taken and the statue was removed on 9 April. The vote in the University Senate was 181 to one. But that lone objector was not the only person trying to resist the firestorm. A former Vice-Chancellor of UCT, Professor Njabulo Ndebele, mused that one could remove a statue of Rhodes "but, like Moby Dick the whale, he will blow."

Professor Sizwe Mabizela, the Vice Chancellor of Rhodes University—whose institution was an even larger potential target for iconoclasts—opposed re-naming it. "The name of Rhodes has now become associated with advancement of education. You think of the Mandela-Rhodes Scholarships . . . It's about excellence in academics."[3]

The decision to remove the statue did not quell the protests. Students continued to occupy UCT's main administration building, demanding the promotion of black lecturers, more enrollments for disadvantaged communities, a more diverse and "decolonized" university curriculum, and the removal of other names that offended them on campus. The protests also spread to other formerly white universities such as

Witwatersrand, Rhodes University, Stellenbosch, and the University of KwaZulu-Natal. In an important concession, Stellenbosch announced in November 2015 that Afrikaans— the language of the old white "masters"—would no longer be the primary medium of instruction.

In Cape Town, the Rhodes Must Fall (RMF) protesters moved on to other subjects. An amnesty was granted to the protesters; but Maxwele was suspended for intimidating a lecturer. He also made hateful statements: "The statue fell. Now it's time for all whites to go" and "We must not listen to whites . . . We do not need their apologies. They have to be removed from UCT and have to be killed." But the High Court insisted that he be reinstated.[4]

Rhodes Must Fall (Oxford)

By then, the "Rhodes Must Fall" flame had spread to Oxford and was focused on a small statue of Cecil Rhodes standing high above the High Street on the façade of a college wing he had funded that passersby rarely ever noticed. Sobered by the pandemonium that had spread worldwide on social media, Oriel College immediately parleyed with the protesters and committed to spending the next six months studying various options: from taking it down altogether to "contextualizing" it by adding an explanatory plaque. That led to a ferocious pushback in the popular press and scholarly journals. Donors, too, were up in arms. Oriel College benefactors threatened to cancel £100 million in funding if the statue was even touched.

Former Rhodes Scholars also considered cancelling their contributions to a recent replenishment of the Rhodes Trust's capital, when they learned that rooms at Rhodes House had been renamed, that a bust and a portrait of the "Founder" had been moved out of sight, and that he was no longer being toasted at dinners there. Almost certainly, most of the 5,000 Scholars still alive are grateful to Rhodes for changing their lives and helping them embark on satisfying and sometimes prominent careers; but some also regret that his wealth was based on minerals extracted in difficult conditions by thousands of African workers.

The Oxford campaign was not the "mass movement" that its leaders claimed it was; nor did it "reinvigorate the academy like no other student movement since the 1960s"[5] But it picked up where the UCT protesters left off and perpetuated the firestorm on social media that introduced Cecil Rhodes to many people around the world for the first time. Like the original protesters in Cape Town, the campaigners in Oxford claimed to be targeting something beyond a statue: an institutional culture and "colonisation of the mind that reaches far [beyond] the figure of one individual."[6]

But appealing to racial guilt and fear was bound to be less successful in Oxford than in South Africa, at least in 2016, given the different nature and history of British society and the more manageable challenge the UK appeared to face in securing greater racial inclusiveness and justice in its universities. That resistance to political pressure may have inflamed spirits and rhetoric further. Black students arriving at the University as late as 2013 found that the African Studies library was located at Rhodes House. To some, this was like forcing young Jews to consult Jewish materials in Hitler House.[7] That reaction may seem extravagant, but the feeling was real and deserved to be taken seriously. Strangely, the parallel was only cited in one direction. When African Rhodes Scholars later claimed that there was no contradiction in accepting an imperialist's money while decrying his "crimes against humanity", few were willing to concede that this was like young Jews accepting a Hitler Scholarship.

Rhodes Must Fall (Oxford) was an ambitious and passionate movement, riven with internal divisions and struggling with some of the same biases that pervade society as a whole. A sub-group called Women of Colour (Asians, Arabs, and others) did not include women of African descent. Because of the prominence of black feminists and queers in the movement, some black men abandoned the cause, feeling that the focus of the campaign was being blurred by "petty" gender issues. Some women campaigners were sexually assaulted and even raped.[8] And, fighting fire with fire, some of the language and concepts used were racially charged. Having whites accept that they are "problematic", said one militant, was crucial, as white power is greatest "when it remains un-antagonised, normalised, and therefore invisible." If whites accepted that they are the problem, he concluded, something more positive could emerge.[9] Depending on one's background, this discourse could seem inspired, a cry of pain, or merely specious.

The beauty of Oxford itself became an issue, even though most of the colleges were founded well before there was a British Empire. "This country, the way it was built, the artistic imagination," said one participant, "was based on plunder . . . I walk around and it's so beautiful it's depressing. Because you know this was only possible if something perverse happened."[10] The Pitt Rivers Museum was described by an African Rhodes Scholar as "one of the most violent places in Oxford" because it housed so many colonial artefacts. Stuffy the Museum may be: its Victorian layout and Imperial flavour have changed so little since 1884 that it is almost "a museum of a museum". Yet, it was already wrestling with how to challenge cultural stereotypes and heal "historically difficult relationships" before the protests broke out.[11]

On 28 January 2016, the Provost of Oriel College announced that the six-month "listening exercise" it had promised the month before was now being wrapped up and that its governing body had decided that the Rhodes statue should stay where it was, with a plaque added to explain its significance. "The College believes the recent debate has underlined that the continuing presence of these historical artefacts is an important reminder of the complexity of history and of the legacies of colonialism still felt today. By adding context, we can help draw attention to this history, do justice to the complexity of the debate, and be true to our educational mission."[12]

Nigel Biggar, Regius Professor of Moral and Pastoral Theology at Oxford, a former chaplain of Oriel College in the 1990s, and head of a five-year research project on "Ethics and Empire", greeted Oriel's change of mind as "very good news": "The bad news is that it nearly didn't. And that fact bears some reflection. Why was it that the Governing Body of an Oxford college—replete with very highly educated and experienced adults—came so close to capitulating to the shouty zealotry of a small group of students?"[13] Anthony Lemon, an emeritus fellow of Mansfield College compared the protesters to the Islamic State and the Taliban destroying archaeological sites.[14] Donal Lowry, Fellow of the Royal Historical Society and an Irishman conscious of his country's own bitter colonial history, asked: "Where would such destruction end? Should the name of Churchill College, Cambridge, be changed, too, because of his associations with imperialism?"[15]

James Delingpole, a libertarian conservative and director of Breitbart (UK), adopted the same condescending and aggressive tone that some of the activists had used towards whites: "Cecil Rhodes's generous bequest has contributed greatly to the comfort and well-being of many generations of Oxford students—a good many of them, dare we say, better, brighter, and more deserving than you. This doesn't necessarily mean we approve of everything Rhodes did in his lifetime—but then we don't have to. Cecil Rhodes died a century ago. *Autres temps, autres moeurs* [Other times, other customs]. If you don't understand what this means, then you should ask yourself the question: 'Why am I at Oxford?'... Scholars have been studying here since at least the 11th century. We've played a major part in the invention of Western civilisation . . . And what were your ancestors doing in that period? Living in mud huts, mainly . . . Understand us and understand this clearly: you have *everything* to learn from us; we have *nothing* to learn from you."[16]

Brian Young, a history lecturer at Oxford, referred to Rhodes Must Fall as an "outbreak of moralizing Maoism". "History and its necessary and highly complex variety is loathed by the terrible simplifiers, whose destructive energy is applied to dismiss rather than to comprehend complicated legacies. And to comprehend is not necessarily to forgive; it is simply and entirely to comprehend."[17]

Inevitably, the Chancellor of the University, Lord (Chris) Patten of Barnes, joined the debate: "If people at a university aren't prepared to demonstrate the sort of generosity which Nelson Mandela showed towards Rhodes and towards history . . . then maybe they should think about being educated elsewhere."[18] Many thought he was adding oil to the flames; many others agreed with him.

After Oriel's decision, the Rhodes Must Fall Oxford campaign petered out. There were two small demonstrations in March and December 2016 and a few postings on their Facebook page in 2017 commenting on distant events like the Free West Papua movement in Indonesia, and little else. But they had made their mark and they could take some satisfaction that people around the world would remember the campaign for years to come.

The movement also had echoes abroad. In August 2017, sixteen months after the protests at UCT, violence broke out in the usually peaceful university town of Charlottesville, Virginia over the proposed removal of statues commemorating the Confederate general Robert E. Lee. In December 2018, students at the University of Accra in Ghana insisted that a statue of the Indian independence leader Mahatma Gandhi be taken down because of disparaging remarks he had made about Africans as a young lawyer in South Africa. Even in Canada, a country proud of its generally peaceful history, statues of the first prime minister Sir John A. Macdonald became controversial as a result of his treatment of the country's First Peoples.

June 2020

Then, in June 2020, out of what seemed a clear blue sky, but for many was the dark cloud of four hundred years of oppression, the police killing of George Floyd in Minneapolis unleashed a storm of opposition to police brutality and systemic racism across the United States that spread to the United Kingdom, to other European countries, and to some African and Asian nations as well. This massive re-igniting of the Black Lives Matter movement shattered smugness about historical "heroes" again and raised the question about how much of the past should be subject to "correction". Once again, monuments became targets, but on a scale almost no one could have contemplated beforehand.

On 7 June, the statue of the former slave trader Edward Colston (1636-1721) was torn down in Bristol and thrown into the harbour, and in London the statue of Winston Churchill in Parliament Square had the word "racist" painted on its base. The next day, a monument to slaveowner Robert Milligan

(1746-1809) outside the Museum of London Docklands was removed by the Canal and River Trust to "respect the wishes of the community" and there were calls to demolish the statue of Robert Clive (1725-1774), the first British governor of Bengal, in Whitehall.

The same day, the Mayor of London Sadiq Khan called for a review of all the city's landmarks, including murals, street art, street names, statues and other memorials, with a view to deciding which legacies should be honoured.[19] On 11 June, the City of Bournemouth, Christchurch, and Poole (BCP) announced that it would remove a statue of Robert Baden-Powell (1857-1941), which it feared would be attacked. Until then, it was to receive 24-hour protection. The founder of the Scout movement, Baden-Powell, has been accused of racism, homophobia, and support for Adolf Hitler.[20]

In Oxford, a thousand demonstrators demanded again that the Rhodes statue on the façade of Oriel College be taken down and the city council invited the College to apply for planning permission to do just that. On 17 June, Oriel announced that it was prepared to accede to these demands and established an independent commission to look into the implications. The protesters also called for the re-naming of the Rhodes Scholarships and Rhodes House and a "public and permanent acknowledgement of the imperial and racist origins" of the Rhodes legacy.[21]

In Belgium, a statue of King Leopold II (1835-1909), under whose rule an estimated ten million Africans may have died in what is now the Democratic Republic of the Congo, was set on fire in the city of Antwerp. Other statues of the man were daubed with red paint in Ghent and Ostend and pulled down in Brussels.[22] In Paris, outside the French Parliament, an activist vandalized the statue of Jean-Baptiste Colbert (1619-1683) because he was the author of the Code Noir (or Black

Code) which regulated slavery and race in France's colonial empire.[23]

In the United States, on 4 June, the Governor of Virginia announced that he would take down the 130-year-old statue of the Confederate general Robert E. Lee in the state capital and put it in storage. A judge blocked the action for a month, pending further hearings, and a lawyer in the case hoped that "things [would] calm down by then."[24] On 13 June, the statue of the former Confederate president Jefferson Davis was removed from the Kentucky State Capitol in Frankfort.

Princeton University—which had wrestled with the issue for years—decided to delete the name of US President Woodrow Wilson (1913-1921) from its School of Public and International Affairs because he had imposed racial integration on several federal agencies. As university president, Wilson had also blocked black students from attending Princeton and spoke approvingly of the Ku Klux Klan.[25] Protesters also demanded the removal of twin Emancipation memorials—one in Washington, DC and the other in Boston—depicting a freed slave grovelling in gratitude at the feet of Abraham Lincoln.

Across the United States, in Tuscaloosa, Birmingham, Indianapolis, Jacksonville, and Raleigh, Confederate statues were removed, toppled, beheaded, or smeared with paint. In the nation's capital, until they were thwarted by police, protesters tried to tear down the equestrian statue of President Andrew Jackson (1767-1845) in Lafayette Square, right in front of the White House, because of his ruthless treatment of Native Americans.

Dénouement

Almost a year after the Black Lives Matter protests and the renewed calls to take down the statue of Cecil Rhodes on the

High Street in Oxford, Oriel College came to a surprising decision. After ten months of work, during which it received more than a thousand written contributions—most of them in favour of retaining the statue—Oriel's Independent Commission of Inquiry supported removing it but made no specific suggestions about how that should be done. It also recognized how complex, costly, and time-consuming it would be to obtain the necessary permissions from local, heritage, and national bodies, especially in the light of the British Government's new policy to "retain and explain" controversial statues and sites.

As a result, the Provost of Oriel College announced on 20 May 2021 that the College had "decided not to begin the legal process for relocation" but instead to "focus its time and resources on delivering the report's recommendations around the contextualization of the College's relationship with Rhodes, as well as improving educational equality, diversity and inclusion". "We know," the Provost continued, that "this nuanced conclusion will be disappointing to some, but we are now focused on the delivery of practical actions aimed at improving outreach and the day-to-day experience of BME [Black and Minority Ethnic] students."[26]

The decision process was serpentine and unsatisfying, but at the same time faithful to the eddies and contradictions in Rhodes's own life.

CHAPTER TWO
A Vivacious Man

IRIDESCENT LIZARDS NOW scuttle across the lichen splotches around Rhodes's grave. Set in the Matopos Hills of southern Zimbabwe, a spot once sacred to the Ndebele people, Rhodes chose it himself for its "World's View" and a nobility worthy of how he hoped to be remembered. Now, there are so few visitors that the Department of National Museums and Monuments does not even bother to keep track. "We have more important issues to deal with in this country," the young caretaker told me, without the slightest trace of sarcasm. The Department's main mission now seems to be to protect the World Heritage site against vandalism around the clock.

Cecil Rhodes's tomb may seem a strange place to begin his story, but death was on his mind most of his life and his resting place is a striking reminder of his faded glory. It may also appear unconventional to focus first on his personality. But as Rhodes is a much-debated figure, it seems appropriate to introduce him as his contemporaries knew him, not as a cardboard cut-out, but in flesh and blood, with strengths and weaknesses, ideas, ambitions, and passions that alternately inspired and disappointed his friends. That is because, like most other human beings and the crystals that made him rich, Cecil Rhodes had many facets.

Lack of Pretension

His most remarkable feature was an almost total lack of pretension. Although he earned about a quarter of a million pounds a year (about £33 million today), he lived on about £600 (the equivalent of £78,000) and dressed for comfort rather than show.[a] He once sent a coat to a tailor to be mended and was told that, except for the buttons, it was worthless and beyond repair. He didn't even wear a watch. He was refused entry to the 1892 Kimberley Industrial Exhibition because he didn't have a ticket or the money to pay for one. Even when Rhodes insisted on who he was, the attendant stood his ground, doubting that a prime minister would dress so shabbily. Rhodes had to wait for someone he knew to arrive and vouch for him. Later, he sent the attendant a sizeable cheque to reward him for his sense of duty.

"The conventions of society merely bore him," recalled a friend. "He cares for realities alone. A man is judged simply for what is in him... Set Mr. Rhodes in a roomful of magnates and you will probably find he has picked out some unknown person to talk to, if, perchance, that unknown person has brains."[1] Some saw him as an eccentric. "Being a man of ideas, a great practical genius in his own way," recalled a friend, "he is out of the common in everything."[2]

---

a   The Bank of England inflation converter suggests that £1 in 1890 would be worth £129.46 in 2019. Hereafter, only current values will be used, except where sterling amounts occur in direct quotations.

It was only late in life that Rhodes acquired a house of his own, apparently feeling that he didn't need one. The lodgings he shared with a friend in Kimberley in the 1880s were known as "one of the sights of the town". In a room said to be smaller than a small dressing-room, Rhodes slept on a trundle-bed intended for servants that was barely large enough for his big body. There, an eye-witness commented, "Rhodes dreamed of annexing, if not the planets in the heavens, at least the planet he dwelt on."[3] While Parliament was in session, he stayed at a hotel in Cape Town or in rooms over a bank.

He was 40 years old when he bought Groote Schuur ("Big Barn") on the slopes of Table Mountain, the awe-inspiring massif towering over Cape Town. First built in 1657, the house was refurbished in the original Dutch style by the architect Sir Herbert Baker, at Rhodes's request. Once it was complete, Rhodes continued living in an outbuilding that had been part of the servants' quarters and only began using his bedroom in the house when he was persuaded that the outbuilding spoiled the view of the Mountain and should be demolished.

But he left most of the walls of Groote Schuur bare, feeling that pictures were too expensive. "If I had a twenty-thousand-pound picture hanging there, the pleasure from looking at it would be spoilt because I would feel: 'There's two miles of my Cape to Cairo railway hanging on my wall.'"[4] He once considered buying a portrait of a dying musician holding an unfinished composition, with the inscription *Ars longa, vita brevis* ["Art is long, life is short"]. Although it probably reminded him of his own race against time, he backed off when he heard the price (£65,000). "I can build a court-house in Bulawayo for that."[5]

His personal finances were a complete shambles, because once he was well-off he seemed indifferent to the details. "He cared about as much for money, so far as avarice went, as a monkey cares for a diamond necklace," said a friend.[6] During the last decade of his life, his chequing account was overdrawn for nine months of the year. The only time he was in the black was when his dividends from De Beers arrived; yet he continued to give away millions of pounds in charity, piling up interest on his overdrafts of as much as £650,000 per annum.[7]

His personal banker, Lewis Michell, was so appalled by his client's habits that, when he was given power of attorney, he confiscated Rhodes's cheque book. But the magnate continued to write cheques on sheets of note-paper, sometimes signing them in pencil. "To a banker brought up on the strictest tenets of his sect," Michell recalled, "[Rhodes] was an undoubted trial."[8] He did not verify the financial statements that Michell submitted to him; did not know what he was worth until he was shown a balance-sheet; and never kept track of the sums he was owed. His securities were sometimes registered in the names of third parties or found in the pockets of disused suits and obscure corners of his desk. Yet, when necessary, he could make long, persuasive, and—to some listeners—mesmerizing presentations at shareholder meetings in London, without notes.

Generosity

As we have seen, he was also a generous man. "It seemed that anyone in Africa who wanted something, from a square meal to a ticket home, had only to go to Groote Schuur to get it," recounted one writer.[9] His friend is feiedHLord Grey once asked him: "Why do you always give away cheques of 20, 30, 50 pounds or more to every ne'er do well who whines to you for help?" "Well," said Rhodes, "a man once came to me in Cape Town and said he was on his beam-ends [wit's end], could I lend him something? I didn't like the fellow's face and refused, and that night he committed suicide. That was a lesson to me; and since then I have never dared to refuse money to folks who are hard up."[10] Even in the early days at Kimberley, he "practised almost indiscriminate philanthropy", paying for medical treatment or trips to the seaside for those needing a change of air.[11]

At the Kimberley Club one morning, he spotted a young man at the front desk in apparent distress. He had been wounded during one of the Ndebele wars and required medical treatment in England if he was not to be permanently disabled; but he could not afford the passage home. Rhodes was upset that he had not written to him for help, but the young man explained that he had gone to Rhodesia of his own free will and, while they had crossed paths there, he had never expected to see Rhodes again. Rhodes insisted on sending him a cheque at the Club by 1pm. Tied up at a De Beers directors' meeting, he asked a colleague to send the cheque instead, then came out again to say, "No. It's not nice for him to have to go and ask for a letter. It's like asking for the money. You go up yourself and give it to him." Then, minutes later: "Look here. Don't write that letter. No one would like to get a letter or a message. It will hurt his feelings. Give me the cheque. I'll go and give it to him myself." Which he did.[12]

Another time, outside the De Beers office, he saw an African who had lost a leg and learned that he had been injured on duty as a member of the Rhodesian "native" police force. For more than half an hour, Rhodes kept colleagues waiting as he talked to the man and arranged for him to be given a horse, saddle and bridle, blankets, food, and enough money to re-establish himself in his home village.[13]

Concerned about the financial losses that "his settlers" had suffered during the 1896 war, he donated more than £2 million to tide them over. He did the same for the Ndebele people who had lost most of their cattle to disease and were facing starvation, sending more than £6 million to buy corn. In his eulogy for Rhodes six years later, the Archbishop of Cape Town referred to these gifts: "Open-hearted, perhaps, to a fault, he said to me more than once, 'I have often told my rich friends that they cannot take their riches away with them when they die, and that they would therefore do wisely to make good use of it while they live.'"[14] According to another close friend, his "generosity to others was suspected to be unstinted. I say suspected, because no man knew. He had mastered the profound secret that a Man's life does not consist in the things that he possesses."[15]

He grew so accustomed to being asked for money that he occasionally gave it away to those who didn't even want it. One bewildered man came away with a large cheque after asking Rhodes for advice about starting a horse-breeding farm. Too impatient to listen to his story, Rhodes gave him the money even though the man intended to fund the scheme himself.[16] A close colleague records how "Rhodes, meeting the most disreputable tramp, invited him to share his own meal. Any unfortunate . . . was always the better for meeting Rhodes in his travels." One day, after he had lunched with a delegation of farmers, one of them picked up a stone on the gravel path as a memento of meeting the statesman. Hearing that, Rhodes sent him an antique silver snuff-box out of his collection.[17]

Sometimes, his kindness did not cost a penny. At the beginning of 1895, on a voyage from Odessa to Brindisi, his ship was caught in a hurricane. After his personal valet John Norris had put him to bed, Rhodes asked him where he would be spending the night. When Norris said "in the saloon", Rhodes suggested that he share the cabin with him. Then, hearing that the economy passengers were being soaked on deck, he asked Norris to bring in as many of them as possible, too. Later,

Norris recalled: "He actually filled his cabin with the most evil-looking human beings I had ever seen, drenched through and through, and stuck it [out] right through the night. Most of them had the most vile-smelling food, which they hung on to in only a very dim light. I never heard Rhodes even mention it but unfortunately for me it took years to shake that night's ordeal off."[18]

At other times, Rhodes's considerateness was tied to a sense of duty. During dinner with the general manager of a steamship company, he learned that two light vessels loading coal onto a ship off Cape Town had been driven from their moorings and carried out to sea. Rhodes's host wanted to cable the naval station at Simon's Town to ask them to intercept the vessels but the local telegraph office was closed and Simon's Town was more than twenty miles away. Rhodes jumped to his feet, drove there in his carriage to alert the Admiral, and joined some of his men on a tugboat in search of the missing vessels. It was a stormy night and water swept the deck from end to the other. Although he was seasick throughout, Rhodes refused to be brought back to port until the nine-hour search was called off just before dawn. (The vessels were rescued by another boat the next day.) His staff at Groote Schuur stayed up all night worrying. But he showed up at Parliament as usual at 2:30 pm looking exhausted but satisfied that he had done what he could in the circumstances.[19]

When his estate on Table Mountain was complete, he opened the grounds to the general public, building roads along the slopes and stocking the grounds with wild birds and animals to please the visitors. It was said that he loved to see the working man, accompanied by his wife and family, come from the crowded parts of Cape Town on a Sunday morning to spend the day on the estate and enjoy the fresh air. According to his secretary Philip Jourdan, "Thousands availed themselves of his generosity and large-heartedness, and it was a genuine pleasure to watch their happy faces." Now and then, visitors plucked flowers or harassed the animals, and Rhodes's steward would suggest that the estate be closed to outsiders. But he would not hear of it. "Why should I punish ninety-nine good citizens because the hundredth does not know how to behave himself?"[20] Later, Rhodes bequeathed the estate to the Cape Colony with a view to making it the official residence of the prime minister of a united South Africa.

Not everyone admired Rhodes's open-handedness. His banker Michell, for one, felt that not all of it was disinterested. "For many years he allowed himself to be persuaded that indiscriminate almsgiving had its reward, that loyalty could be purchased with *largesse*, and that bread thrown upon the waters always returned after many days. But injudicious charity proved at times a curse, not only to himself but to the recipient."[21] His generosity was also linked to his general disregard for money. According to his secretary, he handled money like a child who did not understand the value of it. Paying for cabs in London, he would take a coin out of his pocket without even looking at it. "If it happened to be a gold piece, the cabby would touch his cap gratefully and drive away very pleased with himself. If, on the contrary, his tender amounted to less than the fare . . . the chances were that [the cabby] got a gold coin in addition to the silver."[22]

Of course, it is easy to be indifferent to money when you have a great deal of it and some of the accounts of his selflessness seem a little too saintly. He was certainly aware of the advantages of wealth. Major-General Charles Gordon (1833-1885), the hero of Khartoum, once told him how he had refused a roomful of treasure offered to him by the Chinese government for helping to put down the Taiping Rebellion.

Rhodes was aghast. "I should have taken it and many more roomfuls as they offered me. It is no use having big ideas if you have not the cash to carry them out."[23]

He was even blunter with his banker. "You don't seem to care for money," Michell said. "For its own sake, no," Rhodes answered. "I never tried to make it for its own sake, but it is a power, and I like power."[24] He wrote cheques to buy influence, placate opponents, and even paper over tiffs with his young consorts. And he would not object to reaping benefits from his generosity. "Pure philanthropy is all very well in its way," he said once, "but philanthropy plus 5 per cent is a good deal better."[25]

Reading and Writing

For someone who insisted that his Rhodes Scholars should not be bookworms, he was an avid reader. Early in his career, at a friend's house in the country, he filled a kit-bag with books belonging to the man's wife. "Something to do if I am faced with a weary and boring wait in the veld [open country]," he said. His wife was aghast, as Rhodes had the habit of reading a few chapters at a time and, if he liked them, tearing them out to share and discuss with a companion. "It was the action of a future millionaire," observed the friend, "but hardly good for my wife's little library."[26]

At sea, he spent most of his time immersed in books. His secretary would buy fifty or so before a voyage, mostly about ancient civilizations (including Egypt, Greece, and Rome), modern history, South Africa, and the political questions of the day. He enjoyed sitting in his cabin with the titles scattered on the floor, dipping into them until he found one he liked, then going up to the captain's deck to finish it. Even on land, despite his busy schedule, he made a point of reading in bed for thirty minutes before putting out the light, commenting once on how much one could get through in that way.

Unsurprisingly for an imperialist, his favourite book was Edward Gibbon's *Decline and Fall of the Roman Empire*. He even asked the bookseller, Hatchard's of Piccadilly, to have all the original sources that Gibbon had used, translated into English. The bill had exceeded £1 million before he was persuaded to drop the project. (So much for his frugality.) Those volumes are still at Groote Schuur. He was also devoted to the *Meditations* of the Roman Emperor Marcus Aurelius and was fascinated by Napoleon Bonaparte. He once boasted that he had read every English-language biography of the man.[27] An engraving of the Emperor seizing the crown from a slightly flustered Pope Pius VII at Notre Dame Cathedral and putting it on his own head still hangs in Rhodes's bedroom at Groote Schuur.

If he enjoyed reading, he hated writing, and prepared many of his speeches—including those brimming with statistics and financial data—in his head. He once stuffed a stack of letters into a drawer, with the remark, "Most of them will answer themselves."[28] One of his secretaries suggested that there was more method than impatience in that department. He believed in personal interviews, maintaining that "more could be done by an hour's friendly chat than by months of letter-writing. He believed in seeing people."[29]

Persuasiveness

All biographers agree that Rhodes was persuasive and stubborn. The clearest example of that was the fifteen years he spent amalgamating thousands of diamond holdings into the De Beers monopoly. In the view of one biographer, "he had an hypnotic and persuasive charm—an ability to win people over 'on the personal'."[30] According to Barney Barnato, the last man to stand between Rhodes and total control of the diamond fields, "When you have been with him half an hour you not only agree with him, but come to believe that you have always held his opinion . . . He tied me up, as he ties up everybody. It is his way."[31] He expected his staff to overcome all obstacles. "Every morning when you awake," he wrote in one of his notebooks, "consider whether during the preceding day you have advanced your object in life."[32]

Even in the face of physical danger, he kept his poise. In Stellaland, a short-lived Boer republic (now part of South Africa's North West Province) coveted by both the British and the nearby Transvaal Republic, he met a physically imposing Afrikaner military commander renowned for his cold-bloodedness. When Rhodes first talked to him, the man replied: "Blood must flow." "No," said Rhodes, "give me my breakfast first, and we can talk about blood afterwards." Charmed by his coolness and common sense, within the week the latter-day Goliath asked Rhodes to be godfather to his grandchild. "It was not the only occasion in his life," concluded the writer William Plomer, "on which, having taken a bull by the horns, he first patted it on the head, and then taught it to eat out of his hand."[33]

While few writers have described him as charismatic, one modern scholar has suggested that Rhodes had a peculiar talent for connecting with an audience despite his limited skills as a public speaker and a voice that could trail off into a squeak. "His charisma . . . was born of a unique combination of projection of power and humility and the ability to identify with his followers and to invade and inhabit their innermost personal domains. He, in turn, allowed them access to his own personal domain. It was a charisma that could flourish in the particular frontier ambience of the Cape and southern Africa."[34]

Although he was English, some of that magnetism stemmed from pure blarney. In August 1896, a missionary named Douglas Petty recalled hearing Rhodes talk about the Jameson Raid (the attempted overthrow of the government of the Transvaal Republic) at the officers' mess in Gwelo (Rhodesia). "It was one of the finest orations I ever listened to, and we all thought we had been let into the secrets of the raid! But later, consideration showed us that we had learnt literally nothing."[35]

Joie de Vivre

For someone so busy and powerful, Rhodes had a remarkable sense of fun. One night, in a tent, dressed only in his underwear, he woke his friend Lord Grey so brusquely that the man thought the tent was on fire. "No, no," Rhodes answered. "I just wanted to ask you, have you ever thought how lucky you are to have been born an Englishman when there are so many millions who were not born Englishmen? And that's not all: there you are, over forty, with a clean and healthy body and a sound mind when you might have been riddled with disease. That's all I wanted to say."[36]

On another occasion, he lent a biography of Napoleon to his valet John Norris and asked what he thought of it. Norris noted that the Emperor was fond of women and suffered a great deal from bellyache. Rhodes was shaving at the time and let out such a yell that Norris thought he had cut himself. Rhodes replied that Napoleon was "a most wonderful man" but that unfortunately, at the end of his reign, France was no larger than it had been at the beginning. Norris recalls: "He punished me severely for this remark of mine for on a visit to Paris he made me accompany him to the Louvre and stand for hours gazing at pictures [that] Napoleon took from all over Europe; this happened not once but every day for about a week, and each day for hours."[37]

Another feature of his *joie de vivre* suggests that at least one moral yardstick has evolved over time. As his face was often reddish from poor circulation, casual observers assumed that Rhodes was a heavy drinker. But his secretary Phillip Jourdan judged him a "moderate" one. He imbibed a whisky and soda (or a pint of beer) at lunch, followed by another in the late afternoon. At dinner, he enjoyed a whisky or a couple of glasses of champagne and, if alone, would drink stout, champagne, and two or three whiskies before retiring for the night. The only time he was "jolly" was during his negotiations with the Ndebele in the Matopos, when he downed about six whiskies one evening; but Jourdan attributed this to "pure worry" and Rhodes went back to his wagon unassisted.[38] His valet calculated that Rhodes drank the equivalent of half a bottle of whisky per day, then added: "To a teetotaller this may appear a lot, but to anyone averaging 18 to 19 hours of work and worry per day some stimulant is required."[39]

Like everyone, he had his tics. "His love of cleanliness," recalled a friend, "was very remarkable, and he would not camp out in the veld if a jam tin were found at the place selected"[40] According to an employee, "Mr. Rhodes was very 'fussy' about tidiness and orderliness, though in his own person he was not particularly tidy as to dress, etc. I remember so well when I was a junior in the Gold Fields having to see to the yard at the back of the office building being cleared of all litter or papers each day, particularly when Mr. Rhodes was about."[41] One of the minor triumphs of his life, during the siege of Kimberley, was to put thousands of unemployed mine labourers to work burying millions of discarded tin cans under a long new avenue lined with trees.

Magnanimity

Rhodes could also be magnanimous. In October 1900, during the South African War, when Pretoria fell to the British and the impression was created that the war was virtually over, Rhodes attended a "victory" celebration in Cape Town and told an audience bristling with anti-Boer feelings: "You think you have beaten the Dutch?... The Dutch are as vigorous and un-conquered to-day as they have ever been . . . Remember *that* when you go back to your homes . . . Let there be no vaunting words, no vulgar triumph over your Dutch neighbours; make them feel that the bitterness is past and that the need of co-operation is greater than ever; teach your children to remember when they go to the village school that the little Dutch boys and girls they find sitting on the same benches with them are as much a part of the South African nation as they are themselves, and that as they learn the same lessons together now, so hereafter they must work together as comrades for a common object—the good of South Africa."[42]

Ten years before, when he had occupied part of what is now Zimbabwe against the better judgment of some of his fellow parliamentarians, the head of the Afrikaner party, Jan Hendrik Hofmeyr, told him: "You have got hold of the interior, now be generous, let us down gently." "I will not let you down," said Rhodes. "I will take you with me."[43] And he did. From the very start, Boers as well as English settlers were encouraged to occupy the lands that Rhodes's "Pioneers" had seized in the North.

Endurance

Despite a weak heart, Rhodes was capable of great physical exertion. "He loved nature and the simple life which one led when on the veld," a friend said. "Riding thirty miles a day, and walking another ten miles in pursuit of game, was sufficient exercise to tire the most robust, and the result was that we all retired very early at night. Sometimes at eight o'clock we were all fast asleep."[44] Undoubtedly because of his daily exertions, Rhodes was generally a sound sleeper. He told a friend that, if he received a message when he was going to bed that all Cape Town was in flames, he would still nod off. "Possibly," replied the friend, "but you would be organising relief in your dreams. And what is more, you would know everything that had happened when you came down to breakfast."[45]

That ability to rest, in turn, added to his energy. "Are you the same man I saw as a boy?" asked a doctor who examined him during a visit to England. Rhodes nodded. "Impossible," the doctor replied. "According to my books you have been a corpse these [last] ten years." "Never has there been a more dynamic corpse," commented one biographer, "never a man who, knowing death was near, made greater haste to accomplish his ends."[46] The Ndebele called him Lamula M'kunzi ("He who separates fighting bulls"). In fact, an Ndebele elder once drew a parallel between Rhodes and a well-known African hunter and scout. "Compared to the great white Chief, [the hunter] is only the tick bird that picks the ticks off the rhinoceros."[47] According to an eye-witness of Rhodes's two-month long negotiations with the Ndebele leaders in 1896, "He sat day after day throughout the heat of the day talking to the chiefs and cracking jokes with them until we were tired to death of the sight of them. But his patience and perseverance gained him the day. He inspired the chiefs with confidence, and eventually he was able to meet them all together and concluded the much-needed peace."[48]

But there were other, less pleasant, sides to Rhodes's personality, driven in part by the knowledge that he would not live long.

CHAPTER THREE

Stalked by Death

"EVERYTHING IN THE world is too short," he exclaimed once. "Life and fame and achievement. Everything is too short. From the cradle to the grave, what is it? Three days at the seaside."[1] On another occasion, he reflected: "The great fault of life is its shortness; just as one is beginning to know the game, one has to stop."[2] A few years before he died, he took his banker and future biographer Lewis Michell to show him the spot where he wished to be buried but also to lie down on it "to see how it felt".[3] His keen sense of mortality drove him forward like a man fleeing a landslide, making him impatient and impetuous.

"[His] only method of dealing with a problem," said one associate, "is to carve a path straight through it."[4] Another colleague said that he drove his plans forward with "tempestuous energy", intolerant of delays, red tape, and conventions. "A third of one's life," Rhodes complained, "is lost in waiting for people who have failed to keep appointments and in trying to find out if our friends are telling the truth."[5] "It is a fearful thought," he wrote to his British journalist friend W.T. Stead, "to feel that you possess a patent, and to doubt whether your life will last through the circumlocution of the forms of [the] Patent Office."[6]

Sometimes, Rhodes's impatience turned to ruthlessness. In April 1894, he visited one of the principal traditional leaders of Pondoland, on the eastern edge of the Cape Colony, to tell him that the British Government had decided to seize the area "in the interests of his tribe and of humanity". Naturally enough, the man objected, but he eventually signed the articles of annexation. Rhodes then took one of the leader's advisers aside to warn him that if he continued his "career of murder" he would regret it. "I am now your chief," he said, "and what I say I will do. If you talk mischief, even at night, I shall hear. You will never be safe. I will kill you if you deserve it, as I killed Lobengula [the last king of the Ndebele people]."[7] In fact, he had never met Lobengula and certainly didn't kill him. On another occasion, to persuade a local ruler to cooperate, Rhodes had his men flatten a nearby cornfield with machine-gun fire.

Although he was often a bull dog, he could be disarming, self-aware, and even contrite. Accused once of changing his views rather hurriedly, he replied, 'Yes, as hurriedly as I could, for I found I was wrong."[8] "Every day," he said in his final years, "I try to become humbler, but it is hard."[9] In London, where he had gone to face the parliamentary inquiry into the Jameson Raid, Rhodes confided to the wife of an American friend: "The last time I saw you I told you that I never spent sleepless nights, but I have spent many of them since that time. You have also thought that this setback that I have had in my career would be a good thing for me, as I was getting too arbitrary in my ways of thinking and acting, and I want to tell you that you are entirely right. It is a terrible humbling of my pride, but, in the long run, it will be a splendid thing for me, because it will make me a far more reasonable and considerate man."[10]

Irritability

From 1895 onwards, sensing the horizon shrink on his ambitions, he was frequently angry. Always fond of making mischievous or cynical remarks to provoke debate or unsettle his listeners, he appeared to become more brutal. "I like doctors for my work," he once said, "because when there is blood-letting to be done, they are less squeamish."[11] He was also given to moments of megalomania. Asked how long he expected to be remembered, he answered: four thousand years.

The deforming effects of wealth and power and the constant fawning of sycophants around him also made him prickly. Proud that the word "Rhodesia" was coming into common use ("I find that I am human and should like to be living after my death"), he exploded when a tactless colleague pointed out that Van Diemen's Land in Australia was now called Tasmania.[12] After the Jameson Raid—the 1895 invasion of the Transvaal Republic that led to Rhodes's downfall—his old ally, the Boer politician Jan Hendrik Hofmeyr, sent a messenger to say that his friendship remained intact, even if he could not display it publicly. Rhodes jumped out of his arm-chair: "Go back and tell him that I want friends while I'm alive. I don't want any of his post-mortem snivelling."[13] Later that year, Rhodes took his secretary Le Sueur to the Matopos Hills to show him his intended burial site, asking him to cover his eyes on their way up to the summit. "Now look: what do you think of it?" "Oh, I don't know," the young man answered, "it's rather fine." Rhodes was furious. "I suppose if Jesus Christ were to ask you what you thought of Heaven, you'd say, 'Oh, I don't know, it isn't bad'."[14]

In June 1897, his former business partner Barney Barnato jumped overboard on his way back to England. The news arrived when Rhodes was asleep and his secretary decided not to wake him. The next morning, Rhodes was incensed: "I suppose you thought this would affect me and I should not sleep . . . [Do] you imagine that I should be in the least affected if you were to fall under the wheels of this train now?" His secretary saw through this. "He tried to give the impression of being without feeling, but nothing is more absurd. He was crammed with sentiment to his finger-tips, but adopted a brutal manner and rough exterior to cover up the weakness of sentiment."[15]

Inspiring and Exasperating

Some writers have described Rhodes as an autocrat; yet he inspired great loyalty in those close to him and was a consummate delegator. Contrary to the adage, he was a hero to his valet. "We were an ill-assorted couple," recalled John Norris, "although he never tired of telling me I was too abrupt and more obstinate than a government mule. Why government I don't know. We had great love for each other."[16] Another confidant thought that Rhodes brought out the best in his staff. In the words of his "fixer" Dr. Jameson (who led the disastrous raid into the Transvaal), "He leaves a man to himself, and that is why he gets the best work they are capable of . . . Although no doubt in the Transvaal business he has suffered for this system, still in the long run the system pays."[17]

At the same time, when staff failed him, he could be unsparing. "To those who had not sufficient confidence in themselves to overcome difficulties," said one associate, "he never gave a second chance, and they immediately passed out of his life . . . He liked a man to display the attributes of a man, and despised indecision, weakness, and effeminateness in the male sex."[18] Asked by a young military officer about his professional prospects, Rhodes told him that he was likely to succeed, but only up to a point, because he was always thinking of his career rather than the job he was doing.[19]

Bravery or Bravado?

His peace talks with the Ndebele leaders in 1896 were said to be a mark of his courage. But Rhodes's bravado was more obvious than his bravery. Even staunch admirers said that, as a rule, when danger was brewing, Rhodes preferred to take shelter. A fellow traveller told of taking a journey through country infested with lions and remaining nervous all night despite the campfires lit for protection. Five or six men were huddled in one tent, and when they retired for the night Rhodes instinctively took the middle place so that, if a lion came for a meal, it would not be him.[20] Marching to Bulawayo at the start of the first Ndebele rebellion, Rhodes admitted that he was "in a funk all the time" and "more afraid to be thought afraid". So, he threw himself into action, leading reconnoitering expeditions armed only with a hunting crop and standing out on the front lines in his white flannel trousers.[21]

In his final years, he had wild swings of temper. According to one friend, "There are many people who say that he was harsh and unsympathetic. No man was ever more misjudged in this respect. He had an exceptionally sympathetic nature, but his pride would not allow him to show it, and he always tried to hide it."[22] Another loyalist saw his moods as a natural product of his high ambition and heavy responsibilities. If, in the process, he had wounded a friend, he would go out of his way to be pleasant the next time they met. "That was his way of apologizing."[23]

The ups and downs of Rhodes's character were described by

the artist Mortimer Menpes, who sketched him after the siege of Kimberley and later in Cape Town. "He is the roughest man possible, and amazingly animal, yet as delicate and sensitive as a school-girl, and strongly spiritual. I have never seen a man look more angry than Mr. Rhodes, and almost at the same moment I have seen tears shining in his eyes . . . Mr. Rhodes at heart is an exceedingly shy man . . . But at times he is terribly hard, almost cruel; now and then it is hard to believe that there is any sensitiveness or kindness in his composition . . . He knew what he wanted, and would get it as quickly as possible, without any hindrance."[24]

Others denied that he had a nasty bone in his body. His close friend and financier Alfred Beit reacted sharply when someone asked if Rhodes was difficult at times: "Not at all; never! It is true that you have to know him, but when you know him he is perfectly splendid . . . Sometimes he is rude and sounds dictatorial, but that only means he is very much in earnest and convinced and hates to waste time . . . But in all the big things he is wonderful, and he is one of the most generous and kind-hearted of men."[25]

Intimacy

His mercurial manner may have been caused in part by emotional and sexual frustration. Very often, too, he must have been lonely. At the age of 13, in the words of a childhood friend, "instead of gazing at the pretty girl looking over a gate, he was all eyes for the country he passed through, and always remembered which farm was well cultivated and which slackly managed."[26] He claimed that marriage interfered with professional activity. From Oxford, he wrote to a friend: "I hate people getting married, they simply become machines and have no ideas beyond their respective spouses and offspring."[27] At other times, he suggested that "the consideration of babies and other domestic agenda generally destroys higher thought" and that he had "never yet seen a woman who I could get on in the same house with."[28] He might have subscribed to the French writer's remark: "The heart and the brain are two halves of an hour glass. You cannot fill one without emptying the other."[29] Stating it more positively, he doubted being able to live up to the obligations of marriage. "I have too much work on my hands. I shall always be away from home, and should not be able to do my duty as a husband towards his wife. A married man should be at home to give the attention and advice which a wife expects from a husband."[30]

That Rhodes remained a bachelor did not surprise his family, as only two of his eight siblings married. One biographer speculated that, if he had met the right woman, he would have changed his mind. "She might have saved him from many mistakes of his later years and calmed the fiery outbursts that did him and his cause no good: and there is no doubt that she would have had a most considerate husband."[31] His last secretary imagined that "If he had married a good and strong-minded woman who would have nursed his strength and looked after him, he would in all probability have lived much longer, and... risen to even a higher pinnacle of fame."[32] Another associate referred to his "monastic purity" and another to the all-consuming nature of his hard work and "big schemes": "He makes this sacrifice, as he makes many others, to the ideal of the British Empire, to which his life is devoted."[33] But this was pure fancy. What Rhodes was expressing awkwardly in his words and behaviour was that he had no interest in women.

In due course, his attitude to women became so well-known that Queen Victoria supposedly raised the matter over dinner at the end of 1891. Rhodes's reported answer was: "How can

I hate a sex to which your Majesty belongs?"[34] But that was lame and dishonest—Rhodes would have parleyed with the Devil to get his way—so the conversation probably never occurred. But the story confirms the reputation that Rhodes had acquired.

While it would be extreme to describe him as misogynous, it is clear that he was less engaged and charming with women than he was with men and they reacted accordingly. "He is the most impersonal man I have ever known," recalled the wife of Rhodes's American associate, John Jay Hammond. "The world is his omelette and the men the eggs that compose it. I believe that he would lap human bodies like sandbags to build his fort. Mr. Rhodes is a great man [and his] brain is [as] great and level as Table Mountain. [But] he lives entirely beyond the pale of everyday life. Mr. Rhodes can be as bloodless as Fate when people are not of use to him."[35]

One story handed down by descendants of an 1890 Rhodesian "Pioneer" suggests that Rhodes was capable of gallantry. And, in this case, it may also have saved his life. Rushing to Kimberley for a diamond auction, he found himself on a stage coach which stopped on the banks of a rain-swollen river to allow a pregnant passenger to disembark. Fearing the worst, she preferred to wait for the next coach. Rather than leave the woman alone in the open country, Rhodes decided to stay with her. They were fortunate to have done so, because as they looked on, the coach was washed away in mid-stream, killing everyone on board.[36] The story may be apocryphal, but it implies that not everyone remembered Rhodes as a person who lacked grace in his relations with women. All the same, the evidence that he preferred the company of men is incontrovertible.

In his bedroom at Groote Schuur was a photograph of the first Ndebele king's widow, who helped him arrange peace talks in 1896. Elsewhere was a Joshua Reynolds portrait of a female subject that Rhodes thought captured the essence of womanhood. But, apart from occasional dinner guests, these images were the only feminine presence in the place. He had no women employees of any kind. Even his chef—a largely female role at the time—was a man. Rhodes also surrounded himself with a group of good-looking male secretaries to whom he grew so attached that he was annoyed if any of them married. "He felt certain that bachelors would make the best proconsuls to govern the expanding empire," wrote one historian in 1977. "Yet," the same writer added, "there has never been any evidence . . . that Rhodes was a homosexual."[37]

In fact, the signs that Rhodes was "gay" were strewn about for all to see from the very first biographies and, to the very end, he preferred the company of men. "The Muizenberg cottage [Rhodes's simple seaside house, 26 kilometres from Cape Town, where he spent the last month of his life], with its sick room and dying man," wrote Peter Gibbs in 1956, "was still a bachelor's house, and women had no part in it. It was Jameson who did the nursing, and Rhodes' faithful men friends who were his last companions."[38]

Although there were no explicit references to Rhodes's homosexuality, early on, there are certainly hints of it. His personal banker, Lewis Michell, wrote in 1910: "He took, on occasions, a singularly human interest in the welfare of young men, and read their characters with discernment . . . Once, when twitted [teased] with his preference for young men, he retorted, 'Of course, of course, they must soon take up our work; we must teach them what to do and what to avoid.'"[39] In a vivid account of his nine years working and living with Rhodes, Philip Jourdan set out to refute "serious and unjust misapprehensions" about the man: that he wanted war with the Boers, was a drunkard, engaged in improper financial speculation at the expense of others, was harsh, heartless and unsympathetic, and had "unprincipled" relations with women.[40] Yet, in his opening pages, he mentions that Rhodes "seemed to have a liking for young men". He was particularly partial to men with blue eyes.[41]

Later biographers went to exceptional lengths to deny that there was anything "sinister", "abnormal", or "perverse" about Rhodes's male friendships. "If evidence were wanted that such ideas occurred to no one in his lifetime," wrote his official biographers in 1963, "it might perhaps be found in the story recorded by a woman whose services were once offered to him as a secretary. 'I don't want a secretary,' he replied. 'Can't you find me a nice English boy?' No reasonable person could imagine those words being uttered by a man who was homosexual, unless he was a flagrant exhibitionist, which no one has ever suggested of Rhodes."[42]

Neville Pickering

The great love of his life was Neville Pickering, the De Beers corporate secretary, with whom he lived for almost five years, beginning in early 1881, in a cottage opposite the Kimberley Cricket Ground. This relationship appears to have smoothed some of Rhodes's rougher edges and that, in turn, helped attract some of his staunchest supporters. One writer suggests that Pickering was the prototype for the Rhodes Scholars: "Not a dreamer, not a genius, but a sound honest-to-goodness all-rounder of undeniable masculinity."[43] When they met, Pickering was 23 and Rhodes 27, but biographers have always referred to Pickering as "young" because Rhodes seemed so much older. There is no record of what went on behind closed doors and they had very few visitors, but it would be remarkable if the passion and energy of these two young men, in the privacy of their own home, faltered in the face of Victorian moral standards. While they kept to themselves at night, they were very much in evidence in town during the day working, riding, and shooting together. Within ten months of meeting him, Rhodes bequeathed everything he owned to Pickering.

In June 1884, while riding on the veld, Pickering was thrown from his horse into a clump of thorn bushes, cutting and bruising himself badly. At first, his injuries did not seem serious, but the poison from the thorns apparently affected his lungs and he was bedridden for more than a month. He never really recovered and was sickly for the next two years. When Pickering took a turn for the worse, Rhodes was in the newly opened gold fields, staking claims. Grabbing the last available ticket, he rode fifteen hours on the top of a coach in the bracing southern African winter to be with him. During the two months he spent at Pickering's bedside, some of Rhodes's gold options lapsed, one of which—for the purchase of a £65,000 farm—would eventually yield more than £250 million in ore. One biographer suggests that Rhodes could have become "absolute master of the world's chief source of gold." "It was as if fate itself had intervened, and had made Rhodes for once obey his heart rather than his pocket, as though to limit the power that might be exercised by one man alone."[44] He also kept putting off a board meeting to finalize the new diamond monopoly he and his business associates had agreed to establish.[45]

Dying in Rhodes's arms on 16 October 1886, Pickering whispered: "You have been father, mother, brother, and sister to me."[46] Suddenly alone in the world, Rhodes lost all emotional control. At the funeral, dressed in crumpled old clothes, he went from laughing to crying hysterically. "Nothing in his life," wrote William Plomer, "is more distinguished than his devotion to the dying Pickering [and] the shock of losing this young man . . . may possibly have something to do with his tendency to cultivate more and more a hardness and even brutality of manner which, it was supposed by some, was not natural to him but served to hide his susceptibilities."[47]

Afterwards, unable to bear returning to the cottage where he and Pickering had lived, he moved in with Dr. Jameson.[48] Although Jameson and Rhodes almost certainly never became lovers, they displayed an attachment and loyalty to each other that would last their entire lives. Jameson never married but his biographer suggested that his friendship with Rhodes was to become "as strong as a marriage bond".[49] When Jameson became prime minister of the Cape Colony two years after Rhodes's death, he lived at Groote Schuur (which Rhodes had donated to the nation) and on his own death in 1917 was buried thirty yards from Rhodes.

Secretaries and Bodyguards

After Pickering's death, Rhodes surrounded himself with young men who were variously described as his "bodyguard", "lambs", or "secretaries". He was very possessive of them. "I must not only have you," he told one recruit, "but I must have your heart as well. If your best is to be given to me, my interests must be your interests." When one of them, Harry Currey, announced that he was engaged to be married, Rhodes was furious at first, then reassured him that he understood his decision. But Currey knew that he would have to leave Rhodes's service. At the wedding, according to one account, just after the ceremony had been performed, the guest of honour—who was Prime Minister of the Cape, occasional guest of the Queen, and one of the most famous and wealthy men on earth—approached the apprehensive young bride and told her: "I am very jealous of you."[50]

He was playful and considerate with his young associates, and they responded in kind. When his friend Flora Shaw suggested that Rhodes hire a "real" secretary, he told his companions that he liked the idea as that person would almost certainly show him more respect and call him "sir". Their reaction was predictable. "We immediately 'sirred' him about every five words until he was heartily sick of it."[51]

When Philip Jourdan returned from hospital after being treated for appendicitis, Rhodes offered him a glass of choice Rhine wine. Jourdan did not feel up to it, so Rhodes poured a half glass for himself and threatened not to drink it if the young man left his own glass untouched. "It is very old wine, with plenty of body in it, and it will help to revive you." Jourdan followed orders and admitted that it made him feel better. "I knew it would," Rhodes said. "Now I am going to send the balance of the case to Muizenberg, where you must go for a month. The sea air will do you good, and you must promise to take half a bottle every day." He also sent his cook to look after Jourdan, who later recalled, "He was sweetness himself to me, and no one could have been more tender and considerate."[52]

Although no one ever replaced Neville Pickering, a man named Johnny ("Jack") Grimmer came close. A stable hand at De Beers, Rhodes spotted him one day from his office veranda in Kimberley trying to subdue an unruly horse. Each time Grimmer was thrown off, he climbed back on. "That boy has grit," said Rhodes, "I must speak to him," and from that day on their friendship grew. Thick set and lumbering and not particularly handsome, he was loyal and good-natured and had a soothing effect on his employer. When Rhodes was ill, he always wanted Grimmer to be with him and when the young man was bitten by a scorpion in 1897, Rhodes sat with him all day and bathed his feet in vinegar, hoping it would quell the fever.[53]

As their intimacy grew, there were signs of an abusive streak in the younger man and Rhodes's colleagues were sometimes offended by the tone Grimmer adopted. They bickered over minor matters and, at least once, did not speak for days. On that occasion, Rhodes broke the ice by teasing Johnny about his shooting, and within minutes they were laughing and joking again. A friend described Grimmer as unconventional and seemingly brusque but also as one of "the kindest, most loyal and staunchest of men". One day, in camp, to spare others the trouble, Rhodes tried to do something for himself. Johnny strolled over, took the things from Rhodes, and growled, "Of course, you made a mess of it: why couldn't you give me a call?" An eye-witness reported, "Rhodes dropped the tangle meekly with no more than a grunt; but his face was a study. The look of deep amusement and affection in his eyes and the softened expression on his face spoke volumes."[54]

Grimmer took part in all the major events of Rhodes's final years. He went to Rhodesia as a "pioneer" in 1890, was involved in both the 1893 war and the 1896 uprising, and sat with Rhodes during the lengthy 1896 peace talks in the Matopos Hills. Although they never lived together, three weeks before he died, Rhodes asked for an extra bed to be prepared so that Johnny could be in the same room at the end. Grimmer lived only two months longer than Rhodes. Shortly before he and Philip Jourdan were to embark on a round-the-world trip with the money Rhodes had given them, Grimmer contracted blackwater fever and died within twenty-four hours. He was only 34.[55]

Spirituality

William Booth, founder of the Salvation Army, said that Rhodes "was a great heart hungering for love."[56] It is probably true that he was more often frustrated than fulfilled in his emotional life. But he probably never felt very guilty about loving other men, as he had a very convenient attitude to religion. Although Rhodes was the son of an Anglican priest, his friend W.T. Stead described him as a "Darwinian" rather than a Christian. "He knew there was no Hell. The old faiths were dying out . . . [although] he respected them all with the wide tolerance of a Roman philosopher. If his life were to have a worthy goal, it must be among the living, not among the dead, with the future rather than the past."[57] He told a Jesuit friend that he was an agnostic, but still believed in doing one's best in the world, according to one's own lights, and not harming anyone intentionally. But, like many practical people, he hedged his bets and trusted stubbornly in his powers of persuasion. "If I go before the Almighty to-morrow, and He was to tell me that He thought I had acted very badly at times and had wronged some people wittingly . . . well—I should be prepared to have it out with Him."[58]

Laying the foundation stone of a Presbyterian chapel near Cape Town in 1900, he challenged "any man or any woman, however broad their ideas may be, who object to go to church or to chapel, to say that they would not sometimes be better for an hour or an hour and a half in church . . . There are those who, throughout the world, have [chosen to] devote their whole mind to make other human beings better, braver, kindlier, more thoughtful, and more unselfish, for which they deserve the praise of all men."[59] Addressing a gathering of the Salvation Army in London the year before, he said: "I know this, that in my own [Anglican] Church there are many disputes as to details—disputes as to the use of incense, the use of the confessional, the lighting and non-lighting of candles, and as to the wearing of embroidered garments—but, after all, let us put these details aside. What do we recognise? We recognise this, that they are not doing the work of the ordinary human being. Be he an officer of this organisation, a minister of my Church, or a priest of the Roman Catholic Church, they all have a higher object. They give their whole lives to the bettering of humanity."[60]

Towards the end of his life, his spiritual side—if that is what it may be called—may have altered his sense of priorities. After a visit to a Salvation Army "colony" in England, with a possible inkling of the Rhodes Scholarships in mind, he told General Booth's son: "Ah! You and the General are right: you have the best of me after all. I am trying to make new countries; you are making new men."[61]

Whether riding on the veld for hours or wandering on Table Mountain, which he described as his "church", he followed the advice of his intellectual hero Marcus Aurelius ("to retire into thyself"). According to the journalist W.T. Stead, "He had a mystic side incomprehensible to most of his friends, but it was the sphere in which he really lived." His architect Herbert Baker quoted others about Rhodes's "shy and solitary spirit", his "far-offness, a background of romance", and the fact that "the largest part of his brain was always far away". Even his close friend Jameson confessed that "no one ever knew all that was in Rhodes' mind. Though he talked freely, there were silences when he seemed to rise to some higher atmosphere and no one knew what happened there." "Biographies, therefore," concluded Baker, "even those written by men who were most intimate with him, have not revealed all sides of his full and complex nature."[62]

In his *Meditations*, Marcus Aurelius wrote that "Perfection of character is this: to live each day as if it were your last, without frenzy, without apathy, without pretence."[63] It cannot be said that Rhodes lacked frenzy: his ambitions and projects required energy and drive and inspired haste and impatience. But he certainly was not apathetic and, despite his emotional frustrations, appears to have savoured life, whether lost in the plains of his imagination, engaged in lofty conversations with his close friends, or giving vent to his boyish sense of fun.

The French biographer André Maurois ended his short book on Rhodes with the thought, "Greatness is not the same as virtue, but there is always virtue in it," while Lord Acton believed the opposite: "Great men are almost always bad."[64] Whoever was right, most would see in Rhodes real virtues to be admired and obvious faults of which all of us are capable. He also inspired deep loyalty and affection in his friends. Yet, their voluminous memoirs contain paradoxes, question marks, and touches of self-promotion. Any portrait of the man, therefore, can only be impressionistic. And character by itself does not define a life. While Rhodes's copy of Marcus Aurelius was well-thumbed, he was also very familiar with Christian scripture, including no doubt the passage: "By their fruits ye shall know them." (Matthew 7:20)

CHAPTER FOUR

Achievement

ECIL JOHN RHODES was born on 5 July 1853, at Bishop's
Stortford, in Hertfordshire, about forty miles northeast
of London. He was the sixth of eleven children, two of
whom died in infancy. His father was the Vicar of St. Michael's
Anglican Church, admired for his charity and brief homilies.
He had hoped that his sons would follow in his footsteps; but
none did. The oldest, Herbert, went to Winchester College and
the second son Frank attended Eton, but Cecil was sent to the
local grammar school—probably because the family budget
could not bear the strain of more elite education.

At this stage of life, the founder of the most prestigious
scholarship in the English-speaking world did little to
attract attention. He did not discredit himself, but he did not
distinguish himself either, and while he played some cricket
he was certainly not an outstanding athlete. In fact, his health
was a concern from the start. With a history of tuberculosis in
the family, it was thought natural that Cecil's lungs were weak;
but today it is considered more likely that this was a symptom
of heart disease. Thinking that a sea voyage and dryer climate
would help, and as he had no immediate professional aims,

Rhodes's parents sent him off to join his eldest brother Herbert in South Africa. Herbert was trying to grow cotton in Natal, one of the two British colonies that, forty years later, would join two former Boer republics to create the Union of South Africa.

South Africa

Cecil landed at Durban on 1 September 1870, barely seventeen years old. Herbert was prospecting for diamonds 500 miles away at Kimberley. So, the young man spent his first three months with a family friend, Dr. Sutherland, Natal's Surveyor-General, who predicted that Rhodes would end up as a village parson in England. But Rhodes's immediate challenge was more terrestrial. That year, Herbert's cotton crop had failed almost completely; but the following season, through effort and innovation, the two brothers turned a profit and won a prize at the local agricultural show. Insects and a shortage of water, however, forced them to abandon the farm in October 1871, barely a year after Cecil had arrived in Africa.

Despite the setbacks, Rhodes always saw this time growing cotton in the Umkomaas Valley as a sparkling chapter of his life. Years later, when told that something was impossible, he would say: "Ah, they told me I couldn't grow cotton!"[1] Living alone with about thirty workers (most of them Zulu-speaking), he learned his first lessons in managing people and developed an admiration for Africans, but also some misconceptions about them. Later, as a politician, he used this fleeting experience of agriculture to profess a special bond with Dutch-speaking Afrikaners in the Cape, most of whom were farmers.

Cecil then joined his brother at the diamond mines of Kimberley, carrying with him not just his digging tools but also volumes of the ancient classics and a Greek dictionary, as he had already decided to go to Oxford. The journey took more than a month and, when his horse died, he walked for fourteen miles a day ahead of the ox-cart carrying his personal effects. At Kimberley, he took quickly to supervising the mine work and, between reading and moments of reverie, developed business and bargaining skills that impressed everyone. Soon he began speculating in claims with such success that people started referring to "Rhodes's luck". The three brothers (Herbert, Frank, and Cecil) were now working together, but it was the youngest of the three that drew the greatest admiration. Not content just to work their holdings, Rhodes and his partner Charles Rudd bought an ice-making machine and sold enough ice-cream in three months to pay for it. Then, they won a lucrative contract for pumping water out of the diggings, before they even owned a pump.

Rhodes grew to be large (six feet four inches) but his health did not match his physique. In 1872, at the age of 19, Rhodes had his first heart attack and, to convalesce, Herbert took him on a foray north to some districts of the Transvaal Republic where gold discoveries had been reported. Trekking across the open country and camping under star-filled skies, we are told that he fell in love with Africa. The next year, Herbert went north, spending time in jail in Portuguese East Africa (now Mozambique) for gun-running, then joining a Foreign Office expedition to suppress the slave trade in Central Africa. In 1879, he died in a ghastly accident in Nyasaland (now Malawi) while pouring home-brewed gin in his hut. An ember from his pipe ignited the alcohol and the bottle exploded, setting his clothes on fire. He threw himself into a nearby river but died of his injuries shortly after at the age of 34.[2]

Oxford

Frank and Cecil returned—less eventfully—to England in 1873. Frank joined a cavalry regiment and Cecil sat for his entrance examination at Oxford, where he was accepted at Oriel College in October. Rhodes had hoped to go to University College but was rejected because of his deficient Latin. His friendship in Natal with a young relative of Oriel's Provost Edward Hawkins probably eased his entry into the college.[3] He did not stay long, returning to Kimberley after just one term in December 1873 to recover from a severe chest infection, contracted while rowing for his college on the wintry Isis (the stretch of the Thames at Oxford). Before he left, a doctor gave him only six months to live. Two years later, in April 1876, he returned for seven consecutive terms, before going back to South Africa for five more years. It was not till the autumn of 1881 that he completed his ninth and final term and received his BA and MA degrees on the same day (17 December 1881). By any measure, it was an unusual undergraduate career and, by the time he graduated, he was a rich man and a Member of the Cape Parliament.

If circumstances had been different and his health had been stronger, Rhodes might have completed his Oxford courses like everyone else in three rather than eight years and become a barrister. Instead, his future was being forged in South Africa. In 1874, the diamond industry was at a low ebb and the 21-year-old faced a formidable challenge. Many of the mines had collapsed and then been flooded by torrential rain. Diamond prices were slumping, credit was scarce, and miners were leaving in large numbers. Many people thought that the exhaustion of the crumbly yellow topsoil spelled the end of the Kimberley diamond industry. But Rhodes kept his nerve, discovering that the blue ground underneath, while harder to work, was still rich in potential. Mining regulations were changing, allowing individuals to own several claims at a time, and this encouraged Rhodes to start buying and amalgamating holdings. Meanwhile, individuals who would play important roles in his life were appearing on the scene, including the financier Alfred Beit, who would become a close business partner and trustee of his final will.

Creating De Beers

In August 1877, at the age of 24, Rhodes had a second heart attack, which rattled him so badly that he barricaded himself into his room, insisting that he had seen a ghost. Barely a month later, on 19 September, travelling out on the veld and well before he had enough money to bequeath to anyone, he made his first will. Written hastily on a crumpled piece of paper, it left all his possessions not to his family but to the British Secretary of the Colonies, to be used for "the extension of British rule throughout the world." According to his banker Lewis Michell, if his "daily companions amid the diamond claims and debris heaps of Kimberley had seen this astonishing document, [they] might well have questioned his sanity of mind."[4]

But Rhodes kept his focus and, three years later, with a number of friends, set up the De Beers Mining Company, with the ultimate aim of controlling overall production. It took him just seven more years to achieve that. By 1887, at the age of 34, with the financial help of Lord Nathaniel Mayer Rothschild (1840-1915) and Alfred Beit (1853-1906), Rhodes controlled 90% of the world's output of diamonds. Friends attributed this success to his personal qualities. According to one admirer, "He had to adopt different tactics with each man according to his character as he read it, and in the end, by his tact, his wonderful judgement of human nature, and his dogged perseverance he succeeded in persuading all interested to his way of thinking."[5] Two years later, Rhodes went to London and Paris to set up a diamond-buying syndicate that would purchase the entire output of the mines and sell it at prices that would guarantee an acceptable profit.

His management of the industry attracted admiration and controversy. To reduce diamond thefts, which were costing more than £90 million per year, Rhodes housed the African mine workers in compounds for the duration of their contracts (typically 2-3 months), and prevented them from contacting illicit diamond buyers. This infuriated the shopkeepers in Kimberley who lost the miners' business; but others argued that the camps ensured good food and shelter for the workers at a reasonable cost and prevented them from dissipating their earnings on liquor.[6] The impact for the mine-owners was even clearer: within twelve months, total recovery of diamonds rose from 30% to 95%.[7]

Jealousy and suspicion were also on the rise. There were occasional marches through Kimberley by disaffected diggers who assumed that Rhodes was using underhanded methods to succeed where they had not. Early on, Rhodes was even accused of bribing a rival pumping company not to compete with him, and he may have slipped back to Oxford in 1876 to escape a court case as much as to brush up on his Aristotle.

While Rhodes was still amalgamating the diamond industry, gold was discovered in 1886 on the Witwatersrand, in the neighbouring Transvaal Republic. The displaced diamond diggers of Kimberley began rushing to the mining camp of Johannesburg and already successful men like Rhodes and Beit followed. Rhodes missed several opportunities through bad advice and even more when he rushed to the deathbed of Neville Pickering, but did well overall, with the result that his company The Consolidated Gold Fields of South Africa became one of the richest and most powerful in the industry. The economic impact of the gold rush on the Transvaal was remarkable. In the ten years after the discovery of gold, the total revenue of the Transvaal rose sixteen-fold—from £23 million to almost £400 million.[8]

In 1880, the same year that De Beers was incorporated, Rhodes was elected to the Cape Parliament as the Member for Barkly West, a mining town close to Kimberley. This would be the first step in a political career that led to his becoming Prime Minister a decade later. Despite promoting public service in his final will, his entry into politics was not a shining example of selflessness. He wanted to ensure a rail link between Kimberley and the sea and to encourage tariff and taxing policies that would be favourable to the mining industry.

His new position would also be a listening-post, offering him advance notice of developments affecting his business and the amalgamation of the diamond industry. It would also add to his personal prestige in London, where financial markets regarded mining ventures as highly risky. A year later, he told a friend how difficult it was to sell diamond shares in the City and that "only a small circle have touched the rubbish floated here."[9] But Rhodes persisted, with remarkable results.

One of his key backers, Lord Rothschild, later described the setting up of De Beers as "simply a fairy tale". "You have succeeded in establishing . . . a marvellously steady market for the sale of your production, and [ensuring] that those who are selling diamonds are quite as concerned in maintaining the price as the purchasers."[10] Still, he warned Rhodes against forcing up the price of diamonds too far and using any of the company's money for "imperial" schemes. "We have always held that the De Beers Company is simply and purely a diamond mining company."[11] It is hard to assess now how prudent Rhodes was in pricing production; but, on the second point, he ignored the financier's advice entirely.

Protecting the "Suez Canal"

Rhodes first dreamt of occupying Central Africa as a student at Oxford, walking in Christ Church Meadow—or so he recalled. Yet, except to the few who read his first will and "Confession of Faith", drafted at Oxford at the age of 24, he showed no sign of that ambition in his first decade in South Africa. As an M.P., however, it was inevitable that events on the frontier would give those early musings new life.

His immediate concern was Bechuanaland (now Botswana), which by 1882 was being fought over by four rival African groups, each of which was promising large tracts of land to any European volunteers who would fight on its side. In one historian's words, "It may be imagined what a disorderly crew of shady adventurers, cattle and horse thieves and land sharks had been attracted by this bait."[12] At first, Rhodes opposed establishing a British protectorate over Bechuanaland, preferring that the Cape Colony control the area itself; then, he accepted that a protectorate was the most practical means of keeping a trade and military route open to central Africa. Two years later (in December 1887), with the "Scramble for Africa" among European powers at full throttle, Rhodes grew concerned that that narrow route to the North—which he referred to as the "Suez Canal"—could soon be cut off. The Germans from the West, the Portuguese from the East, and the Dutch from the Transvaal Republic were all courting the king of the Ndebele people, Lobengula, for exclusive rights of passage and trade on his lands. And it was not to be ruled out that the Belgians from the North would also join in the contest.

The Ndebele were an offshoot of the Zulus, who broke away from their parent group during the reign of Shaka Zulu (1787-1828) at about the time the Dutch started moving out of the Cape Colony to escape British control. That "Great Trek" (1836-1854) created new Afrikaner-run republics (the Transvaal, Natal, and the Orange Free State), but also sowed conflict with the original owners of the land, contributing to the downfall of the Zulu Kingdom. In one battle alone, at Blood River in 1837, Afrikaners slaughtered 3,000 Zulu warriors in retaliation for the killing of some 69 *voortrekkers*.[b] Meanwhile, the Ndebele had been making their way slowly from Zululand to the North, taking over other peoples' land in the same way the Boers had done. Now, to avoid the Boers, they were forced to move even further north and seized land occupied by the Kalanga and Shona peoples in what is now Zimbabwe. By 1890, the Ndebele had been there for fifty years and had made Bulawayo their capital.

Some writers have described the Ndebele, like the Zulus, as one huge army, whose very name was derived from their method of fighting: *Those who hide behind the long shields.* Their first king Mzilikazi died in 1868 and, as he had had three hundred wives, the succession was in doubt for a time. But his son Lobengula succeeded him in 1870, the same year Rhodes arrived in Africa. He was a man of commanding authority, intelligence, and some said restraint—which would be tested in the extreme. A large man, he was—in William Plomer's delightful phrase—"every ounce a king". He was also cruel.[c] Pounded and cheated by the British, his dynasty would die with him.

---

b   Boers who participated in the Great Trek.

The Boers of the Transvaal were the first to reach an agreement with Lobengula, perhaps in part because one of their leaders had warned the King against trusting the British: "When an Englishman once has your property in his hand, then he is like a monkey that has its hands full of pumpkin seeds; if you don't beat him to death, he will never let go."[13] In July 1887, the King agreed that the Transvaal should have jurisdiction over their own subjects in Matabeleland and keep a consul at his court. Six months later, on Boxing Day 1887, Sir Sidney Sheppard, Administrator of the new Crown Colony of British Bechuanaland, asked his deputy John Moffat to persuade Lobengula to change his mind. Moffat was in a good position to do so, as he was the son of the missionary Robert Moffat who had been a close friend of Lobengula's father.

It is unclear whether the younger Moffat was fully aware of the scheming he was part of, as he later denounced some of its consequences. If he was, it is hard to imagine a more extreme betrayal of African values of friendship and loyalty. On 11 February 1888, he persuaded the King to disown his agreement with the Transvaal, sign a treaty of "perpetual friendship" with Queen Victoria, and forgo entering into an agreement with any other power without the explicit go-ahead of the British High Commissioner in Cape Town.

---

c   One eye-witness described a man having his nose, ears, lips, and forehead skin cut off for drinking some of the King's beer, while drunk. 'The next day I heard that this unfortunate wretch was still alive. It was awful to see how the king enjoyed the spectacle." (Thompson, pp. 112-113.)

The Rudd Concession

Nothing was yet certain, however. Other countries kept wooing the King and there were doubts even in London about what to do. In mid-1888, putting her signature to a letter drafted by liberal civil servants at the Colonial Office, Queen Victoria advised Lobengula to be wary of any concession and to give away "only an ox, not his whole herd."[14] At about the same time, Rhodes created a syndicate with two close friends, Charles Rudd and Francis Thompson, and sent them to negotiate mineral rights with Lobengula. On 30 October 1888, Lobengula granted the British "exclusive power over all metals and minerals situated and contained in his kingdoms, principalities and dominions" and—purportedly as a favour to the King—the right to expel any rivals from his territory. In return, Lobengula was to receive £13,000 a month in perpetuity, 1,000 rifles, 100,000 rounds of ammunition, and an armed steamer on the Zambezi River.[15] There was no mention of access to land or eventual settlement.

During the next few months, Rhodes worked hard to consolidate his slender hold on the territory. Neither the Cape Colony nor London was prepared to commit large sums to developing it; so, Rhodes decided to establish a Chartered Company (similar to the Hudson's Bay and East Asia Companies) to exploit the new mineral concessions and oversee eventual settlement. Lobengula was wavering again and sent a deputation of two elders to England to meet "the great white Queen". Eventually, the King—who could not read or write—said that he was not aware of what he had signed and demanded that the document be returned to him, so that his advisers could study it again. Anger was building, spurred on by other Europeans in Bulawayo who had learned in foreign newspapers about the concession Lobengula had signed. The

King felt trapped, suspecting that he had been tricked and expecting an invasion at any moment.

In January 1889, in a letter dictated to the international press, Lobengula suspended the so-called Rudd Concession until further notice. That provoked new concerns on the part of "native protection" societies in England and a request from the Colonial Office to see the full text of the Concession. In forwarding it to London, the High Commissioner in Cape Town argued that "the effect of the concession to a gentleman of character and financial standing [i.e., Rhodes] will be to check the inroad of adventurers as well as to secure the cautious development of the country with proper consideration for the feelings and prejudices of the natives."[16] Even at the time, such disingenuous reassurances must have raised eyebrows in Whitehall.

In February 1889, Rudd wrote to the King to reassure him. "I hear white people have been telling plenty of lies about [us] . . . saying we wanted your land. Do not believe them. We want nothing but the right to work for gold and metals and we are the only people who are able to work so large a country and to pay you well for it."[17] In tandem, Rhodes advised Thompson, who was still in Bulawayo, not to underestimate the competition, "Why not offer [rivals] a piece of country on shares, [with us] funding the expenses . . . Remember you have a country as big as one of the Australian Colonies and if we are too greedy we may lose all."[18]

In England, opposition to creating a chartered company was mounting, with some suggesting that direct rule by the Crown would be fairer to the local populations. The London Chamber of Commerce complained that a monopoly over the mineral wealth of an entire country contravened the principles of free trade. The Colonial Office worried about the costs of an eventual war. Missionaries objected to buying mineral rights with guns. Other critics cited the stagnant economy in Kimberley at the time as an example of the risks of putting everything in the hands of one strong company.

However, on 29 October 1889, after an intense personal campaign on Rhodes's part, Queen Victoria granted a Royal Charter of Incorporation to the British South Africa Company, 20% of whose shares were to be funded by De Beers and the rest by individual investors. There were certain conditions. Downing Street reserved a right of supervision. Special clauses protected the indigenous population and stipulated freedom of religion and trade. And the initial term was for 25 years, subject to cancellation in the event of abuses. But the Company was now equipped with most of the powers of a modern state over a very large territory with no explicit northern boundary.

Forcing an Agreement

Fearing that Francis Thompson was not up to the task of reviving the Rudd Concession, Rhodes now sent his friend Dr. Jameson to Bulawayo to meet Lobengula. Naturally enough, the King was suspicious, but the new visitor brought more than his natural charm; he carried morphine to treat the King's gout. In the fanciful words of one writer, "Within moments, Lobengula's pain and anguish of mind evaporated, and perhaps for the first time in his life, he felt at ease in the company of another human being. He would, however, discuss no business."[19] Jameson returned to Kimberley empty-handed but confident that he had earned Lobengula's trust.

The King now called a meeting of all his senior advisers, one of whom had experience of the outside world. He pointed out that mining entailed access to land, even if that had not been made explicit. Where would the newcomers produce food and firewood? Who would work for them? Others at the meeting agreed, and Lobengula's mood darkened. His "prime minister", Lotshe, who had advised the King to sign the Rudd Concession, remained silent. Making a scapegoat of him, Lobengula ordered that he be brought behind the royal enclosure and executed, together with his family, dependants, and livestock. Hearing that other killings were planned, Thompson fled across the border to Mafeking in the Northern Cape and alerted Rhodes.

Aghast at the news, Rhodes sent Jameson back to Bulawayo with Thompson to see the King, who greeted the Doctor like an old friend. But he refused to parley or even accept the first shipment of arms that had arrived for him. Jameson bided his time, spending the next three months in the King's court, being made an honorary chief, and asking occasionally whether he could send a small party of miners into the territory. He may also have been increasing his doses of morphine to advance his purposes. Eventually, the King agreed that Jameson could re-work an old mining concession at Tati on the southern border with Bechuanaland.

At the end of January 1890, a party of Royal House Guards arrived in Bulawayo in full uniform to present gifts and notify the King of the signing of the Royal Charter setting up the South African Company. Together with the official notification came a letter from the Colonial Secretary stressing to Lobengula the importance of the document. Taking no chances, Jameson replaced it with a forgery expressing unqualified support for the Rudd Concession and warning of imminent invasions of Matabeleland from the Transvaal Republic and Portuguese East Africa.

The King was now in a state of despair and insisted on seeing Rhodes; but Rhodes was too busy to visit. When Jameson complained that the miners at Tati had found nothing, Lobengula suggested offhandedly that they should consider searching elsewhere. The Doctor pounced at the "invitation", suggesting that the miners might go east into Mashonaland, and the King did not object. Jameson then asked whether Lobengula could provide the labour to cut the road in that direction and—we are told—he said yes.

Back in Kimberley, Jameson and Rhodes started recruiting "pioneers" for the occupation of Lobengula's land. The King caught wind of this and began realizing to what degree he had been tricked, threatening to expel all Europeans if preparations were not stopped immediately. He was particularly opposed to foreigners entering the eastern end of his territory on their way to Mashonaland, the very route which Jameson claimed Lobengula had approved. The only road he would allow would be straight through Bulawayo so that he could see the "miners" for himself.

Rhodes and Jameson sent the renowned hunter and guide Frederick Courtenay Selous (1851-1917)[d] to meet two royal advisers at the border who were to show him the way. But when they did not appear, Selous entered Matabeleland on his own, only to turn back in fear of his life when he learned that Lobengula was aware of it. The previous year, Selous had offended the King by killing some of his game and had been forbidden to return. So, Rhodes dispatched Jameson again to pressure Lobengula.[20]

Final Meeting with Lobengula

We have Jameson's own description of his last meetings with the King, showing the Doctor's capacity not just for deceit but also desecration. He and an interpreter by the name of Doyle

---

d His adventures are said to have inspired the character Allan Quartermain in H. Rider Haggard's 1885 novel King Solomon's Mines.

arrived at the King's kraal [enclosure] just before dawn. They walked in and sat on the ground. "The old man was asleep," Jameson related, "wrapped in his Karosses [animal-skin blankets]. Presently he woke, bounced to his feet and stark naked raged about the hut. 'Who told Selous he could make that road?' he shouted, and would not listen to a word I said. Still snorting defiance, he suddenly plunged through the door. We tried to follow, but he had bolted into his women's quarters, and we could not follow."

Jameson and Doyle returned to their wagon to await developments. When they learned that the King had gone to worship at a sacred goat kraal ten miles away, they left after dark and again arrived before dawn. "I waited until I saw smoke rising from the Kraal . . . Doyle and I walked over and entered." The floor was covered with dung (a traditional sealant), muffling their footsteps. "In the centre the King was sacrificing; his back was to us: the [animal to be slaughtered] lying on a small altar in front of him and beyond, in a semicircle, his doctors. He quickly saw they were looking at something behind him, and turned around. I never saw astonishment so plainly written on any face. He stood motionless, his jaw dropped, and with wide open mouth he gaped at us. We walked right up to him; as we did so, the doctors, with murmurs of rage and horror at our sacrilege, closed round us. I stopped, he was still motionless, and then I said—'The King told me I might make that road. Did the King lie?' How long the silence lasted I do not know, but at last he raised himself to his full height, looked me straight in the eyes. 'The King never lies,' he said; waved his doctors back to their places, turned his back on us and continued his sacrificing. 'I thank the King', I said."[21] Having eked out the concession, Jameson returned to the Cape Colony and started planning the expedition. It was the last time Jameson saw Lobengula.

CHAPTER FIVE

Five Crucial Years

SIX MONTHS LATER, on 25 June 1890, the "Pioneers" set out on a two-and-a-half month journey north. Rhodes's original inclination was to march directly to the royal capital Bulawayo and occupy Matabeleland itself, but prudence prevailed.

Instead, with the hunter Selous leading the way, the Pioneers hacked a road through forest and brushland to the east of Lobengula's main territory towards Mashonaland which the King also controlled. Although they expected trouble and were accompanied by hundreds of soldiers and police, according to one first-hand account, the only casualties were four wildebeest and a hippopotamus killed for food and a lion shot for its hide. Lobengula sent emissaries twice to urge the settlers to turn back and they encountered small groups of Ndebele warriors along the way, but they never exchanged fire.[1] None of this was the result of British luck or bravery or common sense; all of it was due to the King's restraint and, above all, to his keen awareness that British weapons would overwhelm the Ndebele if they launched an attack.

One man's diary of the trek reads like an English schoolboy's adventure story:

> We had hardly finished drawing up our laager [camp] when 18 Matabele warriors appeared on the scene. They crossed the river and came swaggering into our camp as if they owned it. They were a tough looking lot; big hefty men, variously armed with assegais [spears] and guns of many patterns. They all carried ox-hide shields, the hallmark of the soldier. Borrow took the opportunity of airing his Sindebele [the Ndebele language] on them and chaffed them; which amused them mightily and they roared with laughter at his jokes. The next day our Matabele friends were still loafing about the camp and were becoming rather a nuisance, so we gave them an ox to eat, and told them to go home. They took the ox, crossed the river driving it in front of them, and were seen no more.
>
> On that afternoon we had a football match in the bed of the river. 'B' Troop had challenged the world, that is to say the whole of the rest of the Pioneer Corps and 'A' Troop of the Police. It was terrible work running about in ankle-deep sand, but we managed to get through with it, and the first rugby football match played in the country resulted in a draw, slightly in favour of 'B' Troop.
>
> On July 14th we started in to make a good drift across the river. Selous' patrols returned in the evening and reported that they had not come across any Matabele. They had visited several kraals and had found the Banyai—as the natives in that part of the country were called—in a very miserable condition, mostly living in

holes in the rocks . . . They said that they had been raided some months back by the Matabele, who had killed all the old men and women that they could lay their hands on, and taken away the young men, girls, and cattle. This the Matabele called 'collecting taxes'.[2]

The English were not the only ones who looked back on these events nostalgically. In his vivid 1967 novel, *On Trial for My Country*, the Zimbabwean writer Stanlake Samkange (1922-1988) imagines an afterlife in which Lobengula and Rhodes answer to their respective fathers for their mistakes. "My son," laments the first Ndebele king Mzilikazi, "my heart sinks with sorrow and pain to see what my people are today. No more does the sun rise on the glittering glory of the sharp spears of the Ndebele marching to do battle in yonder mountains. No more does fear of the Ndebele make the Shona sleep like squirrels, huddled up in caves with their cattle and goats. The valleys of the mountains [no longer] echo the thudding hoofs of a thousand, thousand cattle on their way to Ndebele kraals; Shona women and children are no more our slaves. Instead, the Ndebele have become the Shona—the slaves of the white man. They are now scattered all over the land like the dry leaves of a tree in autumn and like the leaves of a tree they only live to fall down, die and be buried."[3]

The First Ndebele War

The first year proved hard for the settlers. They suffered heavy rain, malaria, and blackwater fever, found very little gold, and lost no time in airing their complaints to the Company. They were even upset by the cordoning off of the ancient ruins of

Zimbabwe[e], where an archaeological survey was underway at Rhodes's expense. Some hoped to scour the site for gold objects; but Rhodes wanted to preserve the ruins and any artefacts found there for posterity, declaring that anyone removing relics from the site would be deported immediately.[4] In 1891, Rhodes visited "his dominion" for the first time and calmed tempers to some degree with his optimism and energy. "It is quite a different Mashonaland since you came," wrote one settler, "for now everyone is hopeful." Rhodes even appeased a dour Scot who told him, "I would have ye know, Mr. Rhodes, that we didna come here for posterity."[5]

Over the next two years, an eerie peace prevailed but many knew that it could not last. In a masterpiece of unwitting understatement, a contemporary wrote: "It was not to be expected that a warlike tribe like the Matabele would acquiesce without a struggle."[6] Yet, the war that followed was largely the result of a series of blunders. Rhodes and Jameson were aware that they had strained the patience of the Ndebele to near breaking-point and they did not want to provoke them further. They also knew that the Company could not afford prolonged hostilities.

In July 1893, Lobengula sent about 2,500 warriors to punish Shona people near Fort Victoria for allegedly stealing some of the King's cattle. They had strict instructions not to harm

---

e The palace city of Great Zimbabwe was the capital of the 11th-15th century Shona (or Karanga) empire and its remains are the largest and oldest surviving stone construction in sub-Saharan Africa. Despite Rhodes's strictures to the settlers, he appropriated some of the long-necked soapstone birds (believed to be talismanic images of the African fish eagle) that were found on the site. The "Zimbabwe bird" remains the symbol of The Rhodes Trust and a large copy crowns the cupola of Rhodes House in Oxford.

Europeans but their attacks on the Shona, many of whom now worked for the settlers, caused both groups to flee to the security of the fort. Lobengula's commander demanded that the Shona men, women, and children be handed over for punishment, but the British officer in charge of the fort refused. Jameson, who arrived on 17 July, ordered the Ndebele to return home and sent an armed party after them to ensure their withdrawal. The commanding officer, Captain C.F. Lendy, opened fire on the Ndebele when he found them attacking a Shona settlement. Remarkably, heeding their instructions not to shoot any whites, the Ndebele continued their retreat without fighting back. But Lendy pursued them, killing about twenty of them and wounding many others.

Jameson now reported to the High Commissioner in Cape Town, Sir Henry Loch, that the Ndebele had attacked Lendy's party. Preparing for war, Jameson alerted Rhodes that he might have to attack Bulawayo. Rhodes urged caution, cabling back: "Read Luke XIV:31." ("Or what king will march to battle against another king, without first sitting down to consider whether with ten thousand men he can face an enemy coming to meet him with twenty thousand?") But Jameson was under pressure from the settlers to raise an armed force and he promised land, gold claims, and even a share of the King's cattle to anyone who volunteered. Critics of the Company, including Christian missionaries, now raised an outcry. The British High Commissioner Loch—who, the year before, had urged the Colonial Office to end Company rule and take over direct administration of the territory—warned Jameson to stand down. He also prevailed on Lobengula to be patient, forestalling further violence for several months.

In September 1893, Loch invited the King to send a party including Lobengula's half-brother and two counsellors to discuss peace. But on the way, in a mix-up of identities, the

British killed the two counsellors as suspected spies. Feeling betrayed, Lobengula now recalled 5,000 men who were conducting raids on the other side of the Zambezi River to prepare for war. With Loch's permission, the South Africa Company now raised an armed force, strengthened the police, and—in the words of a contemporary—prepared "to strike a blow for civilization."[7]

The fighting lasted only nine days. On 25 October 1893, on the banks of the Shangani River, 900 of the Company's men were surrounded by 5,000 Ndebele. The Company repulsed three charges, then routed the enemy "with great slaughter". It was the first use of the Maxim machine gun by the British and probably only the second in world history. (The Germans used it to suppress an uprising in northern Tanganyika in 1889.) The commander of the leading Ndebele regiment, Unondo, hanged himself on a tree rather than face Lobengula in defeat. A week later, near the headwaters of the Bembezi River, another 1,000 Ndebele were killed.

On 3 November Jameson entered Bulawayo, where the King had ordered his kraal to be destroyed as he retreated north, pursued by some of Jameson's men. Lobengula sued for peace, sending a large sum of gold in the hands of two settler soldiers as a token of good faith. But the two men kept the money for themselves and did not report it to their superiors. (They were later given long prison sentences.) So, the small column continued to chase the King until they were intercepted and killed by the royal bodyguard near the Shangani River. Strangely enough, given the much larger number of Africans killed in the brief war, white Rhodesians would later regard this moment the way Americans remember the Alamo. (A monument to the leader of that force, Allan Wilson, and his men stands near Rhodes's grave in the Matopos.) Soon afterward, Lobengula was also dead, perhaps from smallpox. It is also possible that he took his own life.[8]

More Expansion

In late 1889-early 1890, as Rhodes was planning the occupation of Mashonaland, he learned that the king of Barotseland, a vast territory north of the Zambezi River (now Zambia), was interested in seeking British protection. Local missionaries, including a Frenchman named François Coillard, had urged the Barotse ruler to do that, as they were converting very few people and thought that better security and postal and transport services would help their cause. "Here they expect to push the railway through to Cairo!" Coillard bubbled.[9] The possibility of such a protectorate was on Rhodes's mind in London as he made the case for a chartered company.

In June 1890, as Rhodes's Pioneers were moving towards Mashonaland, the Barotse leader granted the Company an exclusive monopoly over mineral exploration in his kingdom. Coillard was realistic about what would happen next: "I expect it will prove a mixture of good and bad. But I am more and more firmly convinced that it was the only chance the natives had to escape destruction. The Barotse are always plotting against each other. If the [Company] can give the country some sense of security it will be a blessing hitherto unknown. But we shall have to see whether their dealings correspond with their promises."[10]

In parallel, Rhodes had agents sign concessions with other African leaders between the Portuguese border in the east and the German one in the west. In due course, he had thirteen other agreements in hand, to which local rulers had put their X's almost certainly without knowing to what they were committing themselves. It is doubtful that any of them knew

English and almost certainly none of them appreciated what it meant to have individual "title" to land, as African land tenure was traditionally communal.

At the same time, Rhodes was also negotiating to take over the near-bankrupt African Lakes Company that controlled large areas close to Lake Nyasa. While an immediate concern was to protect English traders and missionaries from Arab slave raiders operating out of Zanzibar, Rhodes's main interest was in acquiring more land in a favourable climate suitable for colonial settlement. Once he had taken over the Lakes Company, he asked the British government to declare a protectorate over the area (now Malawi) and to allow the Company to administer it at its own expense. That was formalized in July 1894.

Most adventurers—let alone statesmen—would now have paused to savour their accomplishments; yet, Rhodes's ambitions at times seemed unquenchable. Great Britain had recognized Portugal's claim to the coast of Mozambique in 1817; but, when the Pioneers left for Mashonaland in 1890, Jameson had instructions to try to break through and seize the port of Beira. The reason was clear. The journey from Kimberley to Fort Salisbury was over 1,600 miles, whereas from Beira it was only 370. In the words of one historian, "the agents of a chartered company were proposing to invade the nearby colony of another European state in order to seize its territory."[11]

In November 1890, an expedition of fewer than twenty soldiers made its way almost undisturbed towards the port. The only casualty was the correspondent of *The Times* who was eaten by a lion. Two days short of their goal, they learned that the United Kingdom and Portugal had agreed to maintain the status quo for six months, pending a final agreement. They also agreed to the construction of a railway from Beira into the interior. Undeterred, Rhodes and Jameson tried to provoke an "insult to the British flag" at Beira in April 1891, hoping that it would trigger a change of mind in London. But, fortunately, the British prime minister Lord Salisbury stood his ground, checking Rhodes's adventurism and almost certainly preventing more bloodshed.[12]

Later that year, the Foreign Office put its foot down again when Rhodes manoeuvred to wrest the copper-rich Katanga region of what is now the Democratic Republic of the Congo from Belgium's Leopold II. Not surprisingly, Lord Salisbury remarked to the Queen at about that time, "The [Chartered] Company as a whole are quite inclined to behave fairly, but Mr. Cecil Rhodes is rather difficult to keep in order."[13]

Prime Minister

In 1890, at the age of 37, Rhodes became prime minister of the Cape Colony and headed a Cabinet said to be the most talented ever to govern the Colony. "In their pleasant little Parliament," wrote one biographer, "Rhodes was as conspicuous as a peacock in a poultry yard."[14] He brought with him the glamour of a wider world, of the Empire, of the unknown North, and of large business organizations. Members were pleased that he talked to them simply and frankly as an equal; and, for now, they were under his spell. Even fierce critics have acknowledged that he was a man of consummate political skill.

During his five and a half years as Prime Minister (July 1890-January 1896), Rhodes balanced his imperial ambitions with a broad range of domestic initiatives. He promoted agricultural production by creating a Ministry of Agriculture for the first time; saving the Colony's orange groves from pests by introducing the American ladybird (ladybug); bringing in experts from California to improve fruit growing and packing;

and reviving the wool trade by passing the drastic Scab Act, which called for the compulsory isolation of flocks infected with that disease. He upgraded the Cape breed of horses by importing Arab stallions and developed an export trade in horses to India. On a visit to Constantinople in 1894, he convinced the Sultan to give him Angora goats to mix with the Cape stock and improve the quality of the mohair already being exported. And he distributed American vines to wine growers in the Western Cape who were being ruined by phylloxera (a plant louse that attacks vines).

He also proposed the creation of a bilingual (English- and Dutch-speaking) university, anticipating the argument he would later make for the Rhodes Scholarships. Its greatest impact, he predicted, would be when the students returned home, "tied to one another by the strongest feelings that can be created [between] the age of eighteen to twenty-one; and they would go forth into all parts of South Africa prepared to make the country."[15] Unfortunately, the idea did not bear fruit, even though it almost certainly would have had positive effects not only in education but also in the political arena.

Rhodes and the Afrikaners

Throughout his career, and even more so as prime minister, Rhodes made a point of nurturing a close relationship with the conservative Dutch-speaking population, involving them in all his projects, including the settlement of Rhodesia. This helped promote his political agenda within and beyond the Cape Colony but often came at the expense of his own principles and the loyalty and admiration of his liberal allies.

Although the Dutch had been in the Cape since 1652 and the British took it over only in 1806, many English-speaking politicians regarded it as a purely British colony and the

Afrikaners as guests in their own homeland. Rhodes never shared that view. As early as 1878, he told Dr. Jameson: "The Dutch are the coming race in South Africa and they must have their share in running the country."[16] In 1882, he supported the use of the Dutch language in parliament, removing a key grievance of Cape Afrikaners. That bill had been proposed by the leader of the Boers' party (the Bond) Jan Hendrik Hofmeyr, who became a political ally and friend. Rhodes also supported the teaching of the Dutch Reformed faith in schools and the banning of public transport on Sundays. Some Afrikaners started praising him in Biblical terms. In 1883, the editor of the Dutch-language paper *Onze Courant* described him as a young man of "Davidian" appearance. "He has about him the air of the woodlands, heaths and hedges of the southern counties of Old England; but much exercise in the affairs of life . . . has made him a very Methuselah in shrewd, business-like qualities."[17]

To court the Afrikaners, Rhodes even converted from being a free trader to a protectionist. In May 1886, he voted with the Bond to abolish the excise tax on Cape brandy. Although Calvinists generally preached temperance, most of the western wine growers were Boers of French-Huguenot extraction and they resented anything that would complicate their sales. The liberal politician John X. Merriman wrote to a friend: "Rhodes's apostasies have made me feel sicker than a stuck hog. Here you have a fellow with the education of an English gentleman offering himself up for sale."[18]

At the suggestion of the Afrikaners, he supported adding a flogging clause to the Master and Servants Act, although Rhodes insisted—rather feebly—that it should only be applied after a second instance of disobedience. The clause had been voted down in Parliament twice before, because while the lashing was to be administered by local magistrates and would replace fines and prison terms that had proved ineffective, the magistrates would in fact have very little discretion and be obliged to accept the word of the employers. Some opponents objected that, while they believed in firmness, servants should still be treated as human beings; others worried that the change would make it harder to hire Africans. One parliamentarian observed that while the clause was intended to apply principally to African servants and "coloured" [mixed race] farm workers, there could not be one law for Africans and another for Europeans. "It was regarded by many," he said, "and I think rightly, as a disgrace to the Statute Book."[19]

Then, more ominously, Rhodes moved closer to the Bond position on African suffrage, which many Afrikaners saw as a long-term threat to their survival. One of the reasons so many of the Boers left the Cape in the 1830s and 1840s to settle in the North was the British abolition of slavery on 1 January 1834. Fifty years later, some Afrikaners were still nostalgic for the days when there was no confusion about the respective roles of Europeans and their African subordinates. But even more of them resented the idea that Africans should now have any political rights at all. In the Boer-run Transvaal Republic and Orange Free State, only Europeans could vote, whereas in the Cape Colony Africans and persons of mixed-race descent had that right, provided they met the same conditions as everyone else (i.e., they owned a minimum amount of property).[f]

Although Rhodes depended on African votes in his own constituency, in 1892 he tightened the voting rules for everyone, tripling the property qualification from £25 to £75 [£3,250 to £9,750 in current values] and adding an education test. Voters

---

f   Voting rights were also limited in the UK, where there was no universal male suffrage until 1918.

would now have to be able to sign their names and write their addresses and occupations. While that new condition applied to all voters, it was especially damaging to the African electorate, as only 4% of African males could read and write.[20] What startled many, however, was the strong language that Rhodes used in justifying these changes.

Afrikaner politicians did not generally voice their reactionary views in public and Rhodes seemed at times to feel that he should be their mouthpiece. "As long as the Natives remain in a state of barbarism, we must treat them as a subject race and be lords over them," Rhodes said in the debate. (For him, the word "barbarism" meant something rather precise: a lack of Western education and a preference for communal over individual land tenure.) Arguing that Africans did not want the vote, he added, "There would be no injustice in refusing the franchise to the natives as a whole." He saw the "native question" as the main obstacle to South African unity and felt that the Cape would eventually have to make concessions to the Boer republics on this point. That would mean a "readiness to take up an Indian despotism [i.e. British imperial practices in India] in dealing with the barbarism of South Africa."[21] But Rhodes could only go so far to appease the Afrikaners on this point, thanks to the Cape constitution, Cape Liberals, and (after 1892) a Liberal government in London.

While this was clearly a Faustian bargain that would haunt Rhodes's legacy long into the future, his alliance with the Boers was central to his success. The English-speaking politician J.T. Molteno claimed that "Without Hofmeyr and the Bond, Rhodes would have been a rich man only, not a world name and an empire-builder . . . [They] were the basis and foundation of [his] political power."[22] Rhodes's definitive biographer Robert Rotberg concedes that Rhodes had yoked himself to "a political ox-cart" which was suspicious of new ideas and of Rhodes's dreams of a united South Africa. "Yet Rhodes was to ride the ox-cart to fame and to power. The oxen came to do his bidding."[23]

Of course, Rhodes and the Afrikaners did not always see eye to eye. In 1895, they were disappointed when he refused to reinstate a magistrate who had been dismissed for his harshness towards Africans. Then, the Colony's sheep farmers—who were more conservative than those producing wine and wheat—reacted bitterly to the Scab Act, complaining that the State, as well as "foreigners", "capitalists", and "merchants", wanted to impoverish them and turn them into labourers. Rhodes also irritated the wine industry by restricting African consumption of alcohol. As an employer, Rhodes had every interest in keeping his workers sober; but the winegrowers saw the ban as a greater threat to the industry than the outbreak of phylloxera that had recently decimated their vineyards.[24]

Rhodes and the Boers were also at odds over what was to be the most momentous legislation of his career.

The Glen Grey Act

In South Africa, like elsewhere in the British Empire, there was an ongoing debate about whether to build upon or simply sweep away traditional institutions and practices. In 1894, a Resident Magistrate in the Transkei region doubted that the "political institutions of the modern British type are the natural and proper terminus of national life in every clime and nation."[25] There were also competing objectives in "native" policy. Some wanted a prosperous and independent African farming class; others sought nothing more than a pool of cheap labour. Many hoped that African and British interests would coalesce as Africans adopted British ways; others insisted that British and African interests would always be at odds. "As soon as a native acquires a little education," wrote one patronizing administrator in 1895, "he deems manual labour beneath him, and his only ambition is to obtain employment as an interpreter or policeman, in some magisterial establishment, or as a teacher in some mission school." Too much education, misapplied, he thought, hindered rather than encouraged "progress".[26]

Rhodes always had a deep personal interest in these subjects and, as Prime Minister, he reserved the portfolio of "native" affairs for himself, resolving to introduce a more systematic policy on matters that had been the object of, at best, benign neglect. The trigger for the new legislation was Rhodes's concern that land already set aside for Africans in the Eastern Cape was becoming overcrowded as a result of high birth rates, better health conditions, and, in the British view, the smaller number of deaths in the once-endless "native" wars. The Act changed the rules for the land reserves in two districts (Glen Grey and Fingoland), introduced private land titles, and launched an experiment in local self government. It also imposed a labour tax on landless or unemployed Africans to force them to seek jobs. This feature of the Act proved extremely controversial and was never implemented.

To prevent the sub-division of land into smaller and smaller fragments and to eliminate quarrelling among survivors, each individual was to receive a plot of about twelve acres, transferrable only to the eldest son on the occasion of the owner's death. To protect families from losing their land to creditors or neighbouring farmers and to keep the community and tenure system intact, lots could not be sold without government consent. Despite its positive intent, this aspect of the law attracted immediate criticism. European farmers who had settled in the area and were now obliged to move out were obviously disgruntled. A group of African small-scale commercial farmers pointed out that restricting the size of holdings would prevent land consolidation and improvement. In the words of one of them: "Surely Mr. Rhodes can't expect that all Natives will be equal. He himself is richer than others; even trees differ in height."[27] Liberals, who had long backed individual land tenure, worried that the lots were too small and uneconomic. Nor did they like the primogeniture rule, making it inevitable that many young men would be forced into the labour market.

The other key feature of the Glen Grey Act was the setting up of local councils, partly elected by Africans and partly nominated by the government, which were authorized to tax residents for building schools, roads, and bridges, tree-planting, and other social purposes. In the words of Thomas Fuller, one of Rhodes's closest political allies, "It was founded on the conviction that the tribal life of the [African] was an organised life; that the [African] for ages had been a born politician in his own sphere, and that the way to bring him into line with civilised life and a true citizenship was to develop and give play to these instincts, and put public responsibility upon his shoulders to the extent to which he could bear it."[28]

The labour tax (or, as some referred to it, the "tax on laziness") required any healthy African who was not a landowner or working at a regular wage for a genuine employer to pay ten shillings [£60] per year to the government. "This was intended," in Fuller's words, "to drive the 'young bloods' out of the location to work, instead of lolling about all day in their blankets, as well as to provide labour for the [European] farmers."[29] Others objected "that the slow but sure absorption of the natives into the great industrial movements of the country was the best education in what Mr. Rhodes styled 'the dignity of labour'."[30]

To Rhodes's annoyance, Fuller proposed exempting Africans from that tax if they were helping other Africans work their plots. When the amendment failed, Fuller voted against the Bill, as he "considered that the balance between white and black had been disturbed, and that the Bill as it finally passed was unfair to native interests."[31] As it turned out, the labour tax was never enforced and was eventually repealed. All the same, it earned the Prime Minister one of the most-cited damnations of his age. "Mr. Rhodes is a very reasonable man," said Sir William Harcourt, the British Chancellor of the Exchequer at the time. "He only wants two things. Give him [Trade] Protection and give him Slavery [the labour tax] and he will be perfectly satisfied."[32]

Despite voting against it, Fuller later described the law as "a great success". About 160,000 Africans were settled in the reserves and thanks to their "excellent administration", schools were built, trees were planted, and social regulations were enforced. "In fact, it was often said that, in their zeal for education and social improvement, the Glen Grey and Fingoland natives put to shame the indifference shown to such matters in some of the northern districts of the Colony."[33] Rhodes regarded the Act as progressive, saying shortly after, "We are prepared to stand or fall by it . . . If [it] is a success, we shall see neighbouring states adopting it . . . I hope we will have one native policy in South Africa."[34]

Others argued that setting up separate institutions for Africans would "hinder their fusion with the life and institutions of the country—a fusion which ordinary methods would in the long run best secure."[35] Although well-intended, the ultimate effect of the local councils was to remove Africans from the wider political processes of the Cape Colony. On top of that, the councils were purely advisory and dominated by traditional leaders who rarely stood up for the people they were supposedly serving. Despite that, another prominent progressive, Sir James Rose-Innes, who opposed the Act, had changed his tune by

1905. "The segregation of the races within certain limits . . . is the policy to aim at in the future."[36] That vision would prove the curse of South African life, for Africans and Europeans alike, for the next one hundred years.

Some historians have cautioned against drawing broad conclusions from a piece of legislation that was meant to resolve issues in one small part of the Cape Colony.[37] But one scholar has described the law as part of "the transformation of Africans into dehumanized cogs in a violent and exploitative industrial machine."[38] What is certain is that, when the principles of the Act were applied more widely in the country, the majority of South Africans were shut out of national politics and decision-making. It was a British government— and a Liberal one at that—not Rhodes, that sealed the fate of the African population in 1910, by agreeing to a fundamentally segregationist constitution for the new Union. But the Glen Grey Act, proud as Rhodes was of it, and the arguments he used in proposing it were key building blocks in the separation of the races.

1895

The next year was pivotal for Rhodes. On 1 January he was named to the Privy Council[g] and was at the pinnacle of his political and financial success. Prime Minister of the Cape Colony, Chairman of the Board of the British South Africa Company, head of the Consolidated Gold Fields Company,

---

g   The Privy Council is a body of advisers appointed by the British monarch, usually as a personal honour, from candidates who have held high political, legal, or ecclesiastical office in Britain or the Commonwealth. (UK Cabinet Ministers become members of the Council automatically.)

and one of the wealthiest and most famous men in the world, he had reason to think "in continents" rather than just about day-to-day matters. When some of his enemies said: "Ignore him," Edward Garrett, the editor of the *Cape Times*, answered, "One might just as well try to ignore Table Mountain."[39] Yet, on 31 December Rhodes was a broken man.

Midway between that peak and abyss, in May 1895, a Royal Proclamation formally gave the name "Rhodesia" to the Company's territories, which were now larger than Spain, France, and Germany combined. Although the announcement pleased him, the name was not Rhodes's idea. He would have been happy with "Zambesia", while Jameson preferred "Charterland". Some had even suggested that the territory be christened "Cecilia". It was the owner of the country's first newspaper *The Rhodesia Herald* four years before who had set the ball rolling.[40]

Expanding the British Empire had been Rhodes's ambition all his life but in just six years he had "painted the map of Africa red" more than anyone before or after him. The distance between Kimberley and the vague northern border of Rhodes's domain was the same as between London and Moscow. Over a large part of the Company's domain, a European colonial form of order had been established and railways and telegraph lines were under construction.[41] Unless India were to be regarded as a single unit, it was the largest British colony in the world and the second largest of any kind. Only the Belgian King Leopold II's grotesquely misnamed "Congo Free State" was larger. Rhodes was undoubtedly proud of his accomplishments and, in Professor Rotberg's words, since his "motives were more for power than riches, and were as much cosmic as crass, his conscience would not have been stained by what he had managed to achieve."[42]

In London, people who had once mocked him as the upstart

son of a country parson now began to bask in the glow of his achievements. He was a favourite among royals but also on the street, where the London carriage drivers waved their whips at him. Some still questioned his loyalty, as he had occasionally denounced the "Imperial factor" (i.e., direct intervention by the British government) when it did not suit his purposes. The same month that Rhodes became a Privy Councillor, he was refused admission to London's Travellers' Club. He liked gentlemen's clubs. "Civilised society," he observed once, "cannot exist without clubs and universities—and if I had to choose between the two I would be tempted to choose clubs. They are the avenues through which man becomes more than a work machine."[43] Nevertheless, he was not too disappointed by the Travellers' decision, having forgotten that a friend, now dead, had nominated him years before. He was already a member of the St. James's and Union Clubs, and the Athenaeum—Pall Mall's most select and exclusive club—elected him shortly after. But it was a sure sign of discord about him within the British Establishment.

In South Africa, too, while he was the darling of most Europeans and respected by many Africans for his stature and power, he was alienating some who used to look up to him. The feminist pioneer Olive Schreiner, whose novel *The Story of an African Farm* (1883) was a worldwide bestseller, had once sought Rhodes's patronage. "He spoke to me more lovingly and sympathetically of [the novel] than anyone has ever done," she recalled.[44] But she was shocked by his support for the flogging Bill in 1890, even though it did not pass. Then, at a railway station, she was dismayed to see him give a warm handshake to his minister of transport who was in the midst of a corruption scandal. That was enough for her. "I turned on my heel, and went to my house."[45]

Then came the Jameson Raid.

CHAPTER SIX

Disgrace

INVADING THE TRANSVAAL Republic was an outrageous idea. But if it had worked, it might have won Rhodes a crown of laurels rather than thorns. It could also have prevented the South African War. Instead, it hung around Rhodes's neck for the rest of his life. And it raised tensions that erupted into war in 1899-1902, killing 80,000 people.

Although he had discussed the possibility a year earlier, while riding with Jameson on Table Mountain, and a few months before that with Jameson and the American mining engineer John Hays Hammond over campfires on a long trip to Rhodesia, Rhodes was not the first to try to put it into practice.[1] It was the British High Commissioner in Cape Town, Sir Henry Loch—the same man who had staved off the fighting between Jameson and Lobengula the year before—who took the first dangerous steps. In July 1894, Loch stationed the Imperial Bechuanaland Police on the Transvaal border, asked the Colonial Office to send five thousand troops as reinforcements, and requested permission to cross over into the Boer-run republic. The Colonial Secretary refused. Rhodes also objected, feeling that South African problems should be resolved among South Africans rather than in London.

Grievances of the Uitlanders

What had provoked this? The gold rush in the Transvaal had attracted thousands of foreigners to Johannesburg, including Boers and English-speakers from the Cape but also Americans and Europeans. By 1890, the *uitlanders* [foreigners], as the Afrikaners called them, were 60,000 strong—twice the white population of the rest of the Republic. Yet, far from appreciating their sense of enterprise and taxes—which funded 95% of its budget—the government saw the newcomers' urban habits, individualism, and materialism as a threat to rural Calvinist values and tried to isolate them. Only foreigners who had been residents for fourteen years—a condition which disqualified most of them—were allowed to vote. A separate legislature was established to deal with Johannesburg and mining matters, and its bills could only become law if approved by the main parliament, the *Volksraad*. To foil any political agitation, meetings of more than six people were forbidden. Yet, though not citizens, the *uitlanders* could be conscripted to fight in the Transvaal's occasional "native wars".

There were other issues, too. Incompetence and corruption in local government, as well as private monopolies, made life and running a business in Johannesburg expensive. Water, rail services, food, and dynamite (important in gold mining) were also costly. State schooling was in Dutch, forcing many English settlers, who were already paying most of the cost of public education through the tax system, to send their own children to expensive private schools. Hotheads talked about an uprising as early as 1890, but there was no widespread discontent. Most *uitlanders* had come freely and were making a better living than they had elsewhere.[2]

Eight years before, Rhodes had foreseen the situation. Writing to Lord Rothschild in January 1888, he said he was satisfied to have completely "shut in the Transvaal Republic so that it cannot expand." "If we leave matters now quietly to work with the development of the gold in the Transvaal, we shall gradually get a united S. Africa under the English flag. The diggers eventually will never endure a purely Boer Government; the whole matter is simply a question of time."[3] In between, Rhodes had done everything he could to persuade the crusty president of the Transvaal, Paul Kruger, to enter into closer economic relations with the Cape, including mutually beneficial railway lines and a customs union.

But, in Kruger, Rhodes's powers of persuasion had met their match. Kruger never trusted him. "This young man I like not," Kruger said once. "He goes too fast for me. He has robbed me of the north. I cannot understand how he manages it, but he never sleeps . . ."[4] Years later, in exile in Switzerland, Kruger was still livid. "Rhodes was Capital incarnate. No matter how base, no matter how contemptible, be it lying, bribery or treachery, all and every means were welcome to him."[5] But, as William Plomer observed in his 1933 biography of Rhodes, "The pot is often a good judge of the kettle's blackness."[6]

Far from cooperating with the Cape Colony, Kruger refused to enter into the Customs Union (as the Boer-run Orange Free State had done) and imposed heavy duties on pigs, brandy, cattle, and coal coming from the Cape. As most of these products were agricultural, the Cape's Dutch farmers were as irritated as Rhodes with the obstinacy of their "cousin" Kruger. His railway policy was also obstructive. At first, he refused to allow rail links between the two territories; then he relented but set rates at an almost prohibitive level.

More broadly, Rhodes saw Kruger as the greatest obstacle to his dream of a united South Africa and this was all the more painful as Rhodes sensed that he had only a few more years to live. Six months before the Jameson Raid, Rhodes told a friend, "The Kruger regime . . . must come to an end."[7] On the eve of the Raid, Rhodes was more precise: "I do not want to annex the Transvaal, but I want to see it a friendly member of a Community of South African States. I want equal rights for the English language, a Customs Union, a common Railway policy, a common Native policy, a central South African Court of Appeal, [and] British coast protection. I have tried to do a deal with old man Kruger and I have failed. I shall never bring him into line... What I want to do is to lay the foundation of a united South Africa."[8]

Preparations

The rest is a tale of dishonesty. Earlier in life, some had suggested that Rhodes was incapable of deception. "He would make the poorest of conspirators," said one acquaintance, "for to simulate what is not, or to dissimulate what is, is against the law of his nature."[9] Rhodes himself encouraged this misconception: "I find in life it is far better to tell the town-crier exactly what you are going to do, and then you have no trouble."[10] In one of his note-books, he claimed not to believe in keeping secrets: "Put yourself in no one's power. Tell no one anything in the strictest confidence. You [had] far better . . . put your confidential communication in the morning papers."[11] But the Jameson Raid proved that he could be an outright liar.

In fact, Rhodes went to great lengths to keep the Raid secret, even though rumours of it were circulating widely in Cape Town and Pretoria [the capital of the Transvaal]. When Rhodes was approached on the subject by a friend (Mrs. Van Koopman), he assured her that it was nothing more than "malicious gossip" and, taking her hands into his, told her that he respected her far too much to want to deceive her. The very moment they were talking, Jameson and his band of adventurers were preparing to cross the border into the Transvaal. Not surprisingly, Mrs. Van Koopman never spoke to Rhodes again.[12]

The supposed objective of the Raid was to rescue the *uitlanders* from political and economic injustice. But, to be credible, the invaders needed to be seen to be supporting rather than provoking a domestic uprising. Jameson later claimed that they did not intend to overthrow the government so much as force it into negotiations with the English-speaking population. By having a large enough force in Johannesburg, they hoped to persuade Kruger to organize a plebiscite of the whole population (Boers and English-speakers alike) on whether he should stay in office or be replaced. Jameson regarded this as "the least violent and safest" way of achieving their objective.[13]

Yet, not all the *uitlanders* were in a revolutionary mood. A petition signed by about 35,000 people—more than half the English-speaking population—was met by jeers in the Transvaal Parliament that if they wanted the franchise they would have to fight for it. The National Union of *Uitlanders*, which had been pressing for equal rights since 1892, remained weak. The mine owners were more interested in reducing the price of dynamite than obtaining the vote. Workers in Johannesburg were unhappy, but they had no leader. And, in November 1895, the head of the new Chamber of Mines appealed for calm: "All we want in this country is purity of administration and an equitable share and voice in its affairs. Nothing is farther from my heart than a desire to see an upheaval, which would be disastrous from every point of view."[14]

Economic motives also played a part. If it was becoming clear that there was little if any gold in Rhodesia—four years of production in Mashonaland had barely matched a day's output in the Transvaal—the long-term potential around Johannesburg remained high. Another consideration was that a more efficient administration of the Transvaal would increase mining profits by up to twenty percent.[15] Given his stake in the industry, Rhodes appears to have convinced himself that any uprising should be on his own terms. Once he embraced the idea, Rhodes went all out, ignoring the National Union of *Uitlanders* altogether, using the Consolidated Gold Fields Company office in Johannesburg and a secret "reform committee" of his own choosing to spearhead preparations, and having De Beers smuggle arms and ammunition to the future insurgents. But, as the appointed hour approached, the scheme began to unravel.

One Mistake After Another

Almost everything that could go wrong, now did. Jameson had planned a force of 1,500 men but had to settle with 500. He thought he could cover the 176 miles from the Bechuanaland-Transvaal border to Johannesburg in two days when—weighed down by equipment and arms and having to care for the horses—it would have been more realistic to plan on 4-5 days. He cut the telegraph lines running south but neglected a crucial link to Pretoria, meaning that Kruger was aware of Jameson's movements by the hour. The secrecy essential to the operation had been blown almost completely, with rumours circulating widely in Pretoria and Cape Town. Worst of all, the uprising that the invasion was meant to support never materialized. Rhodes and Jameson should not have been surprised by this. Rhodes's brother Frank, who was in Johannesburg trying to whip up revolutionary sentiment, had written to him two months before to say that people were more excited about the upcoming Christmas horse races than any personal grievances. "So long as people are making money," he wrote, "they will endure a great many political wrongs. Nothing is being done beyond a few desultory telegrams and deputations."[16]

Jameson, in the meantime, was being over-confident. Warned a month before that the Transvaal Afrikaners would mount a fierce defence, he replied with contempt: "I shall get through as easily as a knife cuts butter. You people do not know what the Maxim gun means. I have seen it at work."[17] In early December, Frank Rhodes cabled him to delay the "polo tournament"; on 18 December the American John Jay Hammond wired Rhodes to say that he should defer the "flotation". On 28 December emissaries from Johannesburg visited Rhodes at Groote Schuur and told him that the plot should be delayed for at least six months. To their great relief, Rhodes said that he would cable Jameson immediately to call everything off. Later that day, he informed a colleague that the "revolution had fizzled out like a damp squib" supposedly over arguments about what flag would be raised afterwards: the British or a republican one.

Jameson was due to cross the border the next day (29 December 1895) and was eager for guidance. He received it from several people, including Hammond in Johannesburg who cabled in semi-code: "Expert reports decidedly adverse. I absolutely condemn further developments at present." Rhodes's close colleague, Dr. Frederick Rutherfoord Harris, sent three telegrams on his behalf saying that all their foreign friends were "dead against" a "flotation" and that "We cannot have [a] fiasco." But there was no direct word from Rhodes that Jameson should return to Cape Town. When Rhodes decided to send a wire himself, he had run out of time, as Jameson had cut the telegraph lines. Some have suggested that Rhodes delayed deliberately, knowing that his message would not get through and that he had written it for posterity if the Raid failed.[18] But this is speculation.

Historians have wondered ever since what was going through Jameson's head. Perhaps he found it hard to believe that Rhodes would abandon a plan which they had prepared together so carefully over the previous year. He may have imagined that the Prime Minister was throwing up a smoke screen with his staff in Cape Town to disguise the hope that his usually reliable lieutenant would pull things off. Almost certainly, Jameson was feeling cocksure, as he and Rhodes had overcome obstacles of all kinds in the past. The lack of any sign of a rebellion in Johannesburg did not seem to matter much to Jameson. He had an undated letter from the "Reform Committee" inviting him into the Transvaal and Jameson now filled in the date. At dusk, he crossed the border and the die was cast.

Back in Cape Town, Rhodes had been entertaining a large group of people at Groote Schuur in good spirits, presumably because he assumed the Raid was now off. But, somehow, word got through to him. At 11 pm, Rhodes called a friend in town to his bedroom to say that Jameson had crossed the border. His face was white. The next morning, still looking ill and drawn—he had probably not slept—he told colleagues: "This is the finish of me," before adding, "The Dutch will never forgive me." Part of him was combative; but he was still distraught and even a little crazed. On Tuesday 31 December, he tried to persuade the British High Commissioner to travel immediately to Johannesburg to plead with Kruger for understanding; but, understandably, the High Commissioner refused. Then, he proposed to take his own special train to Pretoria, but was told that the Afrikaners would hang him. "Hang *me*?" Rhodes is said to have replied. "They can't hang me! I'm a Privy Councillor! There are only two hundred of us in the British Empire!"[19]

By then, it was too late. The Raiders had got as far as Doornkop, fourteen miles from Johannesburg, but were trapped in a narrow valley where their Maxim guns were no match for Boer marksmen up in the hills. Thirty of the Raiders were killed. On Thursday, 2 January 1896, they surrendered and, along with Jameson, and Rhodes's brother Frank, were thrown into prison. Jameson was to be sent back to Britain for trial, while Frank was to be tried for treason in Pretoria. The ringleaders were eventually sentenced to be hanged, but Rhodes bought their freedom.

Aftermath

Rhodes was now a broken man. He barely slept for five days, walking up and down in his bedroom all night or wandering around the mountain refusing to see anyone.[20] "He had altered the map of the world," noted a friend. "He seemed to own, or to be, South Africa . . . Then came the Raid, and within a few hours he was hurled from the pinnacle of prestige to be smashed and trampled in the dirt of exposure, failure and contempt."[21] In the view of his banker Lewis Michell, Rhodes knew that he had reverted to the indefensible "mediaeval right of private war". "Smitten with blindness, like a modern Samson he had essayed to pull down the pillars of an oppressive commonwealth, and, having failed, he must abide the result . . . [If he had] acted throughout on higher authority he would have stood on firmer ground."[22] Rhodes knew that he would have to step down as Prime Minister and cede his corporate responsibilities to others. He also worried that the British government would cancel the Charter of the South Africa Company. He even wondered if Rhodesia would be re-named. He told his secretary Le Sueur: "I have always loved the north—my north. They can't take that away. They can't change the name. Did you ever hear of a country's name being changed?"[23]

On 5 January Rhodes stepped down as premier but did not give up his parliamentary seat. Later in the month, he made a brief visit to England to save his Company's Charter, which he learned was not really at risk. He was still getting over the shock of failure and being abandoned by people he trusted. "His likes and dislikes were more often than not extreme," recalled his valet John Norris. "If he really cared for anyone he always overlooked their faults. Thus, it was very hard for him after the Raid to find his lifelong friends throwing him over. He was so cynical over some that it preyed on his mind to the last."[24]

One person whose faults he ignored was Jameson. His harshest words about him were, "Old Jameson has upset my apple-cart . . . Twenty years we have been friends and now he goes in and ruins me." But, he added, "I cannot go and destroy him."[25] Although they did not see each other for the rest of 1896, as Jameson was in London being tried for mercenary activities and spending several months in Holloway Prison, they remained close. Later that year, in the Matopos, when Lord Grey told him that he had bad news for him, Rhodes was relieved to hear what it was. A fire had destroyed much of his house at Groote Schuur; but Rhodes had feared that Jameson was dead.

The Raid is now largely forgotten, except among students of South African history. Certainly, none of the "Rhodes Must Fall" protesters cited it against him. But it was the main reason Rhodes was controversial in his own day. Jameson was naïve or deluded, or both. Shortly after returning to the UK to face justice at the Old Bailey, he confided to a friend: "When I started it was with the feeling that, if a single shot was fired, I should have failed." (He seems to have forgotten his bloodthirsty remark about cutting through the Transvaal Afrikaners like "butter" with a Maxim gun.) The same friend, the renowned neurologist Sir William Gowers, described the Raid as "the wildest of actions from the purest of motives."[26] Rhodes's fellow-MP, Thomas Fuller, thought the plot "wholly wrong" but "the outcome of mistaken patriotism, and undertaken with the desire to right great wrongs."[27] George Parkin, later the first secretary of the Rhodes Trust, recognized the logic behind the action. "But in doing this," he wrote, "[Rhodes] forgot that he was Prime Minister."[28]

The first formal inquiry into the Raid—by the Cape Parliament—was not completed until July 1896. Its conclusions might have pleased King Solomon. It found that Rhodes was fully informed of the operation but had never intended to invade the Transvaal Republic uninvited. All the same, his role violated his duty as Prime Minister. His former attorney-general, William Schreiner (brother of the novelist Olive), concluded that: "Misguided though they were . . . , I will never be led into the suggestion that his motives were at any time low or groveling or sordid: and I believe that a vast majority of the people, not only in this Colony but throughout South Africa, including the Transvaal, would say the same. The aim of Mr. Rhodes was a high one. I wish it had been a right one."[29] No one on either side of the House rose to continue the debate and the Report was adopted unanimously.

The British House of Commons took another six months to begin its hearings. By then, Rhodes's reputation in South Africa had been restored, largely because of his peacemaking in Rhodesia. In Cape Town, on 6 January 1897, 5,000 people saw Rhodes off to "face the music" in London. He was so moved by the size of the crowd that tears ran down his cheeks and he said to a friend, "Such appreciation as this generally comes after a man is dead."[30]

In London, he admitted that he had placed troops on the

border of the Transvaal—to be used by Jameson in "certain eventualities"—without informing the High Commissioner in Cape Town or the Board of Directors of the British South Africa Company. He also acknowledged that he had thought the people of Johannesburg deserved better treatment, even if that meant resorting to "extra-constitutional means". As for the Raid itself, "I may state that Dr. Jameson went in without my authority."[31] His friend W.T. Stead said later that Rhodes expected to be imprisoned and even planned what he would read in his cell. "I regretted that Mr. Rhodes was not sent to gaol, and told him so quite frankly."[32] But all he got was a slap on the wrist. As one writer put it, "The majority report censured Rhodes for a misuse of his powers but found nothing against his honour."[33] A likely reason for the light treatment was that Rhodes had cables suggesting that the Secretary of State for the Colonies Joseph Chamberlain had given his implicit go-ahead to the Raid. Chamberlain sat on the commission of enquiry and did not want to be exposed. In keeping the messages under wraps, Rhodes was also protecting his Charter, which Chamberlain had the power to revoke.

Lewis Michell thought the Raid a mere "picturesque and irregular episode" in the long tug of war between the Boer republics and the British Empire. Far from causing the South African War, he felt that the Raid had delayed it by embarrassing Great Britain and tying its hands.[34] Rhodes's first serious biographer, Basil Williams (1921) thought differently, suggesting that the Raid almost certainly helped precipitate the conflict four years later by vindicating the Transvaal President Kruger's sense of anxiety and pushing fellow-Boers in the Cape Colony and Orange Free State into his camp. "No one could have guessed that Rhodes could be so reckless or destructive . . . It was also a betrayal of his efforts throughout his political career to reconcile the British and the Dutch."[35]

Rhodes eventually recovered his poise. Fifteen months later, he was sounding philosophical: "I would be a very small human being if I altered through the recent troubles the ideas of a lifetime."[36] But he knew that his name would always be associated with a spectacular act of folly. Far from the public eye, in the calmness of the Senior Common Room at Oriel College, he told his former Oxford tutor A.G. Butler that the Raid had cost him more than £30 million. Butler replied that it would be better understood someday, but Rhodes was not so certain. "Not in my lifetime, perhaps never."[37]

CHAPTER SEVEN

War and Peace

I N MARCH 1896, the Ndebele rose up again in Rhodesia, but this time, rather than sparing the settlers, they killed about 160 men, women and children. By some accounts, infants were crushed alive in traditional mealie (corn) mills. It was hard to document such stories, but they fuelled a sense of vengeance among the settlers that did not subside for a very long time. Even Rhodes's attempt to negotiate peace would be resented by settlers still intent on avenging these wrongs. In June, the Shona, who were still regarded as the docile vassals of the Ndebele, also rebelled, killing European farmers, miners, administrators, and missionaries with surprising cold-bloodedness.

Since the 1893 war, both the Ndebele and the Shona had suffered deeply from the cruelty of the settlers and the "native police" (made up mainly of Zulus from further south). In Matabeleland, Jameson had confiscated up to 200,000 cattle on the grounds that they had belonged to Lobengula and were thus liable to seizure, apparently unaware that much of the herd was held in trust for his people. Large areas of land had been seized as well and given as rewards to settlers who had fought in the war. When the original occupants returned, they found themselves treated like tenants, subject to expulsion and forced labour. Ndebele women had been abused and raped by settlers.

In Mashonaland, a hut tax had been introduced, which many refused to pay; so, collectors used brutal methods to force compliance. While the tax was usually in the form of grain, livestock, or cash, sometimes it was collected as labour and whole villages would be marched off to work on a road, on a farm, or at a mine. Traditional leaders who stood in the way were fined, beaten, and humiliated. On one occasion, even the chief native commissioner for Mashonaland, whose responsibility was to ensure the welfare of Africans, burned down villages to enforce the tax. Drought, locusts, and rinderpest [a cattle disease] added to the misery; so, when Jameson diverted most of the police force to raiding the Transvaal, the Ndebele seized the opportunity to fight back. Difficult as it is to believe, Professor Rotberg suggests that Rhodes was not aware of any of these abuses as he had left the administration of the territory to his subordinates and only learned of them several months later during the peace talks in the Matopos Hills.[1]

For now, peace was the furthest thing from Rhodes's mind and he lost no time in joining "his" Rhodesians in the fight. In an intense battle on 9 May 1896, he found himself under fire for the first time in his life. Despite being outnumbered 2:1, he rode calmly up and down the line unarmed, seemingly unconscious of the bullets falling around him. Some thought him courageous or foolish; others that he was atoning for his recent sins; and still others that he was being theatrical, displaying the fearlessness and fatalism of his hero Napoleon.

Once British troops and artillery arrived at the beginning of June, the outcome was easy to predict. There were only two actual battles after that, on 6 June and 5 July after which the Ndebele fighters retreated to the Matopos Hills, a terrain favourable to guerrilla warfare. Between 20 July and 5 August, the British lost a fifth of their 1,000 men in ambushes, making it plain that the force was too small to prevail during the southern winter. The commanding general Frederick Carrington decided that he needed at least 5,000 troops to complete the operation and withdrew to Bulawayo, intending to resume the fighting in early 1897.

Negotiating Peace

Rhodes now made a decision that few others would have contemplated, let alone acted upon. Most of his biographers regard it, along with his rushing to Neville Pickering's bedside ten years before, as one of the two most remarkable episodes of his life. In the memorial plaque to Rhodes on the wall of his father's church in Bishop's Stortford, there is no mention of the Rhodes Scholarships; only of his role as a peacemaker.

Rhodes was paying for the fighting out of the South Africa Company budget at a rate of about £500,000 per day. Prolonging the war would mean ruining the Company and, if it dragged on for years, could also cause the British government to lose interest in defending Rhodesia altogether. With the fighting now paused, Rhodes passed word to the Ndebele traditional leaders through various intermediaries, including the widow of their first king Mzilikazi, that he was prepared to parley with them unarmed for as long as it took to redress their grievances. A contemporary was less noble in explaining the mission, which he saw as testing whether Rhodes still had "sufficient influence over the *indunas* [military leaders] of the Matabele tribe, to induce them to lay down their arms, and to submit to the future domination of the white man."[2]

General Carrington thought Rhodes was out of his mind and

refused to accept responsibility for the outcome, insisting that Rhodes and his small party would be massacred. But Rhodes went through with it, bringing along his close colleague Dr. Hans Sauer, Johann Colenbrander (an old hunter who spoke the Ndebele language), Captain Stent (a correspondent with the *Cape Times*), and two African guides. When they arrived at the site of the first *indaba* ["discussion"], a natural amphitheatre of granite rising 200 feet on each side, with warriors lining the cliffs, they must have wondered whether the military leaders would be able to restrain the younger fighters. It was Friday, 21 August.

Captain Stent asked whether they should stay on their horses, but Rhodes suggested they dismount. "It will give them confidence. They are nervous, too. How do they know that we have not an ambush ready for them behind the hill?" As they did that, a small group of Ndebele leaders began to approach them on foot. Rhodes was exultant: "Yes, yes, there they are. This is one of those moments in life that makes it worth living." He offered a peace greeting to the elders in their own language, "The eyes are white." They returned the greeting. "Is it peace?" Rhodes asked. "It is peace, father," was the reply.

Then, the lead Ndebele speaker Somabulana summarized the history that had brought them there: "The white man had come again with his guns that spit bullets as the heavens sometimes spit hail, and who were the naked Ndebele to stand against these guns and rifles? So, the white man took from the Ndebele the land, as they [the Ndebele] had taken it from the Shona and their King had been driven into exile. He had sent presents of gold, a peace offering, and the presents were taken and the peace was refused to him . . . You came, you conquered. The strongest takes the land. We accepted your rule. We lived under you. But not as dogs! If we are to be dogs it is better to be dead. You can never make the Ndebele dogs.

You may wipe them out, but the Children of the Stars can never be dogs."

Rhodes asked in what way they had been treated as dogs. Hearing how contemptuous and arbitrary the Zulu ("native") police had been, Rhodes promised to abolish the force. Then, they talked about the behaviour of the settlers and the Chartered Company, leading Captain Stent to report later that "if one-tenth of the stories that we heard were *true*", the case against the settlers "seemed pretty black." "All that is over," Rhodes promised. At that, Somabulana rose, indicating that the *indaba* was now over. They had been talking for four hours. "But is it peace or war?" Rhodes asked again. There was a deep silence before the answer came. "It is peace . . . You have [my] word."

The next day, the journalist Stent—who had been added to the team at the last minute to record events for posterity— rushed back to Bulawayo with his scoop. Years later, in his memoirs, he reported that officialdom reacted to the news of the first *indaba* with "unconcealed relief". But that was not quite true. General Carrington was irritated that a private citizen was negotiating with the enemy in what (despite Rhodes's funding) was officially an Imperial war. The deputy high commissioner in Cape Town, Sir Richard Martin, took no comfort in the news either, as he was still insisting on an unconditional surrender. Stent was on firmer ground in reporting that "Bulawayo [i.e., the settlers] professed profound disgust at any negotiations at all with the 'niggers'."

Persistence

Rhodes took nothing for granted, apparently sensing that he would have to build up confidence on both sides. That would take time. The second *indaba* on 28 August like the first one, opened on a tense note but ended calmly. It was a larger gathering and, this time, some of the younger warriors spoke out. "Where are we to live, when it is over?" asked one. "The white man claims all the land." Rhodes replied: "We will give you settlements. We will set apart locations for you; we will give you land." The young man shouted: "You will give us land in our own country! That's good of you!" When Rhodes asked him to put down his rifle, he replied: "You will have to talk to me with my rifle in my hand. I find if I talk with my rifle in my hand the white man pays more attention to what I say. Once I put my rifle down I am nothing. I am just a dog to be kicked."[3] Rhodes remained calm and at one point crossed over to sit with the Ndebele to continue the conversation at close quarters. He conveyed authority, good will, and even a touch of humour, all of which impressed his listeners.

Throughout September and into October, he made himself available to any of the Ndebele who wanted to speak with him, still camping out in the open, riding for three or four hours in the morning, then devoting the rest of the day to these consultations. Professor Rotberg suggests that Rhodes was listening with a "third ear"—something that no one before had ever noticed in him or, putting it more kindly, "had long lain dormant".[4] Down-to-earth and even cunning as his motives were, it is easy to understand the astonishment of his contemporaries that this hard-driving man, accustomed to giving orders and ultimatums, should have been willing to spend so much time listening to and commiserating with opponents who vastly outnumbered him and could still turn on him at any moment. Here was a man stripped of all formal public and corporate power, risking his life on the tatters of a reputation that still impressed the Ndebele, to bring the war—and the drain on the Chartered Company's resources—to an end.

Two months of persistence had not made much of a difference to some of Rhodes's compatriots. Hearing that the deputy high commissioner Sir Richard Martin was still determined to humiliate the Ndebele and that he would not recognize any agreement reached in the field, Rhodes held firm. "If necessary," he wrote to his friend Earl Grey, now the Administrator of the territory, "tell the Secretary of State [Chamberlain] that I am prepared to go and live in the Matopos with the rebels." Chamberlain had already made up his mind. "There would be great difficulty," he told Grey, "in defending an attitude of less leniency than that advocated by representatives of the . . . Company."[5]

At the final *indaba* on 13 October, the Ndebele leaders submitted their weapons to Rhodes and Grey, who restored some of the authority they had enjoyed before 1893 and promised them salaries as quasi-government employees. Concerned about losing direct contact with Rhodes, they were assured by Grey that he would act as their conduit. But, to their pleasant surprise, it was Rhodes who stayed in touch and later that year it was he who bought 100,000 acres of good land north of the Matopos for himself and a number of the former rebel leaders.

In June 1897, on the occasion of the celebration of Queen Victoria's Jubilee in Bulawayo, Rhodes sat down to hear their grievances again. This time, 150 senior Ndebele explained to him that territorial regulations were interfering with their traditional methods of managing the land. Rhodes promised to look into this. A star-struck reporter from the local paper described the scene: "Coming to speak to the *indunas* [headmen or senior advisers] individually Mr. Rhodes' manner underwent a startling change; it assumed a boyish exuberance and aspect of pleasure, which was immensely gratifying to the *indunas* personally known to him."[6] Later, Rhodes invited

1,200 Ndebele to his 44th birthday party, where two hundred sheep were slaughtered and gifts of blankets and tobacco were offered to the guests.

Incident at Enkeldoorn

Once the *indabas* were complete, Rhodes made his way slowly back to Bulawayo, visiting settlers along the way and explaining the unpopular path that he had taken to peace. But, while the Ndebele had been won over, the Shona rebellion was still underway. At Enkeldoorn, a Boer community, residents complained that a group of rebels living ten miles away were harassing them during the day, firing their rifles, and forcing everyone to stay indoors. What happened next seems out of character, even for a headstrong man like Rhodes, and the original source of the story was notoriously unreliable.[h]

"Well," Rhodes is reported to have said. "I'll assist you. We must go and clear them out." Then, leaving at 3am, he and his party climbed the mountain where the rebels were living and, as day broke, called out to them to surrender. Surprised, the Shona rushed out of their huts, firing their rifles. After twenty minutes of fighting, they fled, leaving seventy dead behind. At

---

h   This version of the story first appeared in Gordon Le Sueur's *Cecil Rhodes: The Man and His Work* (1913). In his introduction, Le Sueur (one of Rhodes's secretaries) admits that the Rhodes Trust regarded him as so untrustworthy that they denied his request to write an official biography of his former employer and confiscated all his materials. Only William Plomer (1933) gave much credence to the incident. It received three lines in Professor Rotberg's 800-page opus on Rhodes as part of the general "mopping up" of the Mashona rebellion. It is included here for the sake of completeness, given the possibility that it is true.

the bottom of the mountain, a discussion broke out about how many Shona had been killed. So, Rhodes volunteered to go back up, all on his own, and count the bodies.

As William Plomer commented in his 1933 biography, it is difficult to imagine the callousness required to do this, when some of the victims were probably still struggling for their final breaths. There is no suggestion that Rhodes killed anyone himself—he was carrying only a riding crop—but, if true, the story suggests a remarkable capacity to shift from peacemaking to vengefulness in very short order. If the ambush happened as described, current-day human rights lawyers would probably view it as a war crime.

"World's View"

From September 1897 to early January 1898, Rhodes was weakened by influenza and fever to such a degree that some friends feared for his life, and Rhodes himself began talking about his desire to be buried in the Matopos. "Lay me there," he would say. "My Rhodesians will like it: *they* have never bitten me."[7] It was during the *indabas* that Rhodes stumbled upon what he regarded as an ideal resting-place. It had an extraordinary panorama, which Rhodes named "The World's View", and had symbolic value, too, because the tomb of the first Ndebele king Mzilikazi was in a similar setting about seven miles away. Out of pure vanity, or as a sign of his domination of this ground sacred to the Ndebele people, or from a fanciful wish to link his history with theirs, Rhodes warmed immediately to the idea.

As in many aspects of his life, there is more than one version of how he found the spot. His friend, Sir James McDonald, claimed that it was in August 1896, when Rhodes was out riding with his friend Earl Grey. They returned excited and went back that afternoon with McDonald to see the site again. "We sat for some time afterwards," he reported, "in the shade of the vast round boulders that seem to have been thrown up from the bowels of the earth and Rhodes was very silent for a time. Then he said to himself really: 'The peacefulness of it all, the chaotic grandeur of it, it creates a feeling of awe and brings home to one how very small we all are'." Then, according to Macdonald, they lost track of the location altogether.

On their return two years later, they found the path overgrown with bush, and five riders searched in all directions for two days without finding it. On the third day, Rhodes was in such a foul mood that McDonald avoided talking to him. Then, the next morning, acting on a hunch, McDonald went off on his own and succeeded where the others had failed. When he returned, Rhodes almost jumped with delight and insisted on galloping back to the spot immediately. "I had to find my hill, McDonald, I had to find it, it has stayed with me since I saw it last. I fear I've been very irritable the last few days, but I had to find it and I shan't forget how you stuck to it."[8]

Politics Again

During those two years that the "World's View" remained undisturbed, Rhodes reasserted himself politically and provided financial backing to the Progressive Party, which included liberals wanting to draw more African and coloured [mixed-race] voters into the political system. Rhodes also backed the redistribution of constituencies to give proper weight to urban areas. In response to pressure from coloured voters, he amended his September 1897 election slogan "Equal rights for every white man south of the Zambesi" to "Equal rights for every civilised man . . . ", in which "civilised" meant being able to write one's name, having property, or being employed. In that election, the Progressives fell just short of winning a majority but the new premier, a Boer, was in such a weak position that he was obliged to agree to new constituency boundaries. That Redistribution Bill would almost certainly have allowed the Progressives to win the next election, but the South African War broke out before that could happen.[9]

According to his generally sceptical biographer John Flint, Rhodes also began to court the African and coloured vote and showed a "newfound tenderness" in trying to reconcile their interests with those of the English-speaking population. Had he had a change of heart? Or had he simply reverted to the liberal instincts he displayed before he entered into a political partnership with the Afrikaners? Many people—including Rhodes himself—fully expected him to be Prime Minister again.

In one of his final speeches to the Cape House, on 4 September 1899, speaking from the Opposition benches, Rhodes opposed the government's efforts to deprive Africans of the vote. "I wish the natives to wake up to the fact . . . I shall fight this clause to the end." Four days later, Rhodes spoke of the importance of "keeping faith with natives". "On 18th September," Michell says, "he again spoke earnestly in defence of the native vote, and reasserted his belief in the principle of equal rights to every civilised man irrespective of colour."[10] The government carried the day with a majority of 11, with all the Boers opposing the vote for Africans and all the English-speakers siding with Rhodes.

Honorary Degree

In June 1899, the University of Oxford awarded Rhodes an honorary Doctorate of Civil Law (DCL). It had first been offered to him in 1892 but he was unable to return to receive it earlier. In between, the Jameson Raid cast a shadow over the decision, causing more than 90 of Oxford's teaching staff, including the renowned historian H.A.L. Fisher of New College and even a recalcitrant fellow of Rhodes's own Oriel College (the economist L.L. Price) to object. Although they represented nearly a fifth of Oxford's teaching staff, it was a very Oxonian kind of protest.

In their letter to the Vice-Chancellor, they recognized that the honour had been agreed upon "before there was anything to cause any important difference of opinion as to his action." "We do not therefore wish to question the decision ... but simply desire that the facts should be fully known; and ... that this letter with our signatures should be published in the [University] *Gazette*." As it was not an official document, the Vice-Chancellor refused their request.[11] At the same time, it was rumoured that the Proctors [senior officers of the University] would block the award at the actual ceremony. Hearing this, Rhodes's fellow-honoree, the military hero Lord Kitchener of Khartoum threatened not to take his own degree and the Duke of York (the future George V) let it be known that his own attendance would also be in doubt. That settled the matter.[12]

That Rhodes's pride was hurt is evident in his almost juvenile reaction afterwards. "I should have been almost nobody if it had not been for this opposition to me. But I can assure you, gentlemen, they gave me a greater reception than Lord Kitchener, and you must remember that they were not mere undergraduates of eighteen, but Masters of Arts, gentlemen with great beards, because after the day's proceedings, the undergraduates numbered 400 and the others numbered 5000. Gentlemen, I mention this because one's troubles have brought out one's friends."[13]

A British society weekly reported that, at first, Rhodes was dumbfounded by the opposition to his degree: "But gradually he discovered that, as he expected, Oxford was sound, and the majority of the members of Convocation [the main governing body of the University] were Imperialists. Never did enthusiasm rise to such a height as it did on that June day in the [Sheldonian] Theatre at the moment when Rhodes was receiving the degree. Oxford had at last produced a real man of action, an Empire-maker, and she was proud of him . . . That day was probably one of the happiest days in Rhodes' life."[14] On his return to Cape Town, he told his friend Thomas Fuller that there was no honour he coveted more. He was also relieved that his Privy Councillorship had been upheld, despite the Raid, not only by the Ministers of the Crown but also "by the gracious favour of Her Majesty."[15]

South African War

In October 1899, war broke out between Great Britain and the two Dutch Republics. In the months leading up to it, Rhodes had strong doubts that the tensions he had helped stoke would result in hostilities. Talking to the Cape House in July, he even belittled the prospect. "I should feel alarmed if I heard that the Czar was going to Peking, or that the French were moving in Newfoundland or in the Niger territories . . . If you were to tell me that the native chief of Samoa was going to cause trouble to the Imperial Government, then I would discuss the proposition that the Transvaal was a danger to the British Empire."[16] He played no role in the negotiations between the British government and President Kruger and, for obvious reasons, was not invited to do so. "I made a mistake with regard to the Transvaal once," he said, "and that is quite enough for me. A burnt child dreads the fire. I keep aloof from the whole crisis, so that no one will be able to say, if things go wrong, 'That Rhodes is in it again!'"[17]

According to Lewis Michell, Rhodes was one of the few people in the Cape Colony who did not expect a war.[18] He even made small bets with friends against one. He was certain that President Kruger would climb down, knowing the strength of British forces and that the only likely outcome of a war would be the annexation of the Transvaal. However, his secretary Philip Jourdan speculated that "in the secrecy of his heart" Rhodes may have favoured war. Time was slipping away; he still wanted a federation of South Africa; and he doubted that any conflict would last very long. He may also have had a guilty conscience about it. Visiting Boer settlers in Rhodesia in 1900, he was surprised by how well he was received, thinking that the war might have biased them against him.[19]

When war broke out, he took the last train to Kimberley to join in the defence of the diamond mines. This took pluck as a rumour was circulating that the Transvaal Afrikaners wanted to capture him and parade him around the Republic in an iron cage. To save money, he suggested that the African mineworkers return home until the war was over but, when several of them were killed trying to break through the Afrikaner lines, he changed course and employed them in public works in the city.

During the months of bombardment, he sheltered residents in the mines. He also made a nuisance of himself with those in charge of defending the city. Rhodes's respect for the military mind was never very high and it was hard for the erstwhile head of De Beers to accept a subordinate role in his own backyard. His very presence in the city is said to have altered overall strategy in the war, obliging the British to assign resources to lifting the siege of Kimberley that they would happily have deployed elsewhere.[20]

Final Days

Once the siege was lifted, Rhodes returned to the Cape. By then, conventional warfare had given way to Afrikaner guerrilla resistance and British scorched-earth tactics which— though devastating elsewhere—had limited impact on the major population centres. Rhodes spent the next two years rebuilding his house at Groote Schuur, serving again on the board of the Chartered Company, supervising telegraph and railway expansion further north, farming again on a large scale, starting irrigation schemes, experimenting with Angora goats, sheep, and fruit trees, and visiting the settlers in Rhodesia.

In June 1897 he had a heart attack in Bulawayo, then a second, more serious one that November, and yet another in 1899 during the siege of Kimberley. At about that time, he told an audience, "You can conquer anything, but time you can never interfere with."[21] Rather quirkily, Philip Jourdan attributed Rhodes's steep decline to his new-found passion for bridge. Playing regularly every night, he slept in and went for his daily ride only after the freshness of the morning had lifted. Sometimes he didn't ride at all. "I could not help noticing that from the time he neglected his riding his heart began to trouble him more frequently."[22]

In 1901, on his final trip to England, his cardiologist told him that he would survive only a few more months if he did not stop working. He had been diagnosed with an aneurysm of the thoracic aorta "the size of a child's head" which pressed not just on his major veins but also on his trachea and lungs. This was confirmed after his death. Not surprisingly, his declining health tempered his behaviour. According to a De Beers colleague, "Rhodes was very amiable for once and as pleased as one could wish. His heart trouble seems to have softened the harshness and bitterness to some extent. And he never once said a disagreeable thing. I may say that we very nearly came to an agreement on all questions."[23]

In August 1901, he rented a luxurious hunting lodge in Scotland and had a stream of visitors, including the young Winston Churchill. Rhodes "admired his intellectual powers which, in conjunction with his dash and 'go' . . . must inevitably bring him to the front."[24] Another visitor was Daisy Greville, the Countess of Warwick, a renowned London socialite who would later become a socialist philanthropist, funding an agricultural college for women, free meals for schoolchildren, and housing and employment schemes for the poor. She told Rhodes that he was a dreamer. "It is the dreamers that move the world!" he replied. "Practical men are so busy being practical that they cannot see beyond their own lifetime . . . If there had been no dream . . . we should still be living in caves, clubbing each other to death for a mouthful of food."[25]

He spent mid-November to mid-December in Egypt, where he narrated the lives of the Pharaohs to friends by heart in almost reverent tones, before returning to South Africa. He decided to go there purely on the advice of his lawyer and against the wishes of his other friends as it was the hottest time of the year in the southern hemisphere. The purpose was to testify against a woman acquaintance, Princess Catherine Radziwill, who had forged his signature on a number of large cheques.

On the way, Rhodes had so much trouble breathing in his cabin that a bed was set up for him on the upper deck. Although the passage was not particularly rough, he was tossed onto the deck at least once and was very weak when he disembarked. During the month of February, he spent the day at Groote Schuur and evenings at his small cottage at Muizenberg, hoping for fresh breezes off the sea. He was in Cape Town one last time on the last day of the month, giving evidence in the forgery case.

From 9 March, he was bedridden and had an agonizing death, struggling for breath for the next two and a half weeks. Although the cottage was facing the sea, it was the hottest summer in years, and a hole had to be smashed into the outside wall of his one-window bedroom to let in more air. His friends went to great lengths to spare him further distress. Jameson installed boxes of ice in the ceiling to provide some form of air conditioning and rigged up Indian-style punkah fans to be operated day and night. The *Cape Times*, which Rhodes owned, delivered special issues each day that left out the medical bulletins about him that the rest of the city was reading.

His intimates said that he bore the pain bravely. He even talked of getting better and insisted that they book him a passage to England for later in the month. It was due to leave the day he died. But he had always been afraid of what was now happening to him. Eight months before, shortly before leaving London for Scotland, he confessed his horror of serious disease and said, "At any rate, Jameson, death from the heart is quick and clean; there is nothing repulsive and lingering about it; it is a clean death, isn't it?" Unable to look him in the eye, Jameson tried to reply matter-of-factly, but his voice betrayed his emotion. Rhodes noticed, roused himself, and laughed the question off.[26]

The last morning, his companion Jack Grimmer thought that he was looking better and told him so. Grimmer even imagined that Rhodes might be able to make the ship home. But he shook his head: "It's over." He died that day, 26 March 1902, at 6pm.

The next day, according to Jourdan, "The whole British Empire was in mourning."[27] Telegrams and cables of condolence arrived from all parts of the world, flags were at half-mast, and Cape Town's principal businesses closed for the day. Tens of thousands came to view his body at Groote Schuur on Saturday 29 March and Monday 31 March. Thousands more paid tribute on 2 April at the Houses of Parliament, where his body had been transferred. Fifteen thousand people turned out at Kimberley as Rhodes's remains were taken by train to Rhodesia. And, at "World's View", Africans outnumbered European mourners two to one and, at a solemn moment in the proceedings, hundreds of Ndebele shouted out "Bayete!", the salute reserved for their royalty.

Olive Schreiner, who had broken sharply with Rhodes, was saddened by his death. "It was a greater shock to me than I could have believed possible . . . When death comes, one forgets all the faults of a life and remembers only the awful tragedy of the individual Soul—a great 'might have been'," she wrote to a friend.[28] The poet Rudyard Kipling visited Rhodes several times as he lay dying. He thought Rhodes "the greatest of living men", admired his humanity, idealism, and simple habits, but wished that the parliamentarian and statesman could have been more articulate. Kipling, the master of words, tried to fill that gap.[i] When Rhodes died, he wrote to a friend: "I feel as though half the horizon of my life had dropped away." He was too upset to attend the funeral in the Matopos, but he joined the procession that accompanied the body from the Houses of Parliament to St. George's Cathedral in Cape Town.[29]

---

i　He did the same for Dr. Jameson, who inspired Kipling's renowned poem *If*.

CHAPTER EIGHT

Judgement

I F RHODES'S LIFE was now at an end, the debate about him had only just begun.

Certainly, based on the facts presented so far, it will be easy to understand why the usually circumspect Warden of Rhodes House could describe Rhodes fifty years ago as a "scoundrel". Many will regard that as an understatement. And, while recent critics have cited his "crimes against humanity" and likened him to Hitler and Stalin, it is ironic that in his own day he was toppled for planning an invasion of the Transvaal Republic that those monsters would have regarded as relatively bloodless.

Range of Criticisms

That paradox is hardly surprising as the range of criticisms that has been directed against Rhodes is truly astonishing. Some have been petty and incomprehensible. "It was somewhat typical," wrote one South African biographer, "that he should have so much liked scentless flowers, hydrangeas, cannas, and bougainvillea. It was typical, too, that he loved the Cape and the view of the sea where two great oceans meet . . . One ocean was not enough for the Colossus."[1] He has been labelled an "ecological terrorist" for introducing foreign plants and animals to South Africa; one import—the grey squirrel—eventually eliminated its local counterpart. And because he founded a large international company, a forerunner of "neoliberal global corporations", Rhodes has even been accused of fomenting the runaway consumerism of today's young people in South Africa.[2]

While Rhodes's homosexuality is little known in the West, some Africans consider it another reason to detest him. When the Governor of Bulawayo Province called for Rhodes's remains to be exhumed in 2016, a blogger on a tourism website supported the idea. "Rhodes was known to be a homosexual, a sexual behaviour that is taboo in Africa," said Stanford Chiwanga.[3] Others have complained that his grave is guarded 24 hours a day while that of the first Ndebele king Mzilikazi, also in the Matopos Hills, is not protected at all. There have also been suggestions that the rains have failed in recent years because the ancestors are unhappy that Rhodes's remains are still there.[4]

If some criticisms of the man now appear far-fetched, some of his reported accomplishments also seem strained. A state senator from Ohio, talking in Cape Town in 1946 on the 44th anniversary of Rhodes's death, suggested that he had "stifled" German aggression in southern Africa and that, but for him, the "cruel" Prussians and later the Nazis would have straddled South Africa. "For all this, the world owes a debt of gratitude to the energy, farsightedness, and vision of Cecil Rhodes."[5] If that were true, three decades before Hitler's rise to power, Rhodes could indeed be credited with a great deal of foresight. Other admirers went overboard, comparing him to Julius Caesar and Alexander the Great.

Fall from Grace

Remarkably enough, Rhodes's star was already falling within twenty years of his death. "To-day," wrote Basil Williams in 1921, "except in his own Rhodesia, the glamour of his great name is somewhat dulled. Many of the faithful friends, men like Jameson and Grey, jealous guardians of the reputation and tradition of Rhodes, which they themselves had helped to form, have passed away." The cataclysm of the First World War also obscured his story.[6] Even Lewis Michell, Rhodes's personal banker, writing as early as 1910, had to tiptoe around an overall verdict on the man. While admitting that not all of Rhodes's methods had been commendable, Michell believed that "a sober narrative of the facts at my command will not lower him in the eyes of discriminating critics, but will demonstrate, not indistinctly, that he was a great man, great even in his faults."[7]

Compared with the idolatrous memoirs of his close associates in the decade after his death, the tenor of books about Rhodes turned sour in the 1920s and 1930s. Two writers, both published in the same year (1933), tore stripes out of the man. In the words of the South African novelist Sarah Gertrude Millin: "Whose little broom could sweep him back? He could afford to be, as he chose, either liberal, romantic, genial, persuasive and conciliatory; or, on other moods, morose, overbearing, cynical, mad, crude to the point of clownishness in his humour. Not only could he do no wrong, what he did became right, it was his duty to do what he wanted."[8]

William Plomer, the London-based South African poet and editor, suggested that Rhodes saw himself as a man of destiny whose "idea" required "the devotion of the best souls of the next 200 years." "It does not seem to have occurred to him," wrote Plomer, "that many of the 'best souls' at any given moment might not be of the English-speaking race and might not be especially keen on the advancement of that race, nor that many of the 'best souls' of our own race might have little interest in trying to dominate mankind . . . No, the 'best souls' seem to have many other kinds of fish to fry."[9]

Devotees were horrified by such irreverence, based on what they regarded as second- and third-hand information. Even while he was alive, they argued, people at a distance misread the man. There are two examples of such impatience in the Rhodes Papers at Oxford. One is a letter from his valet, John Norris, dated 11 January 1939, correcting the largely "garbled" accounts of his employer's life. "I read such a lot of his misdeeds that it gets on my nerves, and most writers of his life keep telling us what they think he should have done, not what he actually did." A month later, Norris was pillorying Lewis Michell's generally positive biography: "I shall probably some day send you Michell's Life of Rhodes if I ever finish pulling it to bits."[10] There is also a 18 January 1934 letter from T.E. Lawrence ("Lawrence of Arabia") to the wife of Sir Herbert Baker, Rhodes's personal architect: "His Rhodes is a real contribution to a difficult and disputed subject. I only wish he had produced it earlier, to be of use to the first generation of those-not-knowing-Rhodes-but-reconstituting-him-from-documents. No matter. He is available for the future—and there are many more books about Rhodes to come."[11]

People were always prepared to think the worst of Rhodes. The night he rushed off to Simon's Town to try rescuing the lost seamen, some of his friends were surprised that he could be so chivalrous and unselfish. But, they also admitted that it was "unthinkable that any man should go through such experiences for a mere stage effect."[12] Those who knew him well were staunch loyalists. According to Basil Williams (1921), "Besides the respect of the community, he had firm friends, who loved him for himself alone and would have stuck to him had all his financial schemes gone awry. They loved him for a boyish and uncalculating enthusiasm for better things than money-making."[13]

"Who shall try to judge . . . the conception of such men, or judge of their motives?" wrote Rhodes's parliamentary colleague, Thomas Fuller. "To say, as I have often heard affirmed, that Mr. Rhodes was inspired by a mere vulgar personal ambition to write Rhodes on the map of Africa and the deeds of Rhodes in its history, was to my mind utterly absurd . . . It was evident to any one who came within hearing and touch of his musings, and almost his soliloquies, that he had no mere vulgar dreams of personal aggrandisement . . . He habitually carried about with him a wide horizon, and saw even minute questions of policy and experience in a large atmosphere."[14]

Historical Judgements

However, it is significant that all professional historians have been critical of Rhodes. His most authoritative biographer Robert Rotberg (1988) did not reach conclusions sharp enough to post on a placard. But John Flint (1974) was categorical: "If Rhodes had never lived, the Boer War might never have taken place, a different form of South African union might have come about peacefully, and the present geo-political situation in southern Africa have evolved on different lines."[15] In his introduction to Flint's book, J.H. Plumb concludes grimly: "The pantheon of great lives contains, as it must, men who, like Rhodes, did evil unconsciously in the wanton pursuit of grandeur. And by that irony in which history delights, Rhodes aided humanity by his death."[16]

It is also telling that the Rhodes Must Fall protesters were not the first to compare Rhodes to Hitler. The South African novelist Sarah Gertrude Millin, who published a life of Rhodes the same year as William Plomer (1933), commented in her 1941 autobiography: "The something that rises in me against Rhodes is the something—unendingly intensified—that rises in me against Germany." Both Rhodes and Hitler, she said, were obsessed with "bigness"; both thought "in quantities"; and both enjoyed grandiose architecture and mountain heights suggestive of their power. They wanted "nothing less than the world" for patriotic reasons but also to fulfill themselves. Millin described the Jameson Raid as a "Hitlerian putsch".[17]

Stuart Cloete, who wrote in the early 1930s but published his book much later (in 1946), also used then-contemporary parallels, calling Rhodes "the prototype of the modern dictator". "A book could be written, 'From Rhodes to Hitler'. . . His hope was for a great British Reich."[18] "Rhodes had the dream of Nordic superiority, a penchant for big blond men, a dislike of and perhaps a contempt for women. Rhodes saw people as masters and servants."[19] William Plomer added: "To realise how little limit there is to . . . individuals who believe passionately in a single and ruthlessly simple political idea, we have only to think of such different figures in our own day (1933) as Lenin, Mussolini and Hitler."[20]

But such parallels were easier to draw before these writers knew the full extent of Nazi savagery. There were also internal contradictions in these accounts. Cloete (1946) excused Rhodes's greatest mistake: "Someone had to destroy the Matabele, who had destroyed hundreds of thousands. Rhodes did this. A regime of barbarous cruelty was destroyed."[21] While likening his methods to Hitler's, Cloete said that Rhodes was "relatively benevolent" and possibly a humanitarian in the long view".[22]

Later historians have also found similarities between Hitler and Rhodes but only in their outlooks and abilities rather than in their impact on the world. The South African-born

American historian Jeffrey Butler (1977) thought that the two men resembled each other in their "racism, strength of will, preoccupation with half-baked ideas, single-mindedness, [and] consummate skill in negotiating". "But," he added, "it is hard to understand [the] judgment that Rhodes was self-deluded and served *only* himself.[23]

Even some of his critics could see that the picture was cloudy rather than clear. Cloete wrote that, like a diamond, "[Rhodes] must be seen in his total brilliance; in the fire of his mind; in the hardness of his determination; in his integrity as much as in his lack of it; in his consistency as much as in his inconsistency; in his faults, which were great as his virtues were great. He was the enemy of the little; a believer in the great. We can see him as . . . the final and completely modernised specimen of the old Elizabethan adventurer. Beyond evil and good in ordinary terms, Rhodes was great, a master of men in a world that even then demanded masters."[24]

In August 1971, BBC television produced a documentary on Rhodes entitled *A Touch of Churchill, A Touch of Hitler,* which portrayed Rhodes as a ruthless visionary who thought that everyone could be bought and had close associates "not unlike Al Capone's gunmen". But the film concluded that it is "impossible to totally dislike Cecil Rhodes", because of his devotion to Neville Pickering.[25] Like Kaiser Wilhelm II before him, Hitler is said to have admired Rhodes and believed that the British should have persevered with his approach. Joseph Goebbels described Rhodes as "a rare force-man" in sharp contrast to the usual British caution.[26]

A Rhodesian historian, Oliver Ransford, writing in 1974, pointed to an ambivalence in Rhodes's character. "He strove for the reconciliation between the Afrikaners and English South Africans, yet greatly hindered it by the Jameson Raid. He was a romantic dreamer and a cold-blooded realist. He was not a race bigot; but he was often compelled to behave like one. He longed to populate the world with British stock, yet never so much as contemplated marriage."[27]

Such even-handedness contrasts with the devotion expressed by his friends in his own day, like James Maguire (1897): "Men of that time who stand on the verge of the twenty-first century, as we on the verge of the twentieth, will wonder at the short-sighted judgment and narrow spirit that failed to recognise the greatness and the patriotism of the statesman and the man, that cavilled at his methods, and lightly esteemed the value of his accomplished work."[28]

But history is not for the fawning and fainthearted. To quote Professor Butler again, "The business and political success of the sickly young man with the squeaky voice is not easily understood . . . Even if he was not a particularly original thinker, he used his power in markedly different ways from his contemporary capitalist colleagues. The attempts of historians and biographers to deal with such figures as Rhodes make clear the impact of politics on writing."[29]

Literary Views

Literary figures have also had their say. "We fight Rhodes," wrote Olive Schreiner in 1897, "because he means so much of oppression, injustice, and moral degradation to South Africa— but if he passed away tomorrow there still remains the terrible fact that something in our society has formed the matrix which has fed, nourished, and built up such a man."[30] Mark Twain (1897) described him as "the only colonial in the British dominions whose goings and comings are chronicled and discussed under all the globe's meridians, and whose speeches, unclipped, are cabled from the ends of the earth; and he is the only unroyal outsider whose arrival in London can compete for attention with an eclipse."[31] Describing him as "Deputy God on the one side, deputy Satan on the other", he thought Rhodes should be hanged. "I admire him, I frankly confess it; and when his time comes I shall buy a piece of the rope for a keepsake."[32]

Arthur Conan Doyle (1902) regarded him as a "strange but very great man . . . a mighty leader, a man of broad vision, too big to be selfish but too determined not to be unscrupulous—a difficult man to appraise with our little human yard-sticks."[33] G.K. Chesterton (1912) was dismissive: "He had only a hasty but elaborate machinery for spreading the principles that he hadn't got. What he called his ideals were the dregs of a Darwinism which had already grown not only stagnant but poisonous."[34] It is awkward to contradict a writer as delightful as Chesterton; but he was one of many who based their views on second- and third-hand accounts rather than on a close examination of Rhodes's actual words and actions. As for the man's supposed Social Darwinism, the only trace of it is in Rhodes's advice on the raising of children. Like many men without offspring, he had strong views on the subject and felt that a good education was essential. "Then kick all the props away. If they are worth anything the struggle will make them better men; if they are not, the sooner they go under the better."[35] Evelyn Waugh (1960) acknowledged that Rhodes was a visionary but "that almost all he saw was hallucination".[36]

Friends criticized him, too. The journalist and editor W.T. Stead disapproved of Rhodes's "piratical streak", which allowed him to use force to gain his objectives, and wanted Rhodes imprisoned for the Jameson Raid like everyone else. As a result, the two men seldom saw each other after that and Rhodes removed Stead as a trustee of his will. Yet, Stead's book *The Last Will and Testament of Cecil John Rhodes*, published three months after Rhodes died, was a clear attempt to rehabilitate his reputation and he continued to explain Rhodes's ambitions and accomplishments over the next ten years, before perishing on the *Titanic*.

A self-styled friend, Princess Catherine Radziwill—who actually tried to bilk Rhodes out of large sums of money towards the end of his life—described him as "a great Englishman in spite of his faults and perhaps on account of his faults." "Beside the genius of a Darwin or of a Pasteur, the talent of a Shakespeare or of a Milton, the science of a Newton or of a Lister, his figure seems a small one indeed, and it is absurd to raise him to the same level as these truly wonderful men." But, on balance, Radziwill remained an admirer. "In Europe Rhodes would never have found the opportunity to give full rein to his faculties of organization and of conquest. He knew no obstacles and would admit none in his way; he was of the type of Pizarro and of Fernando Cortez, with fewer prejudices, far more knowledge, and that clear sense of civilization which only an Englishman born and bred among the traditions of liberty can possess."[37]

Mining Magnate

At least one specific charge against Rhodes can be considered rather briefly. Many people—including Rhodes Scholars— have regretted that he made his fortune in mining and that he subjected his workforce to difficult and even humiliating conditions. It is true that underground mining at the end of the 19th century was hard and debilitating work and it remains so in many countries to this day. By one account, temperatures in the mines at 5-6,000 feet below the surface were as high as 120 degrees Fahrenheit with a relative humidity of 90-100 per cent, leading to many cases of heat stroke.[38] That explained in part why contracts were for 2-3 months at a time rather than for the whole year. But, even before hut taxes were introduced, many workers travelled large distances to earn money in the mines for their own reasons, as it was more profitable than farming or cattle-raising back home. It is true that living in compounds was unpleasant, but the scale of diamond thefts was so high that they could not be ignored and security checks at diamond mines throughout the world remain highly intrusive to this day.

But why should Rhodes have caused anyone to labour in such conditions to produce mere baubles? Diamonds were in high demand, and it would have required a saint—perhaps even an archangel—to resist the chance of making a fortune from them. Thousands of people poured into Kimberley and later Johannesburg (for gold) with the hope of doing just that. Diamonds were for jewellery, especially engagement rings, and did not yet have an industrial purpose; but people were prepared to pay a handsome price for them. Should Rhodes have bought advertising space in the penny journals to persuade readers to use cowrie shells or opals instead and undercut his own market? And if it had not been Rhodes, it would have been someone else who dominated the industry. As for "baubles", his fellow politician Thomas Fuller once heard the explorer Henry Stanley comment on "what blood had been shed in the Arab raids for every elephant's tusk that had been made into the billiard balls and paper cutters of civilisation."[39]

Of course, it may also be held against Rhodes that he was a monopolist. It was an age of cartels and managed production and, significantly, very few people in Kimberley objected to the fact that diamond prices were controlled. It was the collapse of prices in the mid-1870s that worried the town, caused an exodus of producers, and forced the closure of many businesses that depended on a booming mining sector. Given the nature of the product, low prices might also have disappointed customers because diamonds were regarded as a luxury product, a store of value, and a sign of prestige.

Now, let us examine the most serious charges against Rhodes—that he was an imperialist, a white supremacist, a warmonger, and an architect of apartheid—the system of racial segregation and subordination (falsely dignified as "separate development") that existed in practice in South Africa well before the Nationalist Party formalized it into law after 1948.

CHAPTER NINE

Imperialist

G IVEN THE OPPORTUNITY, one did not have to be very willful to be an imperialist in the 19th century. In fact, Rhodes's career coincided almost exactly with the attainment of the high-water mark of the British Empire.

Although the Empire's original purposes were commercial and military, dreamers, idealists, missionaries, and poets followed in its wake. The romance of Empire only began to lift in the first half of the 20th century, when the "white man's burden"[j] became a financial rather than a metaphorical one and no longer a mere apology for dominating others. By the Second World War, dissolving the Empire was more an issue of timing and method than a fight for the national soul. In the words of one historian, "The passionate dedication of imperialists such as

---

j The title of a poem by Rudyard Kipling (1865-1936) that encouraged the United States to assume colonial control of the Philippines for benevolent reasons: "Take up the White Man's Burden/The savage wars of peace/Fill full the mouth of Famine/And bid the sickness cease ... "

Kipling, Milner and Rhodes had become as incomprehensible as the religious devotion of the persecutors and martyrs of the sixteenth and seventeenth centuries."[1]

Imperialism

Yet, imperialism is as old as human history. From the dawn of written records, and perhaps even earlier, one group has always tried to dominate a large number of other human beings for power and profit. The Sumerians, Macedonians, Persians, Chinese, Romans, Mongols, Mughals, Incas, Aztecs, and Turks also convinced themselves—like imperialists after them—that they were improving the lives of their subjects. The Arab armies that swept through the Middle East, North Africa, and Spain in the 8th century fought, killed, and died, spreading a "superior" faith. In western and central Africa, one African empire after another rose and fell. Yet, the "Scramble for Africa" of the late 19th century, involved so many countries (Belgium, France, Germany, Great Britain, Italy, Portugal, and Spain) and fostered expansionism on such a large scale, that ever since imperialism has been generally considered a European sin.

Like the greed, aggression, and nationalism that underlay it, imperialism was an almost natural product of human ambition. It was also an unfortunate consequence of world exploration, which drew on innocent roots, like a sense of adventure, an interest in expanding trade, and a commitment to stretching the boundaries of human enterprise and knowledge. If Africans had had the opportunity and resources to invade a supposedly empty European continent, they almost certainly would have done so, and young English protesters might now be throwing eggs at a statue of some African potentate in Piccadilly Circus. Ultimately, the offence of British imperialism was that it was enduring and successful—not because of superior moral values or intelligence, but because of better technology, including the machine gun.

It is also difficult to separate issues of race from British imperialism. The British writer Aldous Huxley suggested that the world would be a better place if we described skin colour more accurately—as pinkish-grey instead of "white" and chocolate or coffee instead of "black" and "brown". Yellow and red are even stranger ways of depicting human beings. At best, these labels are clumsy shorthand and a poor substitute for geographical or cultural references like "European" and "African". But the targeting of Africans by every other race in the world has given them a particular reason to resent racism.

Some scholars have wondered why the peoples of central and southern Africa did not join forces to prevent the invasion of their lands by outsiders. One explanation is that—just as Europeans and their descendants still do not see themselves as "people of colour"—southern Africans did not regard themselves as African or "black". What bound them together were local ties—to the land, their leaders, their lineage, family and clan, and their particular languages and traditions. It was the British and other colonial powers who introduced them to race and the "colour bar".[2]

That history, and the fact that Europeans maintained a grip on vast areas of the globe and dominated so many other human beings for so long, explain why Africans see white rather than red when the subject of Empire arises. To some, this may seem another form of racism. But people of African descent have a unique and bitter past.

British Imperialism

In the late 19th and early 20th centuries, however, the British ruling class treated imperial administration very seriously. At

Oxford, it was said that graduates with First Class degrees went off to rule India; those with Seconds were assigned to Africa; and the Thirds stayed home to govern England. Benjamin Jowett, who was Master of Balliol College from 1870 to 1893, wrote to Florence Nightingale, apparently lightheartedly, that he "should like to govern the world through my students". Later, he told Lord Lansdowne (one of three successive Viceroys of India he had taught) that: "There is more great and permanent good to be done in India than in any department of administration in England."[3] Trained in the classics, many colonial administrators flattered themselves that they were like the ancient Greeks and Romans. Progressives among them even regretted that, while anyone in the late Roman Empire—black or white, free-born or ex-slave—could rise to be Emperor, the British Colonial Services were reserved for British nationals.[4]

Most English people may have been proud that the Union Jack fluttered over a quarter of the Earth's surface; but there was no consensus, even in Whitehall, about how the Empire should be managed. During the 1860s, successive British governments were wary of expansion, especially in South Africa, which had absorbed a great deal of public funds with apparently little to show for it. Germany's proclamation of a protectorate over South West Africa in the 1880s altered the strategic calculus to a degree; but, even then, decision-making in London remained unpredictable. The Prime Minister William Gladstone told Rhodes: "Fancy being dragged into the centre of Africa [Uganda] and, do you know, it is all due to those wretched missionaries. Our burden is too great; as it is, I cannot find the people to govern all our dependencies. We have, Mr. Rhodes, too much to do."[5]

Even after the opening of the Suez Canal in 1869, Britain's ultimate strategic aim was to protect the Cape, as London was unsure of being able to control the Canal in the event of war. Many preferred to focus on that narrow objective. But others thought that the Cape could only be defended by controlling large territories in the hinterland and protecting British settlers and Africans against the Afrikaners. The key decision-makers— the Colonial Secretary in London and the High Commissioner in the Cape—could not always get their way. Instead, they had to contend with "public opinion", expressed in different ways—through Parliament, the press, the London clubs, and pressure groups as diverse as missionary associations, anti-slavery groups, commercial and shipping interests, and mining corporations.[6]

Of course, there were outright anti-imperialists as well. William Plomer, who was the first writer to cut Rhodes down to size, felt that "it already seemed urgent [in 1933] that the West should pay more attention to deserving goodwill [in Africa] than to annexing territory."[7] Leonard Woolf, who published Plomer's first novels and served as a colonial magistrate in Ceylon in his early 20s, wrote a scalding book about imperialism in 1920, entitled *Empire and Commerce in Africa*. Before that, in 1902 (the year Rhodes died), in his *Imperialism: A Study*, the socialist economist J.A. Hobson denounced empire as "immoral" and perhaps even more compellingly as "unnecessary". "Such works," wrote Plomer, "serve as a reminder that there are level-headed men with colonial, political and literary experience who actually have doubts about the seemliness of 'scrambling' for other people's countries, and clear ideas about the nature and effects of the colour bar."[8] But the anti-imperialists were a lonely group, like the prophets of global warming in the 1970s and 1980s.

Not only was Rhodes an imperialist; he was an exuberant one. "Some collect butterflies or china," he told the Bishop of Cape Town, "and others pictures, and others purchase landed estates or stately mansions, and live like princes there; it has always seemed to me a nobler aim to open out Southern Central Africa to British energy and British colonization."[9] "What are you engaged on at present, Mr. Rhodes?" asked Queen Victoria in 1891 over dinner at Windsor. "I'm doing my best to enlarge Your Majesty's dominions," he replied.[10] That enthusiasm was contagious. When one of his young "Pioneers", Hubert Hervey, was fatally wounded in battle in 1896, he asked to see Rhodes one last time. When his wish was granted, Hervey said, "Who knows but that I may soon be pegging out claims for England in Jupiter?"[11]

Indeed, for a long time Rhodes set the standard for imperialism. The American journalist and humorist H. L. Mencken said of Teddy Roosevelt in 1926: "He was an Imperialist of the type of Cecil Rhodes . . . [believing] strongly in centralized states, founded upon power and devoted to enterprises far transcending mere internal government."[12] But, whereas Rhodes was almost rueful towards the end of his life about some of his misdeeds, Roosevelt's imperialism was unapologetic. "The most ultimately righteous of all wars," he wrote, " is a war with savages, though it is apt to be the most terrible and inhuman. The rude, fierce settler who drives the savage from the land lays all civilised mankind under debt to him. American and Indian, Boer and Zulu, Cossack and Tartar, New Zealander and Maori—in each case the victor, horrible though many of his deeds are, has laid deep the foundations for the future greatness of a mighty people."[13] Roosevelt's predecessor, US President Grover Cleveland (1885-1889, 1893-1897) told a British audience: "For a man like Rhodes to develop their colonial empire, France will pay twenty millions. Germany would pay thirty millions. America would pay sixty millions—you have got him for nothing."[14]

The Ideals of Empire

Rhodes's interest in Empire was not in domination itself so much as in ensuring space for the expansion of the English "race", whose culture and values he thought would benefit everyone. At Oxford, he was inspired by John Ruskin's Inaugural Lecture as the Slade Professor of Fine Art. Although it was delivered in 1870, three years before Rhodes began his studies, he treasured a printed copy of it for years afterwards. It was an odd oration from an art theorist who would later be regarded as one of England's earliest socialists; but it expressed an enthusiasm that infected Ruskin at mid-career. Florid as it now sounds, the intensity of the Lecture is palpable to this day:

There is a destiny now possible to us, the highest ever set before a nation to be accepted or refused. We are still undegenerate in race; a race mingled of the best northern blood. We are not yet dissolute in temper, but still have the firmness to govern and the grace to obey ... Will you youths of England make your country again a royal throne of kings; a sceptred isle, for all the world a source of light, a centre of peace; mistress of learning and of the Arts, faithful guardian of time-tried principles ... This is what England must either do or perish: she must found colonies as fast and as far as she is able, formed of her most energetic and worthiest men; seizing every piece of fruitful waste ground she can set her foot on, and there teaching these her colonists that their chief virtue is to be fidelity to their country, and that their first aim is to be to advance the power of England by land and sea ... If we can get men, for little pay, to cast themselves against cannon-mouths for love of England, we may find men who will plough and sow for her, who will behave kindly, and will bring up their children to love her, and who will gladden themselves in the brightness of her glory, more than in all the light of tropical skies.[15]

In the inaugural issue of his magazine *The Review of Reviews* on 15 January 1891, the crusading journalist W.T. Stead summarized what he and Rhodes felt about the "immense vocation" of the English people: "Imperialism within limits defined by common sense and the Ten Commandments is a very different thing from the blatant Jingoism which some years ago made the very name of empire stink in the nostrils of all decent people . . . What is wanted is a revival of civic faith, a quickening of spiritual life in the political sphere, the inspiring of men and women with the conception of what may be done towards the salvation of the world."[16]

Who, Stead asked, could most promote human progress? "Let all races vote and see what they will say. Each race will no doubt vote for itself, but who receives every second vote? Mr. Rhodes had no hesitation in arriving at the conclusion that the English race—the English-speaking man, whether British, American, Australian, or South African—is the type of race which does now, and is likely to continue to do in the future, the most practical work to establish justice, to promote liberty, and to ensure peace over the widest possible area of the planet."[17]

One can be sceptical now about the motives of 19th century figures who were comfortably sheltered from the day-to-day realities of the Empire. But there are ample examples in our day of the *hubris* of wanting to transform other cultures and countries in one's own image. One of the best books on the failure of Western international development assistance is William

Easterly's *White Man's Burden*.[k] Despite that disappointing record, thousands of graduate students in international affairs and economic development across the Western world have yearned to "serve" in Africa—like latter-day missionaries—more than half a century after those countries achieved independence and well after any of them could be helped by well-intentioned generalists with little professional and life experience.

Western Superiority

That many English people in Rhodes's day believed they were superior to everyone else is not very different from how many Westerners still regard Africa and Asia now. And how was British self-confidence different from German swagger, French hauteur, and American exceptionalism? Pride in the spreading of a *Pax Britannica* was similar to US efforts to promote a *Pax Americana* in the 20th century. And few people outside that country would suggest that the US is still the "leader of the free world" or repeat the 150-year-old claim (as Chief Justice John Roberts did at the first impeachment trial of Donald Trump) that the US Senate is the "the world's greatest deliberative body". How is it greater than the British House of Commons (the "Mother of Parliaments") or the National Assembly of Mali, struggling to keep hopes of democracy alive in the midst of poverty and war?

A belief in the "civilizing" effect of Empire was so tantalizing that even fervent anti-imperialists could change

---

k   Published in 2006, the full title was *The White Man's Burden: Why the West's Efforts to Aid the Rest Have Done So Much Ill and So Little Good*. The title is of course intentionally ironic.

their views over time. Writing to Leonard Woolf on 21 May 1926, William Plomer expressed a certain nostalgia for South Africa: "I know it and love it, and I know the nobility of the natives and their unsurpassable human qualities, but the whites are unspeakable."[18] The year before, he had said: "It will be necessary to learn to recognise every man's human qualities as a contribution to the building up of an indestructible future, to judge every man by the colour of his soul and not by the colour of his skin. Otherwise the coloured races of the world will rise and take by force what is denied them now by a comparatively few muddle-headed money-grubbers."[19]

Yet, a quarter of a century after denouncing Rhodes's imperial ambitions, looking back on his own life in his 1958 autobiography, Plomer was haunted by the image of an African woman found dying in the bush a century before by British missionaries. Despite being pregnant, she had been thrown out of the house by her mother and husband because she had smallpox. She had given birth out in the open, unaided, only to be attacked during the night by a hyena, which dragged her child from her arms and devoured it. Later, the hyena came back. Weak as she was, the mother was able to fend it off but was badly mauled in doing so.

This "hellish happening", Plomer wrote, stuck in his mind as clearly as if he had witnessed it himself. "It is easy enough to remember the wrongs of Europe's incursions into Africa—the slave trade, commercial exploitation, racial contempt, and social injustice; but it is as well to remember that the wrongs done by Africans to Africans, out of greed, cruelty, callousness, superstition, and ignorance, are beyond computing." In language that Rhodes might have penned, he preferred to remember all that made the solitude of that woman under the tree less likely now: "compassion, charity, disinfectants, education, art, literature . . . [and] lives given to understanding, to forgiveness, to moral and material betterment."[20]

Rhodes's Actions

What about Rhodes's land grabbing? Mark Twain, who visited South Africa in May-July 1896, saw an echo there of American policy in the Philippines, which horrified him. England and America had always been kin, he wrote, "kin in blood, kin in religion, kin in representative government, kin in just and lofty purposes; and now we are kin in sin." Yet, Twain had a two-edged view of imperialism: "No tribe, however insignificant, and no nation, however mighty, occupies a foot of land that was not stolen. When the English, the French, and the Spaniards reached America, the Indian tribes had been raiding each other's territorial clothes-lines for ages, and every acre of ground in the continent had been stolen and re-stolen 500 times."[21] Large countries like the United States and Russia were founded on bloodshed, deceit, and land confiscation on a much larger scale than Rhodesia. These precedents do not provide a moral cover for Rhodes's behaviour, but they do suggest that it was not unique or unspeakable, as some now claim.

For Rhodes, the Empire was not just an opportunity to settle English people abroad and help improve the lives of others, directly or indirectly. It was part of England's life blood: "The dons of a college should tell the students once a year that England is not only the British Isles but the world—that our strength lies in keeping the markets of the world open, that we are a small spot on the world's surface but the greatest power as long as we maintain our markets."[22]

The Empire's civilizing mission was more than rhetoric for him. And such cultural arrogance is not the preserve of European imperialists. In a display case at the Bulawayo Museum about the original inhabitants of Zimbabwe (the Khosan or "Bush" people), there is the following caption: "There are only about 25,000 Bushmen left. They live in Botswana and Namibia, having been pushed into the desert by the more progressive Bantu."[23] In financial terms, too, there was nothing personal about Rhodes's occupation of Central Africa. He was already a wealthy man as a result of his successful investments in diamonds and gold. Most of his personal income came from De Beers and, far from adding to it, Rhodes spent much of his wealth on the occupation and settlement of Rhodesia.

The Spanish conquest of Latin America—directly and through the spread of new diseases—led to so many deaths that the very climate of parts of the continent was affected as forest replaced farmland on a vast scale. Would the Spanish have restrained themselves if they had been able to foresee the extent of human destruction they were unleashing? Perhaps not, as many Spaniards questioned whether the "natives" were even human beings. The Dominican defender of indigenous rights, Bartolomé de las Casas (1484-1566), crossed the Atlantic fourteen times to persuade the Spanish government that the so-called Indians had souls.[24]

Yet, at least at the very start, the occupation of what was to become Rhodesia occurred without the loss of a single human life, thanks mainly to the restraint and realism of King Lobengula. It led to two uprisings—in 1893 and 1896-97—which certainly proved bloody. But the human cost was limited compared with the Spanish conquest of Mexico and Latin America in the 16th century or the American takeover of the Great Plains and New Spain (California, Arizona, Texas, New Mexico, etc.) in the early 19th century. It may be argued that one should not compare degrees of evil: if every human life is sacred, every death is significant. But critics of Cecil

Rhodes have not shrunk from sometimes-extreme historical comparisons. Rhodes's contemporaries also engaged in moral accounting and claimed that they had improved the welfare of the territories they occupied by ending the murderous "tax collecting" of the Ndebele people.

This is not to deny that Rhodes was guilty of deceit and arrogance and a sense of entitlement, posing as duty, on a large scale. Plomer was merciless on this point: "A deliberate annexation or conquest . . . would have had strong arguments in its favour, but the British invasion . . . was marked by humbug and dishonesty. Lip-service was paid in London to philanthropic principles . . . . We too have our witch-doctors, and the flutter of a surplice [the white linen vestment worn by Christian clergy] can always be caught sight of between the machine-guns."[25] A member of the House of Lords added at the time: "Throughout the last acts of that conflict, Lobengula made a far better showing for the credit of human character than did the assailants of his domain."[26]

That said, it was a savage age on all sides—if not as savage as the 20th century would turn out to be. Almost a million people are estimated to have died at the hands of Shaka Zulu (1787-1828) and his warriors earlier in the century, while the human cost of the Ndebele raiding expeditions in what is now Zimbabwe was enormous.[27] Rhodes and his associates did not invade Central Africa for humanitarian reasons, but it is probably true that their land seizures involved much less violence, even in the course of two wars of resistance, than the Ndebele had caused over a period of fifty years.

The real tragedy is that Rhodes did not follow up on his promise, during the peace talks in the Matopos Hills in 1896, to guarantee land to more than an Ndebele elite, however numerous it turned out to be. And the Shona people's traditional methods of shifting cultivation and leaving large tracts of land fallow were overturned by the European settlers' habits of fixed properties and farms. Therein lay the seeds of future conflict.[28] The problem had been crystallized years before. Addressing a South Africa Company meeting after the first Ndebele War, Mr. Albert Grey (later Lord Grey) said that the defeat of the Ndebele had allowed "the starved and wretched natives [the Shona] to descend from their mountain fastnesses and build their huts upon the plains, and for the first time in their lives to cultivate their rich fields in security and peace." But, asked later whom they preferred as lords—the Ndebele or the Europeans— some Shona replied: "The Ndebele burn us and rob us and kill us and take our wives, but then they go away. The white people do not go away."[29]

CHAPTER TEN
White Supremacist?

C LOSELY LINKED TO the charge of imperialism is the suggestion that Cecil Rhodes was an outright racist. Rhodes's views on race were more of a muddle than a doctrine, but three things are clear: he was much less of a racist than most of his white contemporaries; he did not believe in any inherent genetic difference between peoples; and, while he could say brutal things in the heat of war, there is no evidence that he ever mistreated people because of the colour of their skin.

Early Impressions

The seventeen-year-old Rhodes described Africans for the first time in a letter to his mother on 11 September 1870, ten days after arriving on the continent: "The Kaffirs[1] rather shock your modesty. Many of them have nothing on, excepting a

---

1 "Kaffir" is derived from the Arabic word for "non-believer" and was regarded as an insult even in Rhodes's day.

band around the middle. They are fine-looking men, and carry themselves very erect . . . The most disagreeable thing about them is their smell. I don't believe anything equals the smell of a party of Kaffir women on a hot day if you pass on the lee side of them." Then, in the same letter: "There is a great satisfaction in having land of your own, horses of your own, and shooting when you like, and a lot of black niggers to do what you like with, apart from the fact of making money."[1]

These were the thoughts of a boastful and impressionable young man picking up objectionable words and stereotypes around him like lint on fly-paper. Did his reference to body odour mark him out as racially insensitive? Hardly. He was not the first or last to react that way in the tropics. An eminent Turkish economist once made a similar remark to me, getting off a crowded elevator in Côte d'Ivoire. Japanese noses have also been offended on visits to Europe and North America. And, for a very long time, well-scrubbed American tourists took a dim view of Frenchmen before the latter discovered deodorants towards the end of the 20th century. Never having managed anyone before, Rhodes must also have found it heady to be able to give people orders.

But as he struggled to run his brother's cotton farm alone with about 30 African workers, he developed an admiration and respect for them, while also absorbing the prejudices of his day. According to some of the early biographers, it was here that he learned to "manage natives". Writing to his mother again on 26 February 1871, he explained that many people avoided growing cotton because of the need for seasonal labour. "Because, though there are any amount of Kaffirs, they are the laziest race under the sun. Their wants are few, and they will only work when they are compelled to it, either by hunger, or else want of money for [the] hut-tax."[2]

Two months later (on 20 April 1871): "I have lent a good

deal of money to the Kaffirs, as it is the hut-tax time, and . . . if you lend it to them, they will come and work it out, besides getting you a very good name amongst them, and Kaffirs are really safer than the Bank of England. Herbert [his brother] for instance when he went to [explore for] Diamonds, actually gave the whole of his gold to one of his Kaffirs, and it will be far safer with him than with Herbert . . . . I make it a rule if I can never to refuse a Kaffir labour, and if I know something about him, never refuse to lend him money; when they want to go to work, they are awful fellows for weighing in their minds the different advantages of the white masters, and of course it is a great inducement if they know that they are always sure of work, or money advanced by the master, because they sometimes come from 20 to 30 miles distant, for work."[3]

Even Antony Thomas, one of Rhodes's more severe biographers, describes his closeness to Africans as a young man. "Rhodes enjoyed an easy, unprejudiced relationship with the local Africans. He was always intensely interested in them (as he was in everything) and quickly appreciated the value that they placed in a man's trust. Before long, he had applied that understanding to the labour problem and introduced the revolutionary scheme of paying his workers in advance . . . Of course, it all worked to Rhodes's advantage, but at this stage of his life one can believe in something beyond self-interest... His friendliness and unfeigned interest in people took him into Zulu villages where he would observe the details of African life and share their food and hospitality."[4]

Rhodes's Views

As he matured, Rhodes prided himself on his personal rapport with Africans and experimented awkwardly with learning their languages. In the words of an early biographer, "Rhodes regarded the native with more humanity than the Dutch and more realism than the missionary. His personal relations with natives were delightfully natural and open . . . He emphasized the responsibility of the European in contact with primitive peoples, whose rights, if unprotected, must perish, whose character, unless safeguarded, would be undermined, and whose land if not secured, would be lost to them. The European must not be a conquistador but a trustee. The native was a child, to be treated neither as a full-fledged citizen nor as though he were incapable of growth."[5]

Referring to Africans as "children" now seems mortifying. But Rhodes meant it literally. With proper education, good example, and the right opportunities, he thought that Africans could be expected to assume increasing responsibilities. He was vague on how long that would take. In one speech, he referred to a hundred years, which made nonsense of the image; but, on that occasion, he was also trying to allay the fears of Afrikaner politicians whose views were less liberal than his. Yet, Rhodes's view must be set against those of others in his day who regarded non-Europeans as sub-human at best.

Rhodes certainly considered the English "race" to be superior, but not as a result of better chromosomes. Instead, he saw English culture, upbringing, and values as the fruit of a favourable history, including four hundred years of Roman occupation, and regarded Africans as the counterparts of his own remote ancestors in ancient Britain, coming to terms with new technology, institutions, and opportunities.[6] One biographer in 1956 was undoubtedly exaggerating when he claimed that, "In time, Cecil Rhodes was to understand the African natives better than any other man in the continent."[7] But it is undeniable that Rhodes reflected hard about "native" policy, as it was called at the time, based on what he regarded as real sympathy and instincts that were not widespread in his day. "I could never accept the position that we should disqualify any human being on account of his colour," he said on one occasion. "In fact, it is not a question of colour at all [and] I think that we have been extremely liberal in granting [Africans] forty or fifty years training of what we have ourselves obtained only after many hundreds of years of civilisation."[8]

Vere Stent, the journalist who attended the 1896 peace talks in the Matopos Hills, recalled that during the first Ndebele uprising three years before he was shocked by the cruelties on both sides. "Rhodes," he said, "showed sympathy, not with the brutalities, of course, but with the fine up-standing fighting man, the [Ndebele] . . . He could not bring himself to regard the natives as so many white men did, and do in Rhodesia. He was wont to say, 'These are children; they are cruel; so are children, sometimes. Have you never seen a child pull off a fly's wing in wanton cruelty? They are children, and we must treat them as children. The first thing you need in treating children, is sympathy."[9]

The British High Commissioner in Cape Town, Lord Milner, who first thought Rhodes "too self-willed, too violent, too sanguine, and too much in a hurry", later described him as "exceedingly conciliatory", especially towards Africans. His architect Herbert Baker reported that Rhodes spent Sundays in Kimberley visiting the mine-workers. Once, when he persuaded the De Beers board to accept a contentious proposal, he went off to their compound to distribute £1,500 among the workers so that they could share in his success. Jameson told Baker that Rhodes "liked to be with [Africans]; he trusted them and they fairly worshipped him." He gave financial support to Lovedale, the missionary college for Africans that later nurtured independence leaders like Kenneth Kaunda (Zambia), Seretse Khama (Botswana), and Julius Nyerere (Tanzania). Rhodes also put Lobengula's two sons through school near Cape Town.

"He treated them," Baker relates, "according to their rank, welcoming them into his house."[10]

Rhodes's paternalism had its particularities. Curiously, he took a dim view of the "decadence" of some of the coloured [mixed-race] population. According to Herbert Baker, "They were so different from the healthy barbarism of the natives, whom he knew and loved."[11] There were also limits to his protectiveness as a "father". Talking to settlers in Bulawayo in 1893, he defended the Chartered Company's right to allocate land in Rhodesia against the views of the "negrophilists of Exeter Hall"[m] who insisted that land grants must be subject to the British High Commissioner's approval.[12]

In August 1897, on a trip to the Matopos Hills, Lewis Michell learned that Rhodes had settled 4,000 Africans on a housing estate, including many leaders of the recent rebellion. "In almost every second hut there was a chief. Every step in the Matabele 'peerage' was represented. Lo Bengula's own brother was there, with several of his wives, children and sisters." Then, they visited the grave of the first Ndebele king Mzilikazi to ensure that it was now intact. During the war, a British soldier had defiled the cairn, intending to sell the dead king's bones as curios; but "Rhodes came down on him like an avalanche", recovered the fragments and called on the Ndebele to restore them to their resting-place with appropriate reverence and ceremony. "It was his intimate insight into their thoughts and habits," Michell wrote, "that gave Rhodes so strong a hold upon all native tribes with whom he was brought into contact."[13] This was gilding the lily, but informative all the same.

---

m Exeter Hall was a large conference centre in London which hosted gatherings of the Anti-Slavery Society and other humanitarian groups. It was replaced in 1909 by the Strand Palace Hotel.

Rhodes and His Contemporaries

Intended to contradict the idea that Rhodes was heartless, such reminiscences combined overstatement with genuine admiration, as few of his associates behaved in the same way. "One of Mr. Rhodes's most prominent characteristics," recalled Dr. Jameson, "is his great liking for, and sympathy with the black men, the natives of the country. He likes to be with them, he is fond of them and trusts them, and they admire and trust him. He had thousands of natives under him in the De Beers mines. He carefully provided for their comfort, recreation and health. He was always looking after their interests. He liked to be with them, and his favourite recreation every Sunday afternoon was to go into the De Beers native compound, where he had built them a fine swimming bath, and throw in shillings for natives to dive for."[14] This last detail is cringeworthy, but with just a little effort it is possible to believe that this was an expression of genuine camaraderie rather than an example of egregious condescension. One thing is certain: very few other European employers at the time deigned to brush shoulders with their African workers.

Such compliments shed a searing light on the attitudes of Rhodes's contemporaries. Rhodes's friend James Maguire thought that the Chartered Company's "treatment of the natives" was "highly creditable". "It would indeed be stigmatized in other parts of Africa as philanthropic to the verge of sentimentality. The use of the lash, for instance, is not permitted at all." Though probably not a teetotaller himself, Maguire praised Rhodes's ban on Africans drinking alcohol, which was "to the great advantage of their health, their morals, and their finances" and "honourably distinguishes the Chartered Administration almost alone among the many other European Administrations in Africa. It may safely be said that the Chartered Company, if it has erred at all in its treatment of the natives, has erred by excess of leniency."[15]

According to Jameson, Rhodes liked having Africans around him. At Groote Schuur, apart from his valet John Norris, there were no European employees and he was very protective of them.[16] He once reprimanded his secretary Le Sueur for using the word "nigger" several times within earshot of his cook Anthony de la Cruz, a man of mixed race.[17] Almost certainly, Rhodes forgot that he had used the same word as a teenager writing home to his mother; or he had stopped using it altogether.

This is far from saying that Rhodes was beyond reproach in every circumstance. War could draw out the worst and the best in him. Asked during the second Ndebele uprising whether prisoners should be taken, he said "You should kill all you can, it serves as a lesson to them when they talk things over at night."[18] But, when the young journalist Vere Stent was concerned that prisoners who were barely fifteen years old had their wrists bound so tightly that they bled, Rhodes went over and loosened the bonds himself, even though some American mercenaries nearby had spurned Stent's request. Rhodes then released them and sent them home with the message that "the white man wanted peace".[19]

Famous Phrases

Three phrases have been cited against Rhodes to suggest that he was an extreme racist. We have already encountered two of them: "Africans are children" and "Kill as many of them as you can." The third is the most famous: "I prefer land to niggers." But this was the invention of Olive Schreiner, who used it in her 1897 novel *Trooper Peter Halket of Mashonaland*, which was a scalding indictment of Rhodes's and Jameson's actions in Rhodesia. It was based on a faulty recollection of an 1892 debate in the Cape Colony Parliament in which Rhodes had said: "You want to annex land rather than natives. Hitherto we have been annexing natives instead of land".[20] Although still objectionable, what Rhodes meant was that it was better to acquire largely uninhabited territory that would be easy to settle, than to take over areas already populated by others.

Another ugly phrase can be found in Rhodes's "Confession of Faith", written at Oxford in 1877, where Rhodes suggested that other parts of the globe were "inhabited by the most despicable specimens of human beings", whom British rule would help "civilize". It was a puerile and rambling document. He was only 24. And he did not use the phrase again for the rest of his life, at least in the written record.

Rhodes did have a fixation on the "idleness" of Africans who were not formally employed, and he had a horror of "loafers" of any race. He once described his own brother in that way and advised a friend at Oxford not to become a writer as that was a "loafer's" profession. And he used a European parallel in describing able-bodied young Africans living with their parents: "Their present life is very similar to that of a young man about town who lounges about at a club during the day, dresses himself up for a tea-party in the afternoon, and in the evening drinks too much, and probably finishes up with immorality."[21]

Glen Grey Debate

Now, we must turn to the most important speech he ever made on "native" policy, in moving the Second Reading of the proposed Glen Grey Act on 30 July 1894. It is a shocking statement, designed in part to pander to Afrikaner opinion which he needed to court at the time. He started by referring to a national railway strike in the United States organized out of

Chicago that had ended just ten days before. During the strike, thirty workers had been killed by railroad agents. Claiming that the dispute had "practically wrecked" the city, Rhodes pointed out how convenient it was that South Africa had a more docile potential workforce at its disposal. "If the whites maintain their position as the supreme race, the day may come when we shall all be thankful that we have the natives with us in their proper position. We shall be thankful that we have escaped those difficulties which are going on amongst all the old nations of the world."

Choosing words that would have delighted later proponents of apartheid, he explained why he was creating reserves. "What I would like in regard to a native area is that there should be no white men in its midst. I hold that the natives should be apart from white men, and not mixed up with them." Driving in that nail, he continued: "We fail utterly when we put natives on an equality with ourselves. If we deal with them differently and say 'Yes, these people have their own ideas', and so on, then we are all right; but when once we depart from that position and put them on an equality with ourselves, we may give the matter up. What we may expect after a hundred years of civilisation I do not know."[n]

Then, he explained what he regarded as the positive purposes of the Act: "We have to find land for these people; we have to find them employment; we have to remove the liquor from them; and we have to stimulate them to work. Do you admit that the native question is most dangerous? Do you admit that you have done nothing for these people?

---

n   The answer, of course, is inclusive democracy. Nelson Mandela became President of South Africa on 10 May 1994, two months short of the centenary of Rhodes's Glen Grey speech.

Do you admit that in many parts of the colony these people have been ruining themselves? Do you admit that century after century these large numbers could not be provided with land? Do you admit that these people are increasing at a great rate?" Finally, he reverted to the position he was more accustomed to expressing in private: "The natives are children, and we ought to do something for the minds and brains that the Almighty has given them. I do not believe that they are different from ourselves."[22]

This zig-zagging around the subject was plainly an effort to convince the Afrikaners in Parliament to overcome their objections to creating reserves, as many white farmers resented being excluded from what was then still fertile land. Rhodes was proud of the Act as a serious answer to issues that he thought Africans were facing and Europeans were ignoring. The alternative would have been neglect and eventually bloody land disputes right across the Colony. Already, in 1883, Africans outnumbered Europeans 5:1 (1,250,000 and 250,000, respectively). Yet, some politicians were indifferent and even cynical about the looming social conflict. In 1887, Rhodes castigated one of them in Parliament for claiming that "it would be better to have a Kaffir war every ten years than keep up the C.M.R. [Cape Mounted Riflemen]."[23]

The Heritage of Racism

All human beings struggle with racism and xenophobia, and the British have a long record of discriminating against people who are different. Over a million Indian soldiers fought for the British in the First World War and about 74,000 died. Many of the wounded were treated in the Brighton Pavilion and Dome Hospital for Indian Troops, surrounded with barbed wire to prevent them from mixing with the local population.

Almost 16,000 West Indians also died in the two world wars. Yet, until recently, neither group was properly recognized for their sacrifices. Instead, as early as 1919, hate crimes and race riots broke out in the UK and as Commonwealth immigration increased—between 1951 to 1961 the Caribbean-born population alone rose from 15,000 to 172,000—so did tensions. To this day, names like Nottingham, Notting Hill, Brixton, and Tottenham echo the heritage of racial violence.[24]

Cecil Rhodes did not invent British or European or any other form of anti-black racism, which existed long before him and persists to this day. Nor was he a particularly virulent example of the strain. Even self-proclaimed progressives had their blind spots. For example, the novelist Olive Schreiner was squeamish about inter-racial marriage and compared the act of destroying "human varieties" to vandals destroying a Gothic cathedral. "The lap-dog on my knee, the mastiff who guards my house, are both so wholly desirable that I wish to see neither of them extinguished. Shall we value our human varieties less than my dogs?"[25]

But, for a man whose every utterance was part of the public record in one form or another and who spawned memoirs and reminiscences from friends and foes alike, the evidence for his being a "white supremacist" in the current sense of the phrase is unpersuasive. If we are to point a finger at anyone, it should be at ourselves as much as at him. And there are better headings under which to condemn or praise him.

CHAPTER ELEVEN
War and Apartheid

R HODES'S ACTIONS, HOWEVER, did lead to thousands of deaths (perhaps 6,000 in the two Ndebele uprisings) and arguably to even greater casualties in the South African War (as many as 80,000). The first two conflicts were rebellions rather than military actions launched by Rhodes; but that is a technicality. Without his occupation of their land and the settlers' subsequent mistreatment of the Ndebele and Shona peoples, there would have been no occasion for bloodshed.

We may wonder why Rhodes and his compatriots were not more ashamed of the deaths caused by their territorial ambitions. Unfortunately, human beings have a remarkable capacity to overlook carnage, especially if the victims are foreigners purportedly killed for our own protection. Few of us would want a single life on our conscience, let alone the 6,000 that were lost in the Ndebele conflicts. But how many people visiting the World Trade Center Memorial in New York City to mourn the deaths of 3,000 people on 9/11 now think of the at least 1.3 million people who have died since then in wars of retaliation in Iraq, Afghanistan, and Pakistan?[1]

Rhodes's Role

Rhodes created conditions that led to wars but he also tried to stop them. We will recall that he restrained Jameson in the run-up to the first Ndebele uprising by cabling him a passage from the Gospel of Saint Luke. The war itself was the product of a series of blunders. At the last minute, Rhodes also ordered Jameson to stand down on the plot to invade the Transvaal Republic. And, during the second Ndebele conflict, he ignored the advice of the military and civil authorities and ventured into the Matopos unarmed for two months to negotiate peace. There, he stood firm against the Deputy High Commissioner Sir Richard Martin's wish to arrest everyone on his "black list" of supposed rebel leaders. Of course, none of them was going to give himself up. As one of Rhodes's friends wrote, "They preferred the chance of being shot on a granite kopje [hill] in the Matopos to the probability of trying the strength of a hemp rope at Bulawayo."[2] Leaving nothing to chance, Rhodes told Martin that if there was further bloodshed, it would be on his hands, and Martin backed down.

Rhodes's actions were not lost on those he saved. In a friend's words, "The Matabele are perfectly well aware to whose clemency they owe their lives, and the rebel Indunas [leaders] especially have good reasons to be thankful that it was the counsels of Mr. Rhodes, and not the hanging orders of Sir Richard Martin, that prevailed in the end."[3] Nor should it be forgotten that Rhodes saved the Ndebele from starvation that winter by donating £6 million of his personal funds so that they could buy corn. Compare that behaviour with the charge made against Rhodes's contemporary, Canada's first prime minister Sir John A. Macdonald (1867-1873, 1878-1891), that he deliberately reduced food shipments to Indigenous people on the plains in the midst of a famine so as to force them into reserves and make way for the construction of a national railroad. [4]

The biographer Antony Thomas, who is no admirer of Rhodes, suggests that Jameson was the ultimate cause of the various "catastrophes" that his friend had to manage. "Although Rhodes was ultimately responsible for the harsh conditions that had driven his black subjects to revolt, his fundamental mistake had been to delegate power and authority to Jameson and to rely on his friend's judgement. Jameson lacked Rhodes's great gifts of insight and perception, his uncanny ability to get inside other people's heads. He was over-confident, reckless and needlessly provocative. These were not Rhodes's faults. Even at his worst, Rhodes could not be accused of gratuitous brutality."[5] Blaming Jameson for all of Rhodes's misdeeds is rather generous—as surely a man who had shared a house and, occasionally, every waking moment with him would have been aware of the lengths to which Rhodes was prepared to go to achieve his ends. But such a judgment, lenient as it appears, confirms the complexity of the story.

The South African War

What about Rhodes's alleged role in provoking the South African War of 1899-1902? As a private citizen and, more than that, a discredited statesman, he was not in a position to affect the negotiations between the British government and the Transvaal Republic that led up to the conflict. And, whatever his private hopes may have been, he was fervent in his public statements that such a conflict could and should be avoided. Scholars are divided on the extent of Rhodes's responsibility for the War but some are clear-cut. In the view of one historian, no single person—with the possible exception of Lord Milner— can be said to have started the War, and even he "helped to stir the pot [but] did not supply the ingredients.[6] His colleague (and future writer of adventure and detective stories) John Buchan was less sparing: "[Milner] was the last man likely to obtain a settlement with Kruger; there was a gnarled magnificence in the old Transvaal President, but he saw only a snuffy, mendacious savage. He detested lies, and diplomacy demands something less than the plain truth."[7]

When it erupted, it was a "white man's war", fought between 88,000 Dutch republican troops and 450,000 British ones. The British decided not to involve Indian personnel in the fighting, as they had in other African campaigns, and neither side enlisted Africans except as scouts, servants, and guards. Neither the British nor the Boers wanted to weaken European control over the Africans. Despite being outnumbered 5:1, the Boers at first had the advantage, with their knowledge of the terrain, their shooting skills, and a keen sense of the justice of their cause. But, as the fighting dragged on, the head of the British forces, Lord Kitchener (who had received his honorary degree alongside Rhodes two years before) set up concentration camps to separate Afrikaner fighters from their families. By the end of the War, 25,000 women and children—more than the number of British dead (22,000)—had died in the camps from hunger and disease.[8]

While there is no evidence that Rhodes manoeuvred behind the scenes to precipitate the War, once it broke out he threw himself fervently into the fray, taking one of the last trains from Cape Town to Kimberley to join in the defence of the diamond fields. He was also incensed about any criticism of the conflict, including that of the journalist W.T. Stead, which he described as "insubordination". "You have never been to South Africa," Rhodes wrote to Stead, "and yet instead of deferring to the judgment of your own boys, you fling yourself into a violent opposition to the war. I should not have acted in that way about an English question or an American question. No matter how much I might have disliked the course which you advised, I would have said, 'No, I know Stead; I trust his judgment, and he is on the spot. I support whatever policy he recommends'."[9]

The horror of that conflict still weighs heavily on Afrikaners and demands proper accounting. In such soul-searching, Rhodes is an obvious target; but some of that criticism is pure invention. "Rhodes," wrote Christopher Hope in 2018, "had been one of the chief manipulators of the push to war, who believed it to be essential that the right sorts of people prevailed over the wrong sorts of people, especially Boers and Blacks who were each as lamentably backward as the other."[10] According to Hope, President Kruger was the only barrier between Rhodes and "the treasures of the Transvaal"; so he decided to get rid of him as he had with Lobengula, who "stood between him and the goldfields of Bulawayo".[11] Yet, Rhodes already had access to the Transvaal goldfields without a war and, as noted earlier, there was very little gold in Rhodesia. The main purpose of occupying Central Africa was to protect the "Suez Canal" to the North that Rhodes needed to promote British control "from the Cape to Cairo".

As for Rhodes's distaste for Africans and Afrikaners, it is worth listening to Jan Christian Smuts (1870-1950) who fought against the British in the War and was South Africa's prime minister in 1919-1924 and 1939-1948. Writing in the wake of the Jameson Raid, he commented, "The Dutch are perhaps a suspicious people, but when they come to put their trust in a man . . . then the trust becomes almost absolute and religious: such was their faith in Mr. Rhodes."[12]

Yet, in South Africa, among many Afrikaners, Rhodes's name is indelibly linked with the War. The first person to turn down a Rhodes Scholarship (in 1903) was Tobie Muller, a graduate of the Dutch-language Stellenbosch College School, who disapproved very strongly of Rhodes. He went on to become a champion of the Afrikaans language but died at the age of 34 during the 1918 flu epidemic.[13]

Over a century later, writing in *The Times* at the height of the 2015 Rhodes Must Fall campaign, ex-President F.W. de Klerk was unequivocal: "My people—the Afrikaners—have greater reason to dislike Rhodes than anyone else. He was the architect of the Anglo-Boer War that had a disastrous impact on our people. Yet the National Party government never thought of removing his name from our history."[14] Rhodes's role was so self-evident to Afrikaners that none of them has ever been tempted to join the long parade of his biographers. His English-speaking contemporaries, however, thought otherwise. His fellow parliamentarian, Thomas Fuller, who was capable of criticizing Rhodes to his face and was firmly opposed the Jameson Raid, was terse on this point: "Mr. Rhodes had nothing to do with [the War's] inception."[15]

What Afrikaners find obvious is confirmed by many historians. Even though Rhodes tried to call it off, the Jameson Raid raised British-Transvaal tensions to such a pitch that war became inevitable. The fact that Rhodes did nothing further to exacerbate those tensions is irrelevant to the verdict. Those intervening four years were like the batting of an eyelash in a Transvaal Republic still reeling from Rhodes's recklessness.

The irony is that he wanted all his life—as documented in his writings as a young man and his series of wills—to be a peacemaker. The final form of that ambition was the creation of the Rhodes Scholarships. He hoped that the spreading of what he regarded as enlightened values through an old boys' network at Oxford made up of Americans, British, and Germans would help promote global prosperity and perpetual peace. Alfred Nobel, another philanthropist who earned his wealth in questionable ways (through dynamite and arms production) took a different tack, creating a prize to support the international peace movement of the 1890s.

But, unlike Rhodes, whose vision now seems simplistic, Nobel's realism was as cold as the Scandinavian climate. "Perhaps," he wrote to a friend, "my factories will put an end to war sooner than your [peace] congresses: on the day that two army corps can mutually annihilate each other in a second, all civilized nations will surely recoil with horror and disband their troops."[16] Later, he thought that the invention of chemical weapons would end all wars. Rhodes may be accused of being naïve, but—unlike Nobel—he had seen war up close and his idealism may be all the more creditable for that.

Architect of Apartheid?

If it is clear that Rhodes did not plan or even want the South African War but contributed to the atmosphere in which it erupted, so too it can be argued that some of his words and actions prefigured full-blown racial segregation at a later date. But calling him its architect suggests a degree of foresight, design, manipulation, and even vindictiveness that is not easily supported by historical evidence.

Although he made shameful concessions to Boer opinion on African voting rights (for which some of his liberal contemporaries never forgave him) and Jan Smuts later linked segregation ("the new orientation of African policy") with the passing of the Glen Grey Act in 1894,[17] it would be hard to demonstrate that Rhodes set the precise course for race relations in South Africa in the decades that followed. Besides, it seems plain that Rhodes was changing course on the subject of African voting rights in his last two years.

Rhodes had been buried five years when the British Liberal

Prime Minister Henry Campbell-Bannerman granted self-government to the Transvaal in 1907 without insisting on votes for Africans, Asians, and Coloureds. Later, in 1910, when the UK Parliament approved the creation of the Union of South Africa, it provided for qualified voting rights for Africans and Coloureds in the Cape only. In the rest of the Union, only Europeans could vote.

In that debate, another Liberal Prime Minister Herbert Asquith declared rather piously that "any control or interference from outside . . . is in the very worst interests of the natives themselves [but] I anticipate that [the Union] will be a harbinger of a native policy more consistent and more enlightened than that which has been pursued by some communities in the past." Then, in his last speech to the House of Commons on the subject, he said: "I am sure our fellow subjects will not take it in bad part if we respectfully and very earnestly beg them at some time, that they, in the exercise of their undoubted and unfettered freedom, should find it possible sooner or later, and sooner rather than later, to modify the provisions.[18] "In this way," wrote the South African historian Leonard Thompson, "the British Government and Parliament finally washed their hands of responsibility for the political rights of Africans, Asians, and Coloured people."[19] Given his evolving views on this subject, it is difficult to know what Rhodes's position would have been in that debate.

In the field of sports, however—an important feature of South African life—Rhodes set an unfortunate precedent as Prime Minister of the Cape that would have lasting consequences. A cricket star named Krom Hendricks, one of the most talented fast bowlers ever to emerge in South Africa, was a natural choice for the 1894 tour of England. But the English players were nervous about facing the "speed merchant", so Rhodes decided that Hendricks—who was of mixed race, a Cape Malay—should not be selected for the team as it would be "impolitic" to do so. It would be another century before African and Coloured athletes could represent their country in international tournaments.[20]

It is impossible to know how Rhodes would have reacted to formalized or "grand" apartheid as institutionalized after 1948. "His moral attitudes apart," suggests one writer with surprising confidence, "one can be sure he would have recognized it as economic madness."[21] Philip Ziegler, in his 2008 book *Legacy: Cecil Rhodes, The Rhodes Trust and Rhodes Scholarships,* thought that there was "no reason to believe that Rhodes was malign in his intentions or that he would have condoned the enormities to come." But Ziegler found it hard to dispute Professor Rotberg's measured conclusion that: "Rhodes's disregard of (antagonism towards is too strong) the human and political value of Africans foreshadowed, indeed prepared the path for the segregationist attitudes and legislation that were so prevalent during the decades of actual union."[22] More recently, in a submission to the Oriel College Independent Commission of Inquiry in September 2020, Professor Rotberg suggested that, while Rhodes was not "personally racist", some of his actions and policies "unwittingly" enabled those who were to oppress Africans.[23] Those are stinging judgements from a liberal American scholar who spent eighteen years preparing the most authoritative biography of the man. But both conclusions fall short of the claim that Rhodes was the "architect" of apartheid.

That has not deterred knowledgeable people from asserting the contrary. When Nelson Mandela agreed to the creation of the Mandela-Rhodes Foundation on the centenary of the Rhodes Scholarships in 2003, Rhodes's 1997 biographer Antony Thomas cried foul. "To link the Rhodes name with Mandela is a blasphemy. It's unbelievable. It's linking the architect

of apartheid with the exponent of its destruction. It shows
terrible insensitivity." Like some African Rhodes Scholars
more recently, Mandela himself apparently shared the Roman
Emperor Vespasian's view that "money has no odour"—an
observation that the Chairman of the Rhodes Trust William
Waldegrave brought to Mandela's attention in Cape Town.
Mandela described combining his name with that of Rhodes
as "the closing of the circle and the coming together of two
strands of our history."[24]

CHAPTER TWELVE
The Rhodes Scholarships

R HODES KNEW THAT his record would be debated.
The day of his honorary degree, he admitted to friends
at Oriel College that, in expanding the British Empire
and, with it "the cause of peace, of industry and freedom", his
methods had sometimes been "rough and ready". But, in South
Africa "laws of right and equity were not so fine and established
as they happily were in this country" and English history was
replete with "men who had done good service to the State
but some of whose actions . . . were hard to justify in a more
peaceful and law-abiding age." It was against that yardstick that
he hoped to be measured.[1]

At about the same time, in Cape Town, he had a soul-
searching talk with his friend Thomas Fuller. "Barbarism,
[Rhodes] said, had held sway in Central Africa for thousands
of years and it was time it was supplanted by civilisation. 'What
sort of civilisation do you propose?' [Fuller] said, half in jest:
'will it be that which employs gunpowder and Cape smoke [a
popular brandy] as its agents—in other words, the introduction
of the vicious habits of the old country [Great Britain]? 'No'
[Rhodes] said, 'nor do I want the natives to ape European dress

or cover themselves with a veneer of sanctity. I want them to learn to work, to feed and clothe themselves decently, to show some concern for each other's welfare, and ultimately to come into "affairs" [by which Rhodes meant acquiring and distributing wealth and organizing life for the better]."[2]

In Scotland, Lady Warwick had asked him whether he had ever been happy. He said that he had always been pleased planning and conceiving of things that could never happen in his lifetime. Warwick persisted. But had he ever been happy with things just as they were? "No," Rhodes replied. "I was too busy when I was young [and] I have had no time since."[3]

During the last decade of his life, however, he did become excited about an idea that had first occurred to him, sailing on the Red Sea, in 1893: a program of scholarships that would draw together the brightest young men of the British Empire and the United States to study at Oxford, building lasting bonds among them, helping them assume positions of leadership and influence back home, and thereby promoting world prosperity and peace. As an idea, it was as daring as the Jameson Raid. But it took a more propitious course.

As I can attest firsthand, until Rhodes Scholars marry or have their first child, the day they are chosen is the happiest in their lives. Even then, because the honour lasts for life, details of that moment lie deep in their memory for decades to come. Still the most prestigious academic award of its kind in the English-speaking world, it confers a sense of immediate importance and accomplishment (even before accomplishing anything) and builds up self-confidence to an almost dangerous degree. That is why jokes have always abounded to take air out of the new Scholars' balloons. "Charming young men with bright futures behind them" is one of them. (Women were excluded from the Scholarship until 1977.)

A more elaborate spoof was spun by E. T. ("Bill") Williams,

who was Warden of Rhodes House in Oxford and chief administrator of the Scholarships between 1952 and 1980: "When he is first awarded the Scholarship the successful Scholar's reaction is nearly always that there must have been a mistake; he cannot possibly possess the semi-divine attributes which Rhodes demanded in his elect. Next comes the realisation that no mistake has been made: Quite a lot of fuss is made of him, particularly locally, and he comes to regard himself as a very remarkable chap, although in most cases he keeps his head about it. Finally, he arrives at Oxford, still conscious of his glory, and finds, in some cases to his surprise, that he is of no importance at all, and the one thing Oxford requires of these leaders of tomorrow is that they should not start leading today."[4]

Rhodes would have smiled at such tales only if he also knew that his idea of a global scholarship had flourished. Otherwise, he would have refused to joke about a subject that he regarded as dead serious—to such a degree that he devoted the bulk of his fortune to it. Every one of Rhodes's wills, from when he had almost nothing to dispose of except ideas, and widening gradually with his wealth and worldview, was inspired by the same central idea: the broadening of Anglo-Saxon influence as a means of securing peace in the world.[5]

Vision

In his youthful "Confession of Faith" (1877), Rhodes talked about British subjects colonizing all of Africa, the Holy Land, the Valley of the Euphrates, the islands of Cyprus and Crete, the whole of South America, the Pacific Islands, all of the Malayan archipelago, and the seaboard of China and Japan, while also recovering the United States as an integral part of the British Empire. This would create "so great a power as to hereafter render wars impossible and promote the best interests of humanity". He also talked about creating a "secret society" like the Jesuits° to help bring the whole of the "civilised" world under British rule. What was needed was "a Church for the extension of the British Empire". The idea never left him. In March 1891, Rhodes asked Lord Rothschild, who was a trustee of his fourth will, to get a copy of the Jesuits' constitution and "insert English Empire for Roman Catholic Religion". Rhodes had Jesuit friends but probably knew very little about the Society of Jesus itself, accepting the general lore that it was powerful, ingenious, and secretive in promoting its aims.

By the 1890s, he still aimed at founding a "society" of men of strong convictions and wealth who would do for the unity of the English-speaking peoples what the Society of Jesus had done for the Catholic Church after the Protestant Reformation; but he now realized that the Americans would probably not join his crusade. To his friend W.T. Stead, he expressed "his unhesitating readiness to accept the reunion of the race under the Stars and Stripes if it could not be obtained in any other way."[6] He spoke of his admiration for American federalism. "If you want to know how it is to be done, read the Constitution and the history of the United States. The Americans have solved the problem. It is no new thing that need puzzle you. English-speaking men have solved it, and for more than a hundred years have tested its working. Why not profit by their experience? What they have

---

o The Society of Jesus was founded by Ignatius of Loyola in 1534. Known as the "Jesuits", they spearheaded papal efforts to restore orthodoxy and initiate reforms (especially against corruption) after the turbulence of the Protestant Reformation. They also became an important teaching and missionary order.

proved to be a good thing for them is not likely to be a bad thing for us."[7]

In the final years of his life, his secret brigade of outstanding individuals evolved into the idea of a more loosely knit fraternity of young people drawn from America and the Empire to study at Oxford. After visiting Kaiser Wilhelm in March 1899, he added young Germans to his scheme. He told Herbert Baker how greatly impressed he had been by "the appearance of manliness and discipline of the German people". "Such a strong race, he thought, must be brought into his idea of allied powers to promote world-peace."[8]

Once he had settled on the plan, he said that the Scholarships were his "best companion" in misfortune and his "solace in dullness", of which politics and war and the resentment of the Afrikaners could never rob him.[9] "When I find myself in uncongenial company," he told the British prime minister Lord Rosebery, "or when people are playing their games, or when I am alone in a railway carriage, I think of my great idea . . . It is the pleasantest companion I have."[10] He also cut back on projects that would drain money from his estate, including improvements to what his architect called his "wretched little cottage" at Muizenberg (where he would die). "During all the years I had previously worked for him," recalled Herbert Baker, "he had always called me 'mean', because I would not spend enough... But in this last phase I became 'damned expensive', [because] of his desire to save all he could for his Oxford Scholarships."[11]

When the English-speaking world learned of Rhodes's Final Will, it took notice. A young Australian remembered how "this great imaginative scheme was on everyone's lips in a country where the name of Oxford had strange magic." Always prone to feeling inferior, the "colonies" "were aware of a high compliment as well as a great opportunity."[12] In 1910, Rhodes's secretary Philip Jourdan speculated that in 50-100 years the Parliaments of the Empire would be largely composed of Rhodes Scholars. "Time alone will prove whether his anticipations will materialize. Certain it is that his Will has created a great stir amongst nations and has started the best brains in the world thinking."[13] The Scholarship also became famous very quickly in the United States. When an African-American named Alain Locke was chosen in March 1907, the *New York Times* carried the headline: NEGRO WINS SCHOLARSHIP, LOCKE GETS THE RHODES AWARD IN COMPETITION WITH FIFTY.

But why did Rhodes insist that the Scholarships be tenable only at Oxford?

Rhodes and Oxford

In the 1870s, Oxford was already one of the foremost universities in the world and was imbued with a mystique that appealed to the dreamer in Rhodes. Sir Leslie Stephen (1832-1904), one of the greatest thinkers of his day (and also the father of Virginia Woolf), described Oxford as "fertile in prophets" who not only spread ideas but also held remarkable personal sway over their disciples. He had never encountered such types at Cambridge. But "Cambridge men were generally inclined to regard their apparent barrenness with a certain complacency . . . They did not deny the existence of the soul; but knew that it should be kept in its proper place."[14] One 19th century wit described Oxford as "the home of dead languages and undying prejudices". But those who came to study there, especially from elsewhere in the Empire, were impressed by its tolerance for any kind of opinion and almost any kind of behaviour, provided it was not antisocial.[15]

Rhodes's Oxford career was not just drawn out; it was also un-distinguished. In fact, some have wondered why he even bothered to complete his degree or thought it worth eight years of a short life to do so. No one appears to have asked him, but almost certainly he saw it as a safety net if his prospecting for diamonds did not pay off; in that case, he would probably have become a barrister. Then, once he was rich, Oxford became a form of finishing school for the kind of gentleman Rhodes wished to be. Given all that he had to juggle as a business man and politician, his resolve to be "polished" was clearly pronounced. He was older than his contemporaries and did not even live in college, even though he regarded the residential system as one of the most formative aspects of the University. Not only did he not live at Oriel; he rarely entered it, and was most remembered for joining select clubs (like Bullingdon, Vincent's, and the Freemasons) and juggling diamonds at lectures to impress his companions.[16] He was 28 when he took his degree in 1881.

Yet, in the words of an early biographer, the Oxford spirit ("so hard to define and yet so easy to recognise") sank into him. Apart from Aristotle and Marcus Aurelius, Rhodes was inspired by Edward Gibbon, author of *The Decline and Fall of the Roman Empire* (1776), and grew to believe that Rome's burden of governing the world had now fallen on England's shoulders. John Ruskin (1819-1900), the leading art critic of the Victorian era, was also an eye-opener, preaching "a new gospel of beauty and public service to an age wearied of ugliness and commercial self-interest."[17] At Oxford, Rhodes seems to have lost some of the hardness and cynicism that friends complained about in Kimberley and he felt indebted to the University for the rest of his life.

He would always be proud of it. "Have you ever thought," he asked a friend, "how it is that Oxford men figure so largely in all departments of public life? The Oxford system in its most finished form *looks* very unpractical, yet, wherever you turn your eye—except in science—an Oxford man is at the top of the tree."[18][p] On another occasion, he talked about "her compelling influences, her wonderful charm."[19] He had the same down-to-earth loyalty to his *alma mater* as most graduates of any university. Asked how he trusted in each day's diamond production, which was weighed and registered by one unsupervised person, Rhodes answered, "Oh, that's all right. Mr. So-and-So takes charge of the diamonds, and he is an Oxford man and an English gentleman. Perhaps if there were two, they might conspire."[20]

According to his friend Thomas Fuller: "It was not as an educational institution only that he referred to it; it was Oxford with its buildings, traditions, its companionships, and its embodiment of English chivalry and honour. How he loved it."[21] In the last year of his life, when he was suffering and demoralized, his face brightened when a visitor quoted the first lines of Matthew Arnold's poem about Oxford: "Beautiful city so venerable, so lovely . . ."[22] For his own part, the only mark Rhodes ever made on the University was his lavish generosity two decades after graduating and the scores of Scholars bearing his name—now about 100 a year—that would charm and challenge and generally cherish the place for at least the next 120 years and beyond.

Designing the Scholarship

Rhodes left an estate of about £650 million in property, stock, and cash (£500 million after death duties), a much smaller fortune than that of his American counterparts John D. Rockefeller,

---

p Of course, the situation has changed since then. Oxford's achievements in science are now world-renowned.

J. Pierpont Morgan, and Andrew Carnegie. Even his friend Alfred Beit was wealthier; but Rhodes had spent considerable sums in Rhodesia and on railway construction.[23] Apart from some small personal and family bequests, he gave £13 million to Oriel College and asked his Trustees to allocate £7 million a year for the scholarship scheme. He proposed a Reserve Fund for the scholarships "as the Diamond Mines cannot last for ever" and suggested that any residue of the estate be used to provide financial support to the Scholars after graduating, "especially if they show indications of higher ideas, and a desire to undertake public duties" supporting the preservation of the British Empire. He was also prepared to fund a political party in the United Kingdom that "without any desire for office, will always give their vote to Imperial Purposes", as well as to support the migration of British nationals, especially women, to Africa.[24] But the scholarship scheme absorbed most of his residual estate.

The Scholarship had its peculiarities. The first was that candidates "shall not be merely bookworms". Instead, they were to be selected for (i) their "literary and scholastic attainments"; (ii) their "fondness of and success in manly outdoor sports such as cricket, football and the like"; (iii) their "qualities of manhood, truth, courage, devotion to duty, sympathy for and protection of the weak, kindliness, unselfishness, and fellowship; and (iv) their "exhibition during school days of moral force of character and of instincts to lead and take an interest in [their] schoolmates, for those latter attributes will be likely in afterlife to guide [them] to esteem the performance of public duties as [their] highest aim". Rhodes even suggested weightings for the four criteria: scholarship (40%), sports (20%), character (20%), and leadership and public service (20%).

In practice, these guidelines had only limited value and selection became more a matter of intuition than weighing credentials. Over time, the Trustees sought candidates who excelled in one of the three principal criteria (intellectual ability, character, and leadership) rather than those with good marks across the board. Selection committees were told to avoid "go-getters", "dilettantes" and "glib-talkers". "For the purposes of the Rhodes Scholarships," said the long-serving American secretary of the Trust, Frank Aydelotte, "glibness is hardly a virtue nor shyness a drawback."[25]

It is too obvious to ask why there was no emphasis on "feminine" values in the criteria. But why sports? According to George Parkin, this was to respect the Roman principle of *mens sana in corpore sano* [a sound mind in a sound body] and also promote moral discipline, fair play, the chivalrous yielding of advantage to an opponent, and "the acceptance of defeat with cheerfulness and of victory without boastfulness".[26] However, by the 1940s, some argued that selection committees (except in South Africa and Australia), were not giving enough weight to athletic skills. Others thought the balance just right: "Neither bookworms nor bruisers."[27] In the end, the Trustees prescribed that no candidate should be given a Scholarship primarily because of athletic prowess, nor denied one for lack of it.[28]

Selection was based on an interview rather than examination and confirmed by the Trustees, after consulting the ministers of education of the various colonies, provinces, states, or territories concerned. The German Scholars were to be selected by the Kaiser himself. The selection process has of course changed considerably since then; most nominations are now decided by committees in the various states and provinces, made up largely of previous Rhodes Scholars. In the United States, eight regional committees choose four candidates each who live or study there. The Rhodes Trust still confirms the selections.

The original provisions led to an imbalance between the US (32) and so-called Colonial Scholarships (20), which the Trustees doubted was Rhodes's intention. There were three for Rhodesia; nine for South Africa (after 1910); six for Australia (one for each colony, which became states after 1901); and only two for Canada (which was already federated), one for Ontario and the other for Quebec. In addition, there was one each for Newfoundland (a British colony until 1949), Bermuda, and Jamaica. By Act of Parliament in 1929, the number of "colonial" Scholarships was increased from twenty to thirty-four and in 1946 two were added for India. Canada's number rose from two to ten; New Zealand was given two, Malta one, and East Africa was assigned one every three years. The total was 68 until late in the 20th century, when a small number of additional constituencies were added. By 2020, the number had risen to 100.

When the details of Rhodes's Will became known, there were doubts about whether Oxford should accept the scholarship scheme. How could the decisions of Rhodes' trustees override the University's prerogatives in ensuring minimum standards of admission? And how could it accept the non-academic criteria set out in the Will? The Oxford Union (the student debating society) condemned the scheme by a large majority.[29] But, after an appropriate period of reflection, the University overcame its doubts and bowed to Rhodes's wishes.

The provisions of the Will inevitably attracted mockery. William Plomer, whom we have encountered time and again in this story, was especially caustic: "What could be more admirable or more rare than a man with a really healthy body, a truly alert mind, and a genuinely kind heart?... This successful footballer and kind *littérateur*, this dutiful hero and moral exhibitionist, this cricketing paragon of muscular Christianity, has none of the splendour of some Greek or Renaissance imagining, but a close relationship to . . . upper-middle-class Victorian manhood, the server of Mammon in the name of God . . . [Rhodes] should have known better than to expect that those 'all-round' young men . . . would be able to fulfil his purpose. As a rule, they neither make history nor do they even make much of their opportunities."[30]

The American novelist William Styron, who applied for a Scholarship in 1947, was gentler in his teasing. He recalled how his English professor had prepared him for the joys of Oxford: "Studying Old Norse and Middle English in the damp and draughty rooms at Merton College—a place which, he said, one grew fond of; drinking sherry and eating scones, or picnicking on plovers' eggs and champagne, as the pale lads did in novels by Aldous Huxley; going *down* to London for week-ends; enjoying summer vacations in Normandy or boating along the Rhine." Even the rigours of the Marine Corps had not prepared Styron for the anxiety he felt awaiting the results. But Styron was not selected and the chairman of the committee consoled him with the thought that none of the hundreds of Rhodes Scholars who had returned home in his time had become a writer. "Most probably, you would have become a teacher—a doggone good teacher, you understand, but not a writer."[31]

Some of the musings of the Trustees were a natural target of fun. Before India was added as a constituency, it was thought that Rhodes Scholars from other countries should be appointed to the Indian Civil Service. "There is nothing more inspiring in the history of the Empire," dreamt Earl Grey, one of the founding trustees, "than the picture of the chariot containing 300 million of mankind drawn by 1,000 white horses."[32] Even when India was awarded two Scholarships in 1946 and there was no doubt about the number of highly-qualified Indian candidates, the Trustees did not rule out selecting a British candidate in the first year or two, until Lord Elton suggested that that would be "unfortunate".[33]

"On Account of His Race"

Rhodes's Will stated that, "No student shall be qualified or disqualified for election to a Scholarship on account of his race or religious opinions." At first, it was assumed that by "race" he meant English-speaking and Afrikaner; but Rhodes's personal lawyer Bouchier Hawksley insisted that it was intended in the broadest sense and that any debate about this was an offence to the memory of the Founder. Jameson, who knew Rhodes like a brother, had no doubt that Rhodes intended to exclude Africans, saying that he "would turn in his grave to think of it." The Canadian historian John Flint suspected that the clause was designed to ensure that Afrikaners and French Canadians would not be excluded.[34] But the considered view of Philip Ziegler, who studied all the related correspondence, is that while Rhodes probably did not expect suitable candidates to emerge quickly from the educational system in South Africa and Rhodesia at the time, he did not intend to rule out Africans.[35] His intentions about creed were certainly ground-breaking—no one at the time was doing any favours to Roman Catholics and Jews—so it is not outlandish to think that Rhodes was prepared to stretch other boundaries as well. What is more important is that—with some ups and downs—the Trustees interpreted the Will as written.

As early as 1904, some American states asked about the eligibility of non-whites and the Trustees affirmed "strongly and unanimously" that they would not interfere with the discretion of the selection committees.[36] In 1908, it seemed possible that Christopher Lobengula, the son of the late Ndebele king, who was studying in England at the expense of the British South

Africa Company, might apply for a Scholarship. The Company asked the Trustees whether he would be eligible and they did not object, provided that the Rhodesian Government agreed. In the end, for reasons that are unclear, Lobengula never applied. In 1910, Jamaica chose a candidate of African descent, Frederick Mercier, and Queensland chose one of mixed race, G.F. Hall.[37] Ironically, it was the mixed-race Norman Manley of Jamaica, elected in 1914, architect of his country's independence from Britain and Chief Minister for seven years, who first succeeded in having the impact in public life that Rhodes had hoped for.[38]

Unfortunately, African Americans had a much more difficult time benefiting from Rhodes's Will.

CHAPTER THIRTEEN
Legacy in Practice

THE STORY OF the first African-American Scholar is so revealing and disturbing that it is worth telling in full. When Alain Locke, a future father of the "Harlem Renaissance", returned to Philadelphia in 1907, his mother was washing the front steps. "Mother, I'm home to interview for the Rhodes Scholarship. Isn't that wonderful?" She didn't even look up. "I don't know why you are bothering to apply. You know they will never give it to a Negro." Locke replied, "I am going to win . . . It is the least that Rhodes can do, considering all the wealth he took out of Africa."

When the Rhodes Trust secretary George Parkin asked the committee why they had selected a "Negro", its chairman William Harrison, Provost of the University of Pennsylvania, simply lied. None of the letters of recommendation, he claimed, had referred to Locke's race and as the committee had decided on him unanimously before the actual interviews, they thought that it would be unfair to change their minds. In fact, the letter from Harvard—where Locke had done his undergraduate degree—described him as "coloured" and the committee had simply decided to overlook that.

The selection made Locke famous, but there were protests in the American South, where it was suggested that interest in the Scholarship would drop off, if it meant crossing paths with blacks in Oxford. Some Southern Scholars even threatened to leave Oxford. Behind the scenes, Parkin had told the Trustees as early as 1903 that black candidates should "share every possible opportunity that the white man has". But this was the first time the issue had become concrete.

Lord Milner and Rhodes's old banker, Lewis Michell, wanted to reject Locke out of hand, but concluded that the terms of the Will made that impossible. Lord Rosebery agreed, even though he worried that the decision would cause an uproar all over the United States: 'The idea that the loathing of bad blood is confined to the Southern States is, I believe, entirely fallacious". Having said that, he saw no reason why the other American Scholars should object: "They need have no contact with the 'untutored mind' or the black body of this American citizen, and I do not see how he touches them in any way."[1] To the outside world, the Trustees presented a united front. When the American Scholars at Oxford sent an emissary to the Trustees to argue against Locke's selection, he was told that there was plenty of "colour" in the British Empire and certainly no British subject would be debarred from the Scholarship on that ground.[2]

Once the decision was made, the Trust had trouble finding a college for Locke. His preferences—Magdalen, Balliol, Merton, Brasenose, and Christ Church—all turned him down and Locke was forced to accept Hertford, one of the newest and poorest colleges. In the meantime, the man charged with looking after the Scholars in Oxford, Francis Wylie, worked on two fronts. First, he arranged for other American scholars to be moved out of Hertford so that they would not have to run into Locke. Then, he dropped hints to British families and teaching staff of the University to invite Locke to dinner and tea, so as to make up for the bad manners of the southern US Scholars. As a result, Locke was so busy socially during his first term that he told his mother that it was interfering with his studies.

But he was still *persona non grata* in American circles. At Thanksgiving, the American Society refused to invite him for dinner, so two US professors boycotted the event and invited him to their homes instead. Then, on 15 March 1908, Locke and the other US Rhodes Scholars were invited by the Rhodes Trust to lunch with the US Ambassador Whitelaw Reid at his London residence. When some of the Southerners told Reid that Locke was black, the ambassador complained to George Parkin about the "impropriety" of expecting Southerners to lunch with a "Negro". Wylie asked Locke to withdraw his acceptance, but he refused, and the Ambassador promised to receive "the gentleman himself with all proper courtesy" so as to avoid unpleasantness and unfavourable publicity. There are two versions of what happened next. One suggests that the dining room was divided into tables of two, and that Locke was left alone at one of them. When the Ambassador walked in, he proceeded directly to Locke's table and sat opposite him. Another version is that Wylie arranged for Locke to be seated next to a friend. Later, Locke wrote that the incident had converted him "from an individualistic aesthete into an ardent but I hope not bigoted racialist".

Not surprisingly, the rest of Locke's time at Oxford was difficult and he left without completing his degree. For the rest of his life, he hid the fact from his family and friends, conscious that he had been a pace-setter for African Americans and he did not want to disappoint them.[3] For his part, Francis Wylie later reflected, "It is rather amusing that this hostility was first shown by Scholars who came from the land where all men are supposed to be 'free and equal'."[4]

Fifty-Five Years Later . . .

Stung by this experience, no US selection committee chose another African American until 1962. There were practical reasons, too. For much of the 20th century, there were very few African Americans in the Ivy League universities. As late as 1967, only 15 out of 820 Princeton freshmen were black.[5] And of the nearly 3,000 Americans selected for the Scholarship between 1906 and 2000, only three came from historically African-American colleges and universities.[6] Then, two strong candidates—J. Stanley Sanders of Whittier College in California and John Edgar Wideman of the University of Pennsylvania— came to the fore in the same year.

Both were from working-class families, combining first-class intellects with outstanding athletic skills. Two days after being selected for the Rhodes Scholars Class of 1963, Sanders was drafted by the Chicago Bears football team. To the surprise of many sports fans, he chose Oxford over Chicago, aware that he and Wideman were making history and wanting "to show the white world that blacks could be more than sports stars and entertainers." Wideman sat for his Rhodes interview in Baltimore but could not stay to hear the results as he had a basketball game in Philadelphia that evening. When the committee secretary called, he asked how the game had gone. "We won," Wideman answered." "Well," the secretary told him, "you won the game down here, too."[7]

African Rhodes Scholars

Yet, if African Americans had trouble winning Rhodes Scholarships, young people in the newly independent African countries had an even higher slope to climb. The only African constituencies in the Will were Rhodesia and South Africa, which were run by white-minority governments until 1980 and 1994, respectively. On top of that, four of the Southern African awards were tied to elite private and government schools that did not admit Africans. This anomaly did not seem to disturb the Trust. Between 1918 and 1945, in the reports of three successive Secretaries, there was not a single mention of selecting Africans. While they were not explicitly ruled out, they did not appear to be on anyone's mind.[8]

Even the ferment of the late 1960s did not ruffle feathers at Rhodes House. The same year that students ruled the streets of Paris and occupied university campuses across the Western world, the 1968 Rhodes Scholars took up arms in their own way. Bill Clinton and a number of his friends slipped into the Barclays Bank branch on Oxford's High Street and sent hundreds of deposit slips fluttering into the air to protest against British investment in a controversial hydroelectric dam in Mozambique. Many of us participated in the then largest-ever demonstration against the Vietnam War in London on 27 October. Then, a few weeks later, about twenty of us (including Clinton) stormed respectfully into the office of the Warden of Rhodes House to demand that the Scholarship program be expanded to independent African countries. "Bill" Williams, who had been Field Marshal Montgomery's chief of staff and intelligence head in the North African campaign, received us with a slightly bemused look. "I suspect that we will have women admitted to the Scholarship before we expand it to black Africans." He was right. The Will was amended by the British Parliament to include women, beginning in 1977, and Scholars from African countries other than South Africa and Rhodesia were only selected on a regular basis in the 1980s.[q]

Impact

The first thorough retrospective study of the Scholars was done in 1944. Of the 2,190 elected up to 1940, 79 had died in the two world wars and another 135 by accident or natural causes (a rather high rate for a cohort averaging 40 years of age). The selection process was working well and there was no "inside track" to a Rhodes Scholarship. Nor did "class" make a difference. Many North American Scholars had worked their way through college and, while some were from well-to-do families, the children of wealthy parents did not generally apply for scholarships, it was said.

Except for New Zealanders and Australians, Rhodes Scholars had not performed notably better than other students at Oxford and Americans did only as well as the rest of the student body. The largest single group (600-650 or 25%) had gone into teaching, including 20 university presidents and 11 full professors at Harvard and Yale alone. By 1932, American Rhodes Scholars alone had already written 453 books. The

---

q A triennial scholarship for East Africa was awarded intermittently between 1933 and 1953, but "native" candidates were excluded on the bizarre grounds that they were not "British subjects". Scholarships for Ghana and Nigeria were established in 1959 but very few were awarded (Kenny, pp. 456-462). The first black scholar from an African country was elected in 1972 (from Rhodesia) and the first black South African was chosen in 1978 (Kenny, p. 64).

next largest group (400-450) chose law as a profession and more than 150 were practicing medicine. In science, Dr. E.P. Hubble (1910) was already one of the most distinguished astronomers in the English-speaking world. There was a large group in business and banking but none had become a millionaire like Rhodes. And there were many civil servants and politicians.[9]

The career distribution of Rhodes Scholars has changed since then—many now join large international consulting firms or technology companies—but most are still university professors. According to a 2015 survey of 2,300 Rhodes Scholars, 73% have worked in education and research, 28% in consultancy, 19% in law, 17% in government and diplomacy, 16% for non-profit organizations, 15% in medicine, 11% in financial services, and 10% in journalism and other literary activities. (The total exceeds 100% because of career changes.)[10]

Would Rhodes have been disappointed that the largest number were academics? It is hard to say. He wanted men of action and public influence, but that was before the advent of "public intellectuals" deeply involved in policy debates as occasional politicians, members of commissions of enquiry, expert witnesses, and commentators in the media. A good example is Robert Reich, one of the most remarkable members of the 1968 class (which also included Bill Clinton). He served as Labor Secretary in President Clinton's first term; taught economics at Stanford; authored eighteen books on public policy; chairs Common Cause (a nonpartisan government reform group); appears regularly as a commentator on cable news; and hosts podcasts on social media.

As a believer in education, Rhodes might also have comforted himself that their long-term influence would be sound. The first organizing secretary of the Rhodes Trust, George Parkin, himself an educator, hoped that US Scholars would aim at high academic positions and become the "creative center for a more enlightened public opinion in America".[11] Frank Aydelotte, who oversaw the US selection committees for more than thirty years, saw education as "another aspect of government".[12]

But a verdict on the overall impact of the Rhodes Scholars is as ungraspable as the horizon. "The influence of the network," wrote one observer unconvincingly in 1986, "has probably been decisive in more crises than will ever be known."[13] It is relatively easy to measure the impact of a person or team that invents a vaccine to end a pandemic. But how can one weigh the contributions of the many politicians who have been Rhodes Scholars? Fame by itself is not enough.

Already in 1910, the organizing secretary George Parkin tried to dampen expectations: "The majority of the Rhodes Scholars will doubtless be ordinary men, doing—with widened outlook—the world's ordinary work . . . But a great idea gives significance to any work or any worker, and he will be a poor Scholar who is not touched with some spark of the divine fire, the devotion to world service, which burned in the heart of the Founder. And we may fairly hope that once in a while there will be found the exceptional man in whom that flame will be brought to a white heat, helping him to lift the world's heart higher."[14]

Thirty years later, Parkin's successor Carleton Kemp Allen was still trying to rein in hopes about the Scholars. Perhaps the majority, he thought, had not become "persons of definite eminence", but how could it be otherwise? "Men of true light and leading will always be in a minority in the world."[15] But he had little doubt that their collective influence had been constructive in ways that Rhodes would have appreciated and that they "count for something in the English-speaking world".[16]

The Scholarship can also be cruel to some who win it. "A

man elected as a Rhodes Scholar," said George Parkin in 1910, "soon discovers that he has assumed a peculiar responsibility, and one from which he will find it difficult to escape during the rest of his life. He becomes the representative, worthy or unworthy, of the beneficent idea of a great man."[17] For a small number, the Scholarship went straight to their heads and never left it; but, for the most part, that natural pride at the start was transmuted into a sense of public service and responsibility that would last their entire lives.

Perhaps ten percent have become influential and even famous in their own societies, as politicians, jurists, and scholars. Most have led lives of quiet achievement and contentment. Some have felt guilty not to have lived up to the "promise" of the Scholarship. And still others have managed to overcome the sense of ambition which led them to the Scholarship in the first place, questioned the very meaning of "achievement", and for example led yoga and wellness workshops in the deserts of the American Southwest. Very few of them have turned out to be "loafers". And Rhodes, who wanted to be remembered, would be proud to have played a central role in their lives.

Rhodes's hope that the Scholars would be touched in a special way by Oxford was borne out. In the words of Richard Symonds, author of *Oxford and Empire* (1986): "If there is any group of heroes in the story, it is the College tutors to whom the colonial students would read their weekly essays and who would shock and stimulate them with unorthodox comments. Their kindness, tolerance and encouragement emerge from the memoirs of almost all colonials who studied in Oxford."[18] That attitude was not always shared by Americans and Canadians, for whom the adjustment to Oxford was particularly challenging; but most enjoyed and profited from the experience, even if some pretended otherwise afterwards.

"Of course, there is good cooking in Oxford," wrote the 1910 American Scholar Elmer Davis, "as there are crossbows and hoop skirts on sale in New York City; but in both cases you must work to find them . . . [I recall] Oxford chiefly as a place where too many bells were always ringing in the rain."[19]

Joking apart, Oxford was a major drawing card for candidates. In 1991, 83% of alumni said that the possibility of studying at Oxford was their main reason for applying; 71% added that they were attracted by the prestige of the Scholarship. And how did applicants learn about Oxford? In the American case, about half had studied under former Scholars.[20]

Strangely enough, given their small number, Rhodes Scholars also helped to change Oxford. In 1919, the University dropped the Greek exam from its admissions process. A month after Rhodes's Will was made public, old Oxford hands saw this coming. "The Rhodes Scholarships," wrote one contributor to the *National Review* in May 1902, "will bring the Greek question to a crisis" and watering down the entrance exam would deprive Oxford of "a unique opportunity of extending her best influence, and imperil the future of Greek, Latin and Christian civilization everywhere."[21]

Two years before that, the University established its own doctoral program (D.Phil.)—a momentous step for an institution that had prided itself on its undergraduate tutorial system. More than the Bachelor of Letters (B.Litt.) and Bachelor of Science (B.Sc.) programs, which had been introduced in the 1890s, this decision reflected Oxford's understanding that a world-class university must promote research as well as teaching. The change was also a response to the complaints of Rhodes Scholars and other Americans who thought that a doctoral degree would be more helpful for their careers. Before the First World War, many Americans went to Germany to pursue doctoral studies but were reluctant to do that after the

War.[22] By 1936, of about 200 research students at Oxford, 64 were Rhodes Scholars.[23] By 1955, the Chairman of the Rhodes Trust, L.S. Amery (1873-1955), suggested that Oxford had gone from serving "one particular country, and, indeed, largely of a limited class" to feeling itself the University of the whole English-speaking world."[24]

Rhodes was a believer in the British Empire but also a federalist. His dream of a united South Africa drove his actions and even some of his folly during his life. He was also a federalist on a larger scale and was even willing to live under the Stars and Stripes, if necessary. And who knows? If he had lived through the bloody 20th century, it is possible that he would have pushed the principle even further and become a world federalist, too. In that case, he would have liked a letter sent to F.J. Wylie (1865-1952), the first Secretary of the Rhodes Trust, by one of the first American Rhodes Scholars: "Oxford has taught me that nations are different rather than superior and inferior; and I do not find myself a worse American for the knowledge, but a better [one]."[25]

Other Global Scholarships

Perhaps the greatest tribute to Rhodes's idea is the number of global scholarship programs that have developed in its wake. In 1945, Senator J. William Fulbright of Arkansas introduced a bill in the United States Congress to create a program for the "promotion of international good will through the exchange of students in the fields of education, culture, and science". On 1 August, 1946, President Harry S. Truman signed the bill into law. Since then, there have been more than 390,000 Fulbright Fellows and the Program still awards 8,000 grants per year in 160 countries.[26]

Fulbright was a 1925 Rhodes Scholar and his time at

Oxford turned a small-town Southern conservative into a life-long internationalist. Arriving there from his hometown of Fayetteville, Arkansas was a "tremendous shock", he later recalled, like Alice in Wonderland. The future Fulbright Scholars, he thought, would be the "grandchildren" of Cecil Rhodes.[27] He had immense influence as the chairman of the Senate Foreign Relations Committee (1959-1974) and, while he remained a segregationist (at least publicly), he opposed McCarthyism and, later, the Vietnam War. His interest, of course, was not in extending the British Empire but rather in fostering what Rhodes might have seen as its logical successor: the liberal international order, including the United Nations, that the US and the UK championed in the wake of the Second World War.

Another echo—and eventual rival—of Rhodes's idea in the United States was the Marshall Scholarship, established by the British government in 1953 as a gesture of gratitude for American help during and after the Second World War. Intended to strengthen the "special relationship" between the two countries "for the good of mankind in this turbulent world", the program allows about fifty young Americans a year to pursue post-graduate work at a British university.[28]

As British nationals were not eligible for Rhodes Scholarships, the Harkness Fellowships were established in 1925 to allow UK graduates—and later candidates from Australia, New Zealand, Canada, and South Africa—to study in the United States. Since 1997, the program has focused on mid-career professionals engaged in health care policy and practice.[29]

Other philanthropists have joined Rhodes in seeing scholarly achievement as just one building block of a successful career and advancing international causes by drawing together intelligent young people from different backgrounds. Both the Gates Cambridge Scholarships for graduate students from around the world (tenable at the University of Cambridge) and the Bill and Melinda Gates Scholarships for minority American high school graduates put a stress on leadership and a commitment to improving the lives of others.[30]

The Schwarzman Scholarships (funded by Stephen A. Schwarzman, Chairman and CEO of The Blackstone Group) are available to "the world's best and brightest students" to do a one-year Master's degree in politics, business, or science at Tsinghua University in Beijing. Conceived with the same strategic sense as the Rhodes Scholarships, the Program is designed to prepare young leaders to deepen understanding between China and the rest of the world.[31]

Since 2018, the Schmidt Science Fellows (named after the former Google chairman Eric Schmidt) have spent their first post-doctoral year with world-class scientists and laboratories fostering greater synthesis among the natural sciences, computing, engineering, and mathematics.[32]

The Atlantic Fellowships, created in 2017 and supported by Charles F. Feeney through the Atlantic Philanthropies, have brought together lawyers, activists, artists, business people, health workers, and academics to develop ways of promoting fairer, healthier, and more inclusive societies.[33] Both the Schmidt and Atlantic Fellows programs are administered out of Rhodes House in Oxford.

Today's Scholars

With improvements in university education, increased competition for global academic awards, and opportunities for travel and communications that were unthinkable 40-50 years ago, some of today's Scholars are even more accomplished than their predecessors. They have written books, produced documentary films, managed start-ups, made their mark in humanitarian work, done ground-breaking research, and published in leading scientific journals before they even set foot in Oxford.

Building on such success and on an expanded endowment funded by past Scholars, and most notably the "Second Century Founder", Canadian philanthropist John McCall MacBain, the Rhodes Trust has expanded the Scholarship program to cover more countries (including China) and has introduced a number of global scholarships that are not linked to particular territories. There are now 100 in all. In the meantime, the purpose of the Scholarships has been broadened to developing and connecting "compassionate, innovative, and public-spirited people committed to solving humanity's challenges."[34]

The new Scholars have an impressive past to live up to, including a large number of politicians and statesmen. Three (Bob Hawke, Malcolm Turnbull, Tony Abbott) were Prime Minister of Australia, while Fred Patterson (1918) holds the distinction of being the only Communist politician ever elected there. Canadian Rhodes Scholars have been in charge at the provincial level (Allan Blakeney, Bob Rae, Danny Williams) but only one in Ottawa (John Turner). However, its current finance minister (Chrystia Freeland) has a strong chance of following in his footsteps. David Lewis (1932), leader of the New Democratic Party in 1971-1975, was probably the best prime minister Canada never had. Norman Manley (1914) was Chief Minister and later Premier of Jamaica (1955-1962) and Dom Mintoff (1937) was Prime Minister of Malta (1971-1984).

In 1944, the Rhodes Trust's secretary joked that they would never be satisfied until a Rhodes Scholar was President of the United States.[35] If so, they fumbled their chance just three years later by turning down a candidate named Jimmy Carter. As a result, the Trust had to wait almost half a century before Bill Clinton was sworn in, and he appointed other Scholars—Robert Reich (1968), Strobe Talbott (1968), and George Stephanopoulos (1984)—to his team. More recently, Cory Booker (1992) and Pete Buttigieg (2005) have run for the presidency and others—like Eric Garcetti (1993), Mayor of Los Angeles—could do so in the future. Rhodes Scholars have also been mainstays of US foreign policy and the national security establishment: Dean Rusk, W.W. Rostow, Richard Lugar, Stansfield Turner, R. James Woolsey, Dennis Blair, Wesley Clark, Susan Rice, Ashton Carter, and Jake Sullivan. Bruce Reed (1982) is Deputy Chief of Staff to President Biden and Gina Raimondo (1993) is the current Secretary of Commerce.

But most Rhodes Scholars have chosen other careers. (For a more complete summary, see Annex A.) Ironically, one of the first, William Miller Macmillan (1903) became an historian of South Africa and a critic of colonial rule in Africa, while Bram Fischer (1931) was a prominent anti-apartheid activist and lawyer. Clifford Durr (1918) defended Rosa Parks and Martin Luther King, Jr. in the bus boycott case of 1955 in Montgomery, Alabama and Benjamin Jealous (1987) headed the National Association for the Advancement of Colored People (NAACP) from 2008 to 2013. Howard Florey (1921) shared the 1945 Nobel Prize for Medicine for the discovery of penicillin. And, at the height of the Covid-19 pandemic, 180 Rhodes Scholars around the world were involved in one way or another in meeting the challenges of the disease.[36]

Some Scholars have left their mark without reaching the finishing line. Lucy Banda-Sichone (1978) returned to Zambia to promote civil rights as a lawyer and journalist and was forced, once, to go into hiding for fear of her life. When her husband died in a car crash, his family confiscated her property, leaving her destitute but not completely demoralized. She established a legal clinic for widows and orphans, but died at the age of 44. Her portrait was the first of a woman unveiled at Rhodes House, until then dominated by images of white men.[37]

Many Rhodes Scholars, too, have been happy with more modest success, serving in international institutions or in their local communities. Cristina Bejan (2004), a playwright and teacher from North Carolina suggested that "we—as a community—would benefit from embracing stumbling [i.e., making mistakes] over career-building ambition."[38] Mary Cleary Kiely (1981) gave up working at the New York City Board of Education to teach third grade, so happily that her husband (a banker) envied her.[39] Kiely's contemporary, Danielle Fontaine from Quebec, went straight from Oxford to being a full-time mother. "Progress," she said, "requires exceptional leadership, perseverance, and dedication at all levels. It takes a whole army to fulfill the Rhodes mission, including a few mothers on the home front."[40]

Some have become peacemakers in the background rather than on a global scale. An inspiring example is Wilhelm Verwoerd, grandson of the actual architect of apartheid, Hendrik Verwoerd, who was South Africa's sixth prime minister from 1958 until his assassination in 1966. To the chagrin of his family, Wilhelm spent his time at Oxford in the late 1980s confronting his country's and his own personal past and returned home to join the African National Congress just as Nelson Mandela was preparing to become president.

In May 2015, a month after Cecil Rhodes's statue was removed from the campus of the University of Cape Town, Wilhelm attended a ceremony at Stellenbosch University to take down a plaque that had once honoured his grandfather. "How do I listen . . . listen . . . really listen," he said that day, "to the heartbeat of untransformed pain behind the clenched fists and bubbling anger of our mostly black fellow citizens? How can I play a positive role with regard to the deeply-seated, unhealed, emotional, moral and soul injuries from our apartheid past?" Later, he would say: "I find it unconscionable to publicly honour those who represent so much pain to the world. You may think you are not responsible for an original wounding, but in continuing to honour people like my grandfather, in not fighting for justice, we are in effect rubbing salt in the wounds, and we ultimately become responsible for the further wounding of our fellow human beings."[41]

That challenge is the subject of the next chapter.

CHAPTER FOURTEEN

Controversial Statues

STATUES HAVE ALWAYS been divisive. The French revolutionaries beheaded the Kings of Israel on the façade of Notre Dame Cathedral, thinking that they were the Kings of France. That distinction was irrelevant to the revolutionaries, as all monarchs were equally contemptible to them. In 1966, on the 50th anniversary of the Easter Rising, the Horatio Nelson Pillar was destroyed in central Dublin, but few people objected as local politicians had been trying to remove it peacefully for decades. Even in countries that did not experience revolutions or civil wars, some statues have attracted resentment. But, where political divisions are deep and violent, monuments are an obvious target.

South Africa

South Africa is a particularly dangerous place for statues, as few countries in the world are so divided economically and emotionally. "As the Berliners did," observed the South African writer Christopher Hope in 2018, "we are discovering that you can forget about the wall but it does not forget about you: you can pull down the barriers . . . but it is very much harder to get rid of the wall in the head."[1] Visiting the Nelson Mandela statue in front of the Union Buildings in Tshwane (Pretoria), Hope found a white woman sitting cross-legged below the huge monument, taking pictures of other visitors. "I'm an early warning system," she said, nodding towards the statue. "From time to time these guys come here and, because I'm White and they speak in Sesotho, they think I don't know what they are saying. Twenty years after liberation, they say, they have no land and no jobs and no hope. Mandela must fall, they say. It's time for action. White men must go. They killed us. And Mandela, he let us down. Throw Mandela on the scrap heap . . . '"[2] Later, Hope encountered an Afrikaner woman in a traditional lace cap and long skirt protecting the statue of Paul Kruger in Church Square. When I visited both places in January 2020, neither woman was still there; but a security fence now sealed off the Kruger memorial.

Hope also discovered that a bust and memorial garden in Kwazulu-Natal dedicated to Oliver Tambo, long-time president of the African National Congress, had been destroyed, reportedly by people from a neighbouring village jealous of the government's largesse towards Tambo's hometown. "Where will it stop?" a villager asked. In a single town in Limpopo province, more than twenty schools had been destroyed in the belief that the government would pay no attention until "we burn things". In shantytowns across the country, hospitals, clinics, and libraries had also been set on fire, apparently for the same reason. At Port Elizabeth, students promised to kill a zebra a day at a nearby nature reserve until the administration acceded to their demands.[3]

In February 2016, a statue of the first president of the Republic of South Africa, Charles Robberts Swart, on the campus of the University of the Free State in Bloemfontein, was destroyed by members of the Economic Freedom Fighters (EFF). Swart was in office during the Rivonia Trials, that led to the imprisonment of Nelson Mandela and others.[4] Angry Afrikaners have also tilted at statues. Some years ago, a memorial to the 19th century Venda king Makhado was plastered with the colours of the old South African flag, just days after it was unveiled.[5] In such an atmosphere, the demand that Rhodes's statue be removed from the University of Cape Town (UCT) campus seemed almost natural.

The Shadow of Orwell?

But deep social cleavages are not a prerequisite for arguments about memorials. The Rhodes Must Fall movement had repercussions in some unlikely places. In Vancouver, British Columbia, the school board covered up a stone plaque bearing Rhodes's name that had been preserved when an older school had been demolished. The board described Rhodes as "a leader in the establishment of systemic and institutional racism towards black people in Southern Africa" and said that "any further upholding of names like Cecil Rhodes in our district makes us complicit in his legacy." Yet, there was a strong pushback against the decision, even in a place remote from Cape Town and Oxford.

On-line reactions to the story deplored the decision: "Soon all our past will be gone, this is scary stuff people". "Hmmm ... Tommy Douglas and Lester B. Pearson [two of Canada's most respected politicians] probably said something in their life and career which isn't right by 2019 standards ... I guess they too should be covered up and erased." One respondent quoted George Orwell's *1984*: "Every record has been destroyed or falsified, every book has been rewritten, every picture has been repainted, every statue and street and building has been renamed, every date has been altered . . . history has stopped. Nothing exists except an endless present in which the Party is always right."[6]

Inevitably, many people interpret History, at least in part, through the prism of their own personal ones. It is not hard to understand being offended, walking past Rhodes House in Oxford, if you are an African or West Indian conscious of how the British treated your ancestors. It is immaterial to that person that Cecil Rhodes had nothing to do with slavery and was relatively enlightened on issues of race in his day. Similarly, many of those hurt by Lord Patten's apparently dismissive reaction to the Rhodes Must Fall Movement, saw him not just as a former chairman of the Conservative Party but also, more importantly. as the last governor of Hong Kong— an actual latter-day "imperialist". Never mind that Patten went to great lengths to enshrine the political freedoms of the territory's citizens before handing it back to China. To some, his ability to understand the protests was compromised by his own personal background. Media and academic reactions to the Rhodes Must Fall (RMF) campaign reeked of paternalism, elitism, and racial insensitivity. While commentators insisted that their skin colour had nothing to do with their opinions, it was hard for them to put themselves in the protesters' shoes. Even white students deeply involved in the RMF movement confessed to the challenge of participating in its internal discussions with the proper humility, sympathy, and objectivity.[7]

Selectiveness

Yet, there is an unfortunate selectiveness in our approach to monuments, very few of which would survive the intensive moral vetting demanded in some quarters today. As Charles

Conn, the then-Warden of Rhodes House, pointed out a year after the 2015 RMF Movement subsided, "If we are being systematic (and certainly moral reasoning requires treating likes alike), that means evaluating the legacies and artefacts associated with all these important historical characters on the same basis (a project that could encompass every place name, street name, building name, room name, portrait, and statue!)."[8] For example, from 1789 to 1849, eighteen US presidents owned slaves. Why is the focus on George Washington or Thomas Jefferson? Is it because more is expected of them than from other human beings?

That said, should the principle of equal treatment of statues prevent action on the most hurtful ones? Certainly not. Especially if appropriate channels are established to come to sound decisions. Unfortunately, many controversies are decided by *ad hoc* panels operating with rough and ready procedures rather than overarching principles connecting them with other cases. And even obvious solutions can have their pitfalls. To quote Charles Conn again, re-naming the Nobel Prizes or Rhodes Scholarships could be seen as "a disingenuous attempt to hide a fundamental truth, a way of rainbow-brushing the past, while still taking the prestige and money."[9]

Can Colonial Statues Be Useful?

Strikingly, some Africans have argued that colonial statues serve a useful purpose. At the start of the Rhodes Must Fall campaign, Cont Mhlanga, a playwright and head of the Amakhosi Trust in Bulawayo, argued that all colonial monuments, including Rhodes's grave, should remain in full sight until the country had recovered its plundered wealth. Colonial symbols were painful but necessary reminders of the reparative work that remained to be done. "The Rhodes Trust has been operating under the radar," he said. "We are helping the foundation by hiding Rhodes from the public eye . . . In the years to come children will forget about him. But if his symbols remain, our children will ask pertinent questions."[10]

The Zimbabwean blogger Patience Rusare, mixing history and homophobia, agreed with Mhlanga, suggesting that the "well-maintained grave of Rhodes and his homosexual friend [Jameson] tell the story of conquest and of the subjugation of African people . . . These reminders of a brutal era can be removed but we choose not to as they are relics which remind us of the evil colonial past."[11] Or, as Christopher Hope suggested while touring his native South Africa, "We should preserve embarrassing monuments—bad memories can be a precious resource."[12]

An African writing in the Johannesburg newspaper *The Sowetan* in 2015 sounded very much like the English commentators who denounced the RMF movement that year. "One has to wonder what the next demand will be. Perhaps the removal of Cecil Rhodes's descendants from South Africa?... The crucial question is, after the fall, how does that improve the lives of our people? All these years down the line we still have the worst maths and science performance, a dwindling economy, a growing inequality rate, corruption, etc. Where are the black institutions of excellence? Black people have achieved little in 21 years [after majority rule]. And they are venting their anger on statues. Let them shelve their education and bring each and every statue down and let's see what the next scapegoat will be."[13]

Of course, statues convey different meanings, depending on what we know about them. At the beginning of Chapter One, we came across George Watt's "Physical Energy", an equestrian monument dominating the Rhodes Memorial at Cape Town, that Prime Minister Godfrey Huggins of the Federation of Rhodesia and Nyasaland in the 1950s likened to the Federation's policy of racial partnership, with blacks as the horse and whites as the rider. He made his views even more explicit in a speech to the Federal Assembly on 28 July 1954 against a motion to enforce equal treatment of the races: "You cannot expect Europeans to form in a queue with dirty people, possibly an old *mfazi* [woman] with an infant on her back, mewling and puking and making a mess of everything."[14] If there were evidence that Cecil Rhodes shared that odious view, there would be a *prima facie* case for removing the Watt statue.

The Purpose of Monuments

Memorials record people or events that we think deserve to be remembered. But the "we" does not include everyone and the planning of memorials involves ethical and political choices every bit as important as the aesthetic ones. It is quite possible to have successful and even beloved monuments on very controversial subjects. The Vietnam Memorial in Washington, DC is as moving to those who demonstrated against that war as it is to veterans of the conflict. It does not impose a "narrative"—apart from the obvious one that it commemorates only the 58,000 Americans who died rather than the nearly two million Vietnamese. Instead, it allows visitors to bring their own memories, values, and even ideology and come away feeling edified.

Another example is the beauty of the battlefield at Gettysburg, vast enough to absorb a large number of visitors without disturbing the sanctity of the place and to encompass 1,328 monuments, markers, and memorials that appeal to the full range of sympathies and origins of those touring the site. The possible bitterness at seeing a Confederate general (or

Union commander, for that matter) on a pedestal is allayed by the pleasure of seeing one's own heroes celebrated elsewhere on the same ground.

But other monuments express privilege and power so blatantly that they can incite resentment and even violence among people who feel left out of the story. The Rhodes Must Fall campaign is an example of that, as are statues that commemorate individuals now generally regarded as indisputably evil, like Lenin and Stalin. No time was lost in demolishing those testaments to the past. Most statues, too, have been inherited and, although many of them were erected by "public subscription" (i.e., by local notables, supported by small contributions from other citizens), very few went through a process of proper community consultation. Even when they did, the results were not always respected.

For more than a hundred years, passersby have wondered why there is a statue of Oliver Cromwell on the grounds of the Palace of Westminster. The only self-appointed dictator in modern British history, who sealed the fate of Charles I and spearheaded the brutal takeover of Ireland, he hardly seems the kind of man to be celebrated there, even if he championed Parliament against the monarchy. When the Liberal government of Lord Rosebery proposed such a monument in 1895, Parliament and public opinion strongly opposed it and the government withdrew the project. But the statue went up anyway in 1899, funded by an anonymous donor—who later turned out to be the former prime minister himself.[15]

But whom should we celebrate and how do we do that properly? Even with the best intentions and procedures, selection is difficult. In 2007, English Heritage, the organization responsible for the program of blue historical plaques in London, turned down a request to commemorate Wallis Simpson, the wife of Edward VIII, who abdicated the throne rather than end his relationship with her. A recent biography of Simpson had suggested that she had passed vital war-time information directly to the Nazis; hence, she would not meet the criterion that the honoree had made an "important and positive contribution to the welfare or happiness of humanity." (There was some uncertainty, too, about how to describe her occupation.) Yet, there was already a blue plaque in Holborn honouring Hiram Maxim, the inventor of the first fully automatic machine gun.[16]

Then, what should we do with the embarrassing ones? Ideas of "greatness" evolve over time and historical distance can remove scales from our eyes. The British doctor Edward Jenner invented the smallpox vaccine but experimented on children in poorhouses without any form of "consent". There is no doubt that he made a major contribution to the well-being of the world, but we now question his methods. Similarly, Marion Sims, a white Alabama doctor, developed a treatment for fistulas by operating on enslaved African-American women without their explicit agreement (and sometimes without anaesthesia). He is now an object of controversy even though he was once lauded as the "father of gynaecology". It is possible that some of his patients knew and appreciated what he was doing; but we have no proof of that and his contribution to humanity must therefore be clouded. As a result, in April 2018, a bronze statue of Sims was re-located from New York's Central Park to the Brooklyn cemetery where he is buried.

The Teddy Roosevelt Statue in New York City

Sometimes, embarrassment is in the eye of the beholder. In 2019, the American Museum of Natural History in New York City inaugurated a display ("Addressing the Statue") explaining the history of the large monument to Theodore Roosevelt outside the building. The former president is seated on a horse, high above a Native American and what is generally assumed to be an African American standing half-naked on each side of him. The implication of racial hierarchy is so blatant that the monument has stirred debate for years. In 2017, it was one of four controversial memorials reviewed by a city commission. As its members were divided, the city decided to preserve the statue and explain its origins to the public.

In fact, one of the two figures in the monument is an African rather than an African American and the sculptor wanted to emphasize the nobility of both of them, representing Roosevelt's guides and gun bearers on hunting expeditions on the two continents. The sculptor did not intend them to look vanquished. Instead, the design was meant to express Roosevelt's supposed "friendship" with foreign races rather than any contempt for them. Roosevelt actually had a low opinion of Africans, but he was the first US president to dine at the White House with an African American (Booker T. Washington) in 1901. Newspapers in the South described this encounter as "political suicide".

But the language and shades of meanings of the time have faded and to anyone unaware of that background the sculpture, magnificent as it is, tells a very different story.[17] In June 2020, conscious that its efforts to straddle the historical fence had failed, the Museum received the city's permission to remove the statue. In the words of a prominent art critic that week, "One look at the monument tells you that it's a problem, one that no extenuating information can make right."[18]

The Museum's original decision to engage with the controversy set a good example. Tiffany Jenkins, author of *Keeping their Marbles: How the Treasures of the Past Ended Up in Museums—and Why They Should Stay There* (2016) has suggested that "Throughout history, harm has been done; but it cannot be 'repaired', only studied and understood."[19] Writing in *History Today* (March 2016), Alex van Tunzelmann added: "In much of the criticism of Rhodes Must Fall, the question echoes: Where will it stop? Who will be next? The answer is that it will not stop. Future generations can and will interrogate the past. Whatever happens to Rhodes' statue, it is a sign of healthy public engagement . . . Monuments to historical figures and regimes stand not by divine right, but by the grace of those who live alongside them. No vision of the past can be set permanently in stone."[20]

Mahatma Gandhi

Even "saints" are now subject to re-evaluation. During his two decades working as a lawyer in South Africa (1893-1914) Mahatma Gandhi showed little if any compassion for Africans and his political activities were focused on the interests of the Indian community. In 1893, he complained to the Natal parliament that "a general belief seems to prevail in the Colony that the Indians are little better, if at all, than savages or the Natives of Africa." To a health officer in Johannesburg in 1904, he urged the removal of Africans living in a slum alongside Indians: "About the mixing of the Kaffirs with the Indians, I must confess I feel most strongly." In 1905, during an outbreak of the plague in Durban, Gandhi insisted that it would not be stopped while Indians and Africans were being "herded together indiscriminately at the hospital." When he was locked up with Africans in the same cells, he protested that "native prisoners are only one degree removed from the animal".[21]

Gandhi's grandson and biographer, Rajmohan Gandhi, admits that his grandfather was "at times ignorant and prejudiced about South Africa's blacks" but believed that his struggle for Indian rights in South Africa prepared the way for Africans' own fight for independence. Gandhi was an imperfect human being, but at the same time "more radical and progressive than most contemporary compatriots". The author of *The South African Gandhi: Stretcher-Bearer of Empire* disagrees. "Gandhi believed in the Aryan brotherhood," Ashwin Desai told the BBC in September 2015. "This involved whites and Indians higher up than Africans on the civilised scale." As for preparing the ground for African resistance to colonialism, that had begun well before Gandhi set foot on the continent.[22]

It is ironic that the moment which Gandhi later described as a turning-point in his life and which others regarded as the origin of *satyagraha* (his philosophy of non-violent resistance) was the collision of two acts of racism. At Pietermaritzburg station on 7 June 1893, Gandhi was evicted from a train for refusing to leave the first-class carriage, which was reserved for white passengers. He would not move to the second- or third-class compartments as he was holding a valid first-class ticket and, almost certainly, he had bought it to avoid brushing shoulders with Africans.[23]

Should all statues of the father of Indian independence outside India be taken down because of his views of Africans at the turn of the 19th and 20th centuries? It is certainly understandable that students at the University of Accra in Ghana demanded that this be done in December 2017. But most people remember Gandhi positively, even if some Pakistanis resent his condoning the break-up of India into two countries that led to up to a million deaths and the displacement of 12 million people in 1947. Like all great men and women, and most of the human race for that matter, Gandhi can be viewed from several angles.

The American Civil War

If the treatment of famous individuals is subject to winds of fashion or the results of the latest research, major events like the American Civil War (1860-1865) pose endless opportunities for continued strife. Although the Rhodes Must Fall (RMF) movement claimed responsibility for inspiring the Gandhi protests in Accra and a related one at Harvard Law School, the protests in Charlottesville, Virginia against the removal of Confederate statues in August 2017 were the work of white supremacists who stood for everything that the RMF opposed. When a Virginia judge ruled that the statues were war memorials protected by state law, the city council changed tack and replaced the annual Thomas Jefferson holiday with a Liberation and Freedom Day commemorating the end of slavery in 1865.[24]

After Charlottesville, the American Historical Association suggested that removing memorials to "Confederate generals and officials who have no other major historical accomplishment" did not create a "slippery slope" towards removing all monuments to national figures who were known to be flawed. "There is no logical equivalence between the builders and protectors of a nation—however imperfect— and the men who sought to sunder that nation in the name of slavery."[25] But that judgment seems too cut-and-dried. Not every historian, let alone American, would reduce the Civil War to a fight about slavery. And exempting the winners from being challenged appears too convenient.

There is only one monument in the entire United States to the divisiveness of the Civil War itself: the Eternal Light Peace Memorial at Gettysburg, dedicated in 1938 on the 75th anniversary of the battle. But even this "universal" memorial had its limitations. In his remarks at the ceremony, in the interests of "reconciling" North and South, President Franklin Delano Roosevelt made no mention of the main outcome of the War: the freeing of two million slaves.[26]

When Black Lives Matter protesters filled American streets in May-June 2020, more than 700 Confederate monuments were still standing (including 100 each in Georgia and Virginia alone) and there were hundreds of offensive road, school, and park names across the American South. In the year following the death of George Floyd, at least 167 Confederate symbols were removed or renamed, compared with 58 between 2015 and 2019.[27] Towns and cities across the country looked hard at whom they were honouring and not all the issues they faced were purely American.

Slavery

Slavery provokes difficult memories on both sides of the Atlantic. In Fredericksburg, Virginia, a stone block in the town centre was once used to display men and women for sale at slave auctions. In 1924, the Chamber of Commerce tried unsuccessfully to remove it. More recently, there have been calls for putting it in a museum, while others have suggested keeping it where it is but protecting it with plexiglass. Some see it as a reminder of an ugly past; others think it should stay for the same reason.[28] In February 2020, a memorial to another slave auction site, in Charlottesville—a plaque in the sidewalk so small most people walked over it without noticing— disappeared. Someone later admitted to removing the plaque because he thought slaves and their descendants deserved a more prominent memorial.[29]

To most people in the United Kingdom, the heritage of slavery seems very remote or is associated proudly with the effort to abolish it—the first international humanitarian campaign in history—spearheaded by British idealists like William Wilberforce. But, to Britons of West Indian or African descent, that legacy is still vivid and it survived until recently on the government's books. When slavery was abolished in 1833, the slaveowners were compensated with about 40 percent of the national budget. Even that was not enough, and freed slaves were taxed to make up for the shortfall. That public debt was only completely paid off in 2015.[30] In a pluralistic society, such conflicting memories need to be respected in re-considering our public depictions of the past.

Many people in the United Kingdom feel that the country has yet to "come to terms" with its colonial past. What that means is not always clear, as one person's acknowledgement or apology can seem to others like papering over a wound. Efforts in that direction range from self-justification to self-flagellation. In 2019, Oxford's Ashmolean Museum displayed shattered teapots and cups to remind visitors that "every sip" of the national beverage connected them to the British Empire and—if they liked their tea sweet—to transatlantic slavery (as sugar was once produced by slaves in the West Indies). The objective of the exhibition was to "explode" the idea of a "nice cup of tea'" and explore the legacy of exploitation and violence behind it.[31]

Endangered Donors

If South Africa is a dangerous place for statues, the United States is tricky ground for donors. In December 2019, Tufts University in Boston removed the Sackler name from its medical buildings to distance itself from a pharmaceutical dynasty accused of abetting and profiting from the opioid epidemic. Jillian Sackler, the widow of the man who had given Tufts most of its money, complained: "The man has been dead for 32 years. He did not profit from [opioids], and none of his philanthropic gifts were in any way connected to opioids or to deceptive medical marketing . . . It deeply saddens me to witness Arthur being blamed for actions taken by his brothers and [others]." For more than a year, the dean of the medical school tried to explain the distinction between the family branches to his colleagues on the governing bodies of the University, to no avail. Oddly enough, Tufts did not return any of the Sackler money, even though half of it was still unspent.[32]

In July 2019, Warren B. Kanders, a vice-chairman of New York City's Whitney Museum of American Art, was forced off the Museum's board because one of his companies produced the tear gas used against migrants at the US-Mexico border. Protesters crowded the Museum lobby, marched on the man's Greenwich Village home, and prevailed on artists to withdraw from the Whitney's all-important Biennial exhibition. Other donors wondered who would be next. Someone from the pharmaceutical industry, a chemical company, or Facebook?[33] Such actions put more than the donors' reputations at risk; it threatens museums' budgets, which in the United States depend on their board members for up to a fifth of their annual resources.

Resentment of the rich is hardly surprising, with disparities in income now among the widest in a hundred years. But it is difficult to understand why some millionaires should be targeted more than others because of the sources of their wealth. Certainly, earnings from illegal activities (like the drug trade) should not result in public acclaim or be recycled for public purposes. But such extreme cases are rare and almost all wealth is obtained in ways that someone else will find disappointing.

Certainly, philanthropy can be exploited to repair or enhance the reputation of donors. But much of it is also inspired by the same values that motivated the Rockefellers, Carnegies, and Fords of another era: the desire to "give back" to the society that made it possible for them to be successful and a sense of duty and responsibility inculcated in them at an early age or acquired in the ups and downs of a long life. As government funds will never be enough to meet all the cultural and educational needs of a society, complicating donor efforts to support public causes or serve on boards to attract gifts from others can be short-sighted and self-defeating.

The purpose of such gifts is also key. If Cecil Rhodes had devoted his wealth to commissioning operas that vaunted his virtues or to purchasing armaments to defend Rhodesia, he might have been a forgotten by now. But his commitment to promoting global prosperity and peace by educating future leaders makes it easier to argue that his aims were honourable and that he set an example that should be followed. Of course, as a politician and businessman in a tumultuous era, Rhodes's legacy is more complicated than that of other donors. So, it is still fair to ask why and how we should commemorate people like him. Or, more specifically, what should be do with troublesome statues?

CHAPTER FIFTEEN

What to Do with Them?

R ESPECTING OR RECONCILING different viewpoints are essential in a healthy society. So, how can we ensure that statues do not get in the way of that or, even better, support the process? Here are twelve suggestions:

Try a Little Humility

David Cannadine, Editor of the *Oxford Dictionary of National Biography* and president of the British Academy, suggests that "The besetting weakness of every generation is to suppose that it is the wisest, the most sophisticated, the most moral and the most high-minded of any that has ever lived... Like many generations that have gone before, we may think ourselves superior to our forebears... [but] should we not at least entertain the possibility that future generations may take an equivalently disapproving view of us?"[1]

People condemning historical figures must be able to put their hands on their hearts and swear firmly to themselves that in the same circumstances, or given the same opportunities, they would have behaved differently. Owning other human beings seems heinous to us now but it was commonplace in what we still regard as highly civilized societies like ancient Athens and was referred to almost casually in the Christian gospels, before "slavery" became synonymous with the sale of Africans. And, a hundred years from now, people may scarcely believe that we killed ten billion animals a year for food in North America alone and that we continued to use plastics long after we knew how damaging they were.

How many of us, regardless of our race, can be certain that we would have acted differently from Cecil Rhodes? In talking to the departing South African Rhodes Scholar class in September 2020, the former Justice of that country's Constitutional Court, Edwin Cameron, said: "We are all flawed, soiled by moral compromise. Our hands, every one of us, are grubby from questionable moral choices, from our indecisiveness, from our greed, from our yearning for comfort, from our overweening egos, from our lack of purposeful commitment. We are all complicit in the conditions of our time, where there is no moral purity but only the grubby complexity of ordinary life. In seeking our heroes, it is impossible to separate villains from saints."[2]

Delay Irreversible Decisions for 2-3 Years

Try stretching out the decision-making process as long as possible until the public mood has settled. It was Afrikaner students in the 1950s, associating him with the South African War, who first demanded that Rhodes's statue at the University of Cape Town be taken down. Their ire passed. Tearing down statues is like burning books. Unless they have been put up recently without much public debate, to sow division or wound particular groups, monuments should be seen as historical artefacts in themselves, to be debated and set in context, but not destroyed. We should *respect* history and not gloss over its complications.

To quote Justice Cameron again, "The University of Cape Town's Vice-Chancellor said this week that we must 'erase all traces of the past's injustices.' My point is simple, even prosaic: we cannot. Not only that we cannot—we should not. The past is there not as history, but as present. It challenges our present complicity in injustice—by reminding us of what others, but also we, are capable."[3] Better to erect more statues to enlarge the story than to extinguish these records of the past. But, where public sentiment is firm after a reasonable period of debate and decision-makers are convinced that widespread hurt is being caused by these relics of history, then clearly the public interest must be respected.

Temporizing may seem a luxury in an age when social media can whip up public fury instantly and protesters can take matters into their own hands. In 2020, between 15 and 26 million people joined in Black Lives Matter protests across the United States. Their impact was palpable, with one poll finding that 76% of Americans now considered racism and discrimination a "big problem", up 26% since 2015.[4] But even at the height of one of the most intense political moments in American history, the *New York Times* art critic Holland Cotter appealed for calm: "In the current, healthy drive to neutralize assaultive images, it is necessary, for history's sake, that we first stand back, look hard, sort them out."[5]

Some would argue that forgetting is just as important as remembering. In Spain, following the death of General Franco, his name and those of his close associates were removed from avenues and boulevards across the country but not replaced by the names of Republican martyrs of the Spanish Civil War. Instead, paralleling the restoration of a constitutional monarchy, some street names now echoed a royal past. The *Pacto del olvido* [Pact of Forgetting] made political sense at the time as a way of countering anti-democratic sentiment within the military, but it was not universally popular. Thirty years later, it was formalized as the Law of Historical Memory (2007), which ordered the removal of any remaining memorials that "exalted the Civil War or the repression under the dictatorship" between 1936 and 1975.[6] Letting matters rest allowed a firmer political consensus to take hold. Of course, opinion could have moved just as easily in the opposite direction and insisted on paying due homage to the men and women who had given their lives to preserve Spanish democracy.

Put Up More Statues

Many monuments commemorate people whose military, political, or business records are debatable, so there is a case for recognizing people whose fame is less established but also less tainted. New York City will soon put up a statue near Grand Central Terminal to Elizabeth Jennings Graham, a 24-year-old Manhattan schoolteacher who in 1854—a hundred years before Rosa Parks—refused to get off a trolley because it was reserved for whites. Her family sued the streetcar company successfully, leading to the desegregation of New York mass transit. Another statue will be erected on Staten Island to Katherine Walker, a widow who ran a lighthouse in the early 20th century until she was 73 and rescued more than fifty people by rowing to their rescue when their boats were sinking in rough waters. "See?" writes Gail Collins, the *New York Times* columnist, "This is the sort of thing you learn when you get to see monuments that don't involve generals on horseback. There needs to be a statute of limitations on statues of guys in stirrups."[7]

Consult Widely

Edward Mortimer, Distinguished Fellow of All Souls College (Oxford), journalist, historian, and former director of communications for UN Secretary-General Kofi Annan, has seen his share of controversies. "I am not in favour of obscuring the past," he says, "or of destroying the evidence of what people in past generations said and thought. But in the way we arrange our public spaces today, and the names by which we designate our great buildings and institutions, I think we owe it to ourselves, to our contemporaries, and perhaps even to future generations to make it clear where we stand."[8] Doing that, however, is not straightforward. We must try hard to understand how other people feel; be fair to the past as well as the present; and balance reason and emotion. Fuzzy facts and hearsay must also be rooted out.

Following the violence in Charlottesville, New York City decided to fast-track a number of public monuments depicting women and people of colour, but ran into controversy. The public's number-one choice for a statue was Frances Xavier Cabrini (1850-1917), a Roman Catholic nun who ran health and social welfare programs for poor Italian immigrants and was made a saint in 1946. But she was not included in the first set of people to be honoured. A planned monument to the women's suffrage movement at first excluded black women; but when Sojourner Truth (1797-1883) was added, scholars pointed to the strong differences she had with her white "sisters" on a number of subjects and suggested that it was wrong to paper over them for sentimental reasons.

But at least there had been public consultation. "There is no perfect process when it comes to choosing public art," said the chairman of the City Council committee that oversees cultural affairs. "The community has to be involved at all levels, but there are going to be cases where it's impossible to find consensus."[9]

Consider How Substantial or Immediate the Harm Is

It is easy to understand why Saddam Hussein's statue was torn down in Baghdad when American forces entered the city in March 2003 without first submitting a proposal to a duly appointed committee. But no one would march in Rome to take down a statue of the truly terrible Emperor Nero. Somewhere in between there are thousands of memorials that hurt some people, often among the most informed and idealistic in a society, and the challenge is to examine their case without offending an even larger number of individuals or setting unfortunate precedents. The 2015-2016 debate about Rhodes's statue at Oriel College was more balanced than the noise suggested. A resolution at the Oxford Union to remove the statue passed by only a small margin (245-212) and an on-line petition to keep the statue where it was attracted more support than the one Rhodes Must Fall Oxford had posted.

The location and scale of monuments must also be considered. Vancouver is an odd place to commemorate Cecil Rhodes. But erasing his memory in Cape Town would be like flattening Table Mountain, half of which he bequeathed to the nation and would now be blighted by urban development if he had not done so. Until it was swept up in the June 2020 Black Lives Matter protests, a statue to Robert E. Lee in Richmond, Virginia, which was the capital of the Confederacy, seemed historically defensible. But the one in New Orleans, that was sixteen feet high atop a sixty-foot column, seemed less so. It was removed in May 2017.

Create Context

Rather than remove statues, one should first consider adding others to round out the story. For example, some would argue that the bust of Rhodes that used to sit on a window-sill on the main stairwell of Rhodes House should be put back. Removing it satisfied a small number of current Rhodes Scholars who were uncomfortable with it, but disappointed a much larger number of alumni who still felt gratitude for their benefactor's legacy. The removal of that bust also disappointed some Rhodes House staff, one of whom feigned illness that day so as not to be part of the "cleansing" process.

Perhaps another bust should be put next to it. Lobengula would not qualify as he probably did greater harm to his subjects than Rhodes. It could be the wife of Lobengula's father, Mzilikazi, who helped Rhodes arrange the peace talks with the Ndebele in 1896. Or perhaps it could be Rhodes's friend Dr. James Stewart (1831-1905), head of Lovedale Missionary Institute, the African college that Rhodes supported, symbolizing their joint commitment to education and a better future for Africans. Or it could be Nelson Mandela, linked with Rhodes there as he already is in the Mandela-Rhodes Foundation in Cape Town.

Try Some Imaginative Captioning

At the cottage in Muizenberg where Rhodes died—a veritable temple to the memory of the man—one panel reads: "Power, the way it tends to do, went to Rhodes' head. The patient negotiator became impatient, then seen as a forceful developer, now more often as a ruthless land-grabber. After the notorious Jameson Raid, Rhodes was held responsible, by many, for the tragic outbreak of war between Britain and the Boer republics . . . The emphasis shifted from the romance and benefits of empire to its negative and domineering aspects—racial arrogance, exploitation, the hubris of pride that preceded a fall." Even his sexuality is handled forthrightly. "It has been suggested that Rhodes was homosexual. If that was his underlying orientation, he seems to have suppressed it on the day to day level. Maybe sexual repression liberated his imperial energies? At any rate, sex didn't seem to play a role in his life—he was married to his ideas and ideals."[10] While Rhodes has had many hagiographers, those preparing these displays preferred balance to bedtime stories, knowing it was more powerful.

An alternative is to use innovative techniques, such as light displays, to challenge the one-sidedness of some monuments, like projecting the Bill of Rights on the statues of Confederate generals who fought to deny such liberties to large numbers of their fellow citizens.

Don't Destroy

In June 2019, after fifty years of inconclusive debate, the San Francisco Board of Education decided unanimously to whitewash thirteen murals depicting the life of George Washington at a high school named after him. The murals depicted slaves working for him and a dead Native American lying on the ground as Revolutionary troops march by. The painter, a Russian émigré and Communist, was commissioned to do the work in 1935-36 under Franklin Delano Roosevelt's job creation program. His very purpose in including these figures was to draw attention to the ugly aspects of American history rather than to suppress or glorify them. Yet, more than eighty years later, they were seen by some as disrespectful. The art critic Roberta Smith suggested that, instead of painting over them, they should be covered up with felt or some other opaque fabric. Future generations of students, including African and Native Americans, she pointed out, could well demand that the murals be uncovered. "They will want to see what all the fuss was about, and dissect and analyze them all over again. Human curiosity works that way."[11]

Be Honest

It would be better to sell Rhodes House and move into a faceless office block than give it a new name and pretend that it was built for other reasons than to honour and, yes, glorify, a flawed human being. The Scholarships could be renamed Mandela-Rhodes, giving emphasis to the man more people admire, while remembering that many of those who dislike Rhodes in South Africa also resent Mandela. But the source of the money will not have changed. Or they could be named the Rhodes-MacBain Scholarships, in honour of the "Second Century Founder" John McCall MacBain who contributed $120 million in 2013 to secure the future of the Scholarships. But removing Rhodes's name altogether from an award he created deliberately to promote world prosperity and peace would be hypocritical and serve notice to future donors in all walks of life that their generosity could one day backfire.

Try Sculpture Parks

Following the collapse of the Soviet Union, the new governments of Czechoslovakia and Hungary created sculpture parks where the effigies of Lenin, Stalin, and others could be deposited rather than destroyed. A statue of Ghana's first president Kwame Nkrumah, which was decapitated when he was overthrown in 1966, is now in a large memorial park in Accra, still in two pieces, next to a newer one, echoing a turbulent time and inviting visitors to draw their own conclusions.[12] And we have already seen how the newly independent government of Zimbabwe moved statues honouring Cecil Rhodes to the gardens of the National Archives.

Learn from Controversy

Following the removal of the Rhodes statue in Cape Town, a "National Dialogue on the Transformation of the Heritage Sector" (April 2015) called for recognizing the heroes of the liberation struggle, without being "triumphalist" about it. In re-interpreting existing memorials and deciding on additional ones, the group appealed for an inclusive consultative process that would avoid combativeness while still acting with urgency.[13] In parallel, the Heritage Western Cape Guidelines suggested that "it is better to re-interpret than relocate and better to relocate than recycle or destroy."[14]

Be Understanding of Donors

With necessary exceptions, benefactors of educational and cultural institutions deserve understanding. The donors at Oriel College who insisted that Rhodes's statue be kept in place were not just protecting a distant alumnus; they were also wary of having their own lives dissected in public forums. Re-naming institutions and programs because the source of their funds is now considered objectionable would mean removing Nobel's name from the Nobel Prizes because he earned his fortune producing dynamite. Real malefactors should not be allowed to "launder" their misdeeds through philanthropy. But identifying them requires due process. Pointing fingers should not be enough.

Conclusions

ECIL RHODES WAS a complex man. He was a bully and
buccaneer, but also kind to the unfortunate and tender
to those he loved. He was a capitalist, though not a
particularly crooked one. In his own time, he was considered
a hero, even though he never saved anyone from drowning
or invented penicillin or the polio vaccine. As a politician,
he often favoured expediency over principle. He believed
in the superiority of British culture and institutions and in
spreading them as widely as possible. He was a racist but not
to the same degree as many of his contemporaries. Instead,
he was paternalistic, believing that with proper education and
direction Africans could assume increasing responsibility in
society. Nor is there any record of his treating anyone unkindly
because of the colour of their skin.

Like many successful entrepreneurs, Rhodes could be
hard-driving and ruthless. Some of his plans—which he knew
were dangerous—were thwarted by a more prudent Imperial
government in London. And he was controversial in his day for
two very specific reasons:

- Swindling the Ndebele people out of their land by
  telling them that he was only interested in prospecting
  for minerals, and

- Secretly planning the invasion of an independent Afrikaner state (the Transvaal Republic) while he was prime minister of the Cape Colony.

Those defending him now would say that he only occupied land that the Ndebele themselves had seized violently seventy years before and that the so-called Jameson Raid was well-intended. Neither of these defences holds much water now as deceit is deceit, regardless of the details. While Rhodes added three quarters of a million square miles to the British Empire, that achievement made him glorious only in the eyes of those who felt entitled to occupy other people's lands, especially if those people looked different from themselves. Rhodes also clothed his dishonesty in the language of duty, a "civilizing mission", and the march of "progress".

Many of today's criticisms of Rhodes, however, are just as shaky as past defences of the man. He stopped Jameson when he wanted to precipitate the First Ndebele War, until a series of blunders led to it erupting anyway a few months later. He was reckless in planning the Jameson Raid; but the record shows that he tried to call it off. Despite that, he accepted responsibility for it and stepped down as Prime Minister. He participated wholeheartedly in the Second Ndebele War, infuriated by the atrocities done to settler men, women, and children and apparently unaware of the brutal treatment that the Ndebele and Shona peoples had suffered beforehand. Yet, he stepped in at great personal risk to negotiate peace and prevent British troops from causing even greater bloodshed the following year. He remained loyal to his friends, including Jameson, and respected his enemies. He adopted Lobengula's two sons and put them through school in Cape Town and London. He protected the ruins of Great Zimbabwe and restored the defiled grave of the first Ndebele king, Mzilikazi.

And, towards the end of his life, he appears to have been changing his views on the political role of Africans. He was a captive of his time, ideologically and politically, but also substantially ahead of it.

Taking these points into account implies giving Rhodes the benefit of the doubt, just as most of us would like to be judged one day. Cecil Rhodes can and should be criticized. It is hard to believe that the same man who sheltered "evil-looking" strangers in his cabin on the high seas would be capable of intimidating an African traditional leader by flattening a cornfield with machine-gun fire. Human beings act differently at different moments in their lives, and sometimes abominably in times of stress, and they are not always proud of the consequences. Yet, in the case of famous people, those missteps are recorded in excruciating detail.

Looking at the same facts, reasonable people can come to very different conclusions. They may give Rhodes credit for what were relatively progressive positions in his day or they can point out that there is no such thing as degrees of racism. Murder is murder, whether you use a knife or a gun. One can argue that, if Rhodes had not developed the diamond and gold fields of South Africa, someone else would have done so; or you can insist that it was Rhodes rather than some imaginary figure who did, and it is right to judge how humane his conduct was. The same applies to his occupation of much of central and southern Africa. If his "Suez Canal" to the North had been blocked, the Germans or Portuguese or Boers of the Transvaal would have invaded those lands instead, and none of those actors has gone down in history for their benevolent treatment of Africans. The British occupation led to thousands of deaths but may also have prevented many more by putting an end to inter-ethnic blood-letting. The first can be documented, while the second is almost completely hypothetical.

Some deeds are absolutely wrong; but nothing Rhodes did can be compared with the Spanish Conquest, the trans-Atlantic slave trade, or the Holocaust. No one need feel sorry for Cecil Rhodes, but, to a considerable extent, he has been the target of hearsay. Denouncing him as an "imperialist" is like challenging someone's patriotism today. He is accused of being a warmonger but his life's work was aimed at uniting people, particularly English- and Dutch-speaking South Africans. He promoted federalism in his own region and also more widely in the Empire, as a means of fostering a more prosperous and peaceful world.

He created a country (Rhodesia) that was largely reserved for whites, but so did the founders of Australia, Canada, and the United States. He did not own slaves, like sixteen US presidents. He did not make his fortune from colonialism, as most of his wealth was earned in the diamond and gold mines that existed before he invaded Central Africa. If he is guilty of running underground mines, he must share that opprobrium with every similar mine owner since. More than most of his contemporaries, he cared about what was called "native" policy and introduced measures which he thought would help Africans. And, unlike others, such as Canada's Sir John A. Macdonald, he used his personal resources to save people from famine rather than exploit it as a political weapon.

Rhodes's first serious biographer Basil Williams (1921) said that he "was cast in a large mould, with enormous defects corresponding with his eminent virtues."[1] The author of the most definitive analysis, Robert Rotberg (1988), concluded that Rhodes was "magnificently multifaceted". "He *was* larger than life, and the favor and enmity that his name evokes are appropriate responses."[2] Even severe critics have refused to make a pariah of him. In 1933, William Plomer wrote, enigmatically: "We find ourselves abandoning all question of the supposed rightness or wrongness of his thoughts and deeds ... The more we learn of him the nearer we come to the end of all knowledge, which is a sense of overwhelming wonder and of utter ignorance."[3] For Christopher Hope (2018), "Rhodes stood for something and the ferocity of the detestation many now feel for him is a measure of how profoundly he affected the life and times of the entire country, and still does ... His money and his scholarships changed lives. Others made fortunes from gold and diamonds ... but left nothing behind. No libraries, hospitals, opera houses, art museums or colleges carry their name. The one university that commemorates a mining magnate is named for Cecil Rhodes."[4]

Historians have a duty not to take things at face value; but occasionally they ignore facts that are staring them in the face. Rhodes's dream of a more orderly world inspired by friendship among the most powerful nations has been described, time and again, as naïve. But the fact that his vision never wavered from his early 20s to the end of his life and was expressed in six successive wills, attests to how profoundly he believed in it.

He told his friend W.T. Stead: "You must be an Imperialist, not from mere lust of dominion or pride of race, but because you believe the Empire is the best available instrument for diffusing the principles of Justice, Liberty, and Peace throughout the world. When Imperialism involves the perpetration of Injustice, the suppression of Freedom and the waging of wars other than those of self-defence, the true Rhodesian must cease to be an Imperialist."[5] His vision may or may not have been simplistic; but it was certainly different from the Social Darwinism that was fashionable at the time and that he has been accused of believing in, as well.

Rhodes devoted his wealth to an important cause: promoting

a better world through closer ties between the English- and German-speaking peoples. In that respect, he failed utterly, as the First World War broke out just twelve years after his death. But it would have been vain to expect a scholarship scheme to have immediate effects. Nor could a coterie of like-minded individuals schooled at Oxford brake the forces of nationalism and resentment that exploded in 1939. However, it could be argued that Rhodes's vision of international understanding and cooperation came into its own after 1945 when English-speaking nations—particularly the US and the UK—led efforts to create global institutions like the United Nations, the World Bank, and the International Monetary Fund.

Rhodes's vision of the spreading of liberal values and knowledge has also been echoed in a host of similar scholarship schemes created since the Second World War, including the Fulbrights, the Marshalls, and more recently the Schwarzmann, Schmidt, and Bill and Melinda Gates awards. Almost certainly, Rhodes would have regarded his own Scholarships and their offshoots as his ultimate contribution to humanity.

Not everyone today will identify with Rhodes's vision. Some would argue that his internationalism was a confederation of the powerful and that the "neo-liberalism" underlying free trade and economic growth in recent decades has done more harm than good. But, like John Ruskin, Rhodes's response might have been: "You think that an impossible ideal. Be it so; refuse to accept it if you will, but see that you form your own in its stead. All that I ask of you is to have a fixed purpose of some kind for your country and yourselves; no matter how restricted so that it be fixed and unselfish."[6]

In dedicating a tablet to Rhodes in Oxford in 1906, Lord Rosebery suggested that "in this ancient University his truest and noblest monument will be the career, the merits, and the reputation of the Scholars whom he has summoned within these walls."[7] In 1987, Brian Roberts concluded that no Rhodes Scholar, however bright, had ever made the outstanding contribution to the world that Rhodes envisaged. "In many ways what Rhodes, for all his idealism, effort and ruthlessness, had built was no more than an elaborate house of cards; a house that has been blown away by the winds of history."[8]

More than thirty years later, that verdict seems premature. The Rhodes Scholarship is still the most sought-after academic award in the English-speaking world and recent secretaries of the Rhodes Trust have gone to great lengths to broaden the reach and impact of the program, nurture professional links among the thousands of past recipients around the world, and leverage the network to confront pressing global issues.

The fact that Rhodes's greatness is still being debated is reassuring to those who see history as complicated rather than as a straightforward morality play. It is also a reminder that, in assessing controversial figures from the past, we should look at the facts rather than accept uncritically what others have said about them. There is also a case for humility as none of us knows for certain how we would have behaved in the same circumstances. And how we assess the past is a reasonable proxy for how we deal with the present and with each other.

Annex

Famous Rhodes Scholars

Statesmen and Politicians. In addition to those listed in Chapter 13, Jan Hofmeyr (1910) was a South African liberal politician. Roland Michener (1919) was Governor-General of Canada (1967-1974). Arthur Porritt (1923) served in the same role in New Zealand between 1967 and 1972, as did Zelman Cowen (1941) in Australia from 1977 to 1982. Carl Albert (1931) was Speaker of the US House of Representatives (1971-1977). J. William Fulbright (1925), Richard Lugar (1954), Paul Sarbanes (1954), David Boren (1963), Larry Pressler (1964), Bill Bradley (1965), Russ Feingold (1975), and David Vitter (1983) were US Senators. Marcel Massé (1963) was Clerk of the Privy Council and President of the Treasury Board of Canada. Cyrus Habib (2003) was Lieutenant Governor of the State of Washington and the first Iranian-American elected to state-wide office in the U.S.

Canada's Arnold Smith (1935) was the first Secretary-General of the Commonwealth (1965-1975) and Manmohan Malhoutra (1958) was Assistant Secretary-General. Another Canadian George Ignatieff (1936) was president of the UN Security Council in 1968-1969. Montek Singh Ahluwalia (1964) was the Deputy Chairman of India's Planning Commission, Shahid Javed Burki (1960) was Pakistan's Minister of Finance and Wasim Sajjad (1964) served as interim president of Pakistan and chairman of the Senate.

Political Activists. Other Rhodes Scholars have been prominent in public causes without attaining political office. Isaac Shongwe (1989), a businessman, and Ndumiso Luthuli (2000) ffollowed in the footsteps of Bram Fischer (1931) in challenging the human rights record of the South African government both before and after majority rule. (Luthuli is now the regional secretary for the Rhodes Trust in Southern Africa.) Others fought for social justice in their own ways. Adam von Trott zu Solz (1931) participated in the July 20th 1944 plot to assassinate Hitler and was executed afterwards. Arthur Mutambara (1991) was active in Zimbabwe's Movement for Democratic Change, while Kingwa Kamencu (2009) was a candidate in Kenya's 2012 presidential election.

Law. Frank Holman (1908) was president of the American Bar Association in 1948. Edmund Herring (1912) served as Chief Justice of the Supreme Court of Victoria from 1944 to 1964. John Marshall Harlan II (1920) was an Associate Justice of the US Supreme Court (1955-1971), as were Byron White (1938) from 1962 to 1993 and David Souter from 1990 to 2009. Wilbur Jackett (1934) was Chief Justice of the Federal Court of Canada (1971-1979). Nicholas Katzenbach (1947) was US Attorney General (1965-1966) and Daryl Williams was Attorney General of Australia (1996-2003). Gérard La Forest (1949) and Jean Beetz (1953) served on the Supreme Court of Canada. The South Africans Leonard Hoffmann (1954) and Johan Steyn (1955) became UK Lords of Appeal in Ordinary. Dyson Heydon (1964) and Kenneth Hayne (1970) were High Court judges in Australia and John Doyle (1967) was the Chief Justice of South Australia. William A. Fletcher (1968) was on the US Court of Appeals for the Ninth Circuit. And Edwin Cameron (1975) served on South Africa's Constitutional Court.

Business. The American billionaire John Templeton (1934) earned his fortune in mutual funds and was a philanthropist himself, founding Templeton (now Green Templeton) College, Oxford. William Vaughn (1925) was Chairman and CEO of Eastman Kodak; Frank Wells (1953), the president of Warner Brothers (1973-1982) and the Walt Disney Company (1984-1994); and Rod Eddington (1974), CEO of British Airways and a director of the News Corporation. The Canadian Dominic Barton (1984) headed the international management consulting firm, McKinsey & Company, and his compatriot Patrick Pichette (1987) was Chief Financial Officer at Google.

Medicine. Medical pioneers have included the Canadian neurosurgeon Wilder Penfield (1914), the Australian pharmacologist Howard Florey (1921), and John Eccles (1925), who won the Nobel Prize for Medicine in 1963. Eric Lander (1978) chaired President Obama's Council of Advisors on Science and Technology and founded the Human Genome Project. Siddhartha Mukherjee (1993) teaches at Columbia Medical School and is the author of *The Emperor of All Maladies: A Biography of Cancer*, which won the 2011 Pulitzer Prize for general non-fiction.

University Administration. George Paton (1926) was Vice Chancellor of the University of Melbourne (1951-1968), while Rex Nettleford (1957) headed the University of the West Indies and Richard Deane Terrell (1959), Australia's National University. Neil Leon Rudenstine (1956) was president of

Harvard from 1991 to 2001 and Joseph Nye, Jr. (1958) was Dean of the Kennedy School of Government there. The Australian John Hood (1976) was Vice-Chancellor of Oxford. John Robert Evans (1955) and David Naylor (1979) were both presidents of the University of Toronto. Deepak Nayyar (1967) was Vice Chancellor of Delhi University. Colin Bundy (1968) and Loyiso Nongxa (1978) headed Witwatersrand University (Johannesburg) and Max Price (1982) was Vice Chancellor of the University of Cape Town. Marc Tessier-Lavigne (1980) was president both of Rockefeller University and Stanford and Christopher Eisgruber (1983) headed Princeton.

Scholarship and Letters. Marius Barbeau (1910) was a Canadian ethnographer and folklorist. The historian George F.G. Stanley (1929) designed the Canadian flag. Two Scholars headed the Library of Congress for forty years: Daniel J. Boorstin (1934) was the Librarian from 1975 to 1987 and James H. Billington (1950) from 1987 to 2015. The American writer John Edgar Wideman (1963) was awarded the PEN/Faulkner prize twice. The New Zealander Robert Burchfield (1949) was editor of the *Oxford English Dictionary*. There have been two Poet Laureates, one in the United States (William Jay Smith) and the other in Jamaica (Mervyn Morris), and other poets as well: the Americans John Crowe Ransom (1910) and Robert Penn Warren (1928) and the South African Chris Mann (1971). Edward De Bono (1953) is a Maltese writer, psychologist, and author.

E.F. Schumacher (1930), a German economist and social theorist, was the author of the highly influential book *Small is Beautiful: Economics as if People Mattered.* (1973), while the Canadian A. Michael Spence (1966) won the Nobel Prize for Economics in 2001. Jonathan Kozol (1958) wrote *Death at an Early Age* (1967), which sold more than two million copies in the U.S. and Europe, and is still active in fighting educational inequalities in the United States. Richard Flanagan (1984), an Australian environmental activist and novelist, won the 2014 Man Booker Prize for *The Narrow Road to the Deep North*, while the Indian writer Neel Mukherjee (1992) was long-listed for the same prize that year. Naomi Wolf (1985) is an American author, feminist, political adviser, and social critic. There have also been several philosophers: Charles Taylor (1952), John Searle (1952), Ronald Dworkin (1953), Michael Sandel (1975), and David Chalmers (1987).

Media. The American Howard K. Smith (1937) became a nationally known broadcast journalist. Boisfeuillet Jones, Jr. (1968). was publisher and CEO of *The Washington Post*. Michael Kinsley (1972) founded *Slate* magazine and was editor of *The New Republic*. Walter Isaacson (1974) was managing editor of *Time* Magazine and CEO of CNN. Nicholas Kristof (1981) is a Pulitzer Prize winning reporter and columnist with the *New York Times*, while Atul Gawande (1987) is a surgeon and medical writer for the *New Yorker* magazine. Rachel Maddow (1995) hosts her own public affairs program on the US cable-news network MSNBC. Fasi Zaka (2001) is a Pakistani political commentator, columnist, radio talk show host, and TV anchor. Ronan Farrow (2012) won a Pulitzer Prize for his exposé of Hollywood producer Harvey Weinstein, that was instrumental in sparking the worldwide "Me Too" movement. Even in the arts and entertainment, Rhodes has had a presence. Kris Kristoffersen (1958) was an American singer and songwriter and Terrence Malick (1966) a ground-breaking American film director.

Sports. Appropriately, Scholars have also thrived in "manly outdoor sports"—as well as gender-neutral indoor ones. The

New Zealander Jack Lovelock (1931) won the 1,500-metre gold medal at the 1936 Berlin Olympics and Annette Salmeen (1997) was an American gold medallist swimmer at the 1996 Olympics. Bill Bradley (1965) was a star of the National Basketball Association (and later US Senator for New Jersey in 1979-1997). Chris Laidlaw (1968) played rugby with the New Zealand All Blacks but then (like Bradley) took his talents into other directions, becoming a diplomat, Member of Parliament, talk-show host, and Human Rights Commissioner. Yifan Hou from China (2018) is a former women's world champion in chess and Madison Tung (2019) was the first woman wrestler and wrestling national champion at the US Air Force Academy.

Bibliography

Books

Alexander, Peter F.

William Plomer: A Biography. Oxford University Press: Oxford and New York, 1990.

Aydelotte, Frank

The Vision of Cecil Rhodes: A Review of the Forty Years of the American Scholarships. Oxford University Press: London, 1946.

Baker, Herbert

Cecil Rhodes: By His Architect. Oxford University Press: London, 1934.

Baxter, Peter

Rhodesia: A Complete History 1890-1980. Peter Baxter History: Portland, Oregon, 2018.

Calderisi, Robert

Earthly Mission: The Catholic Church and World Development. Yale University Press: New Haven and London, 2013.

Cary, Robert   *Charter Royal.* Howard Timmins:
                                  Cape Town, 1970.

Chantiluke, Roseanne et al.   *Rhodes Must Fall: The Struggle
                                  to Decolonize the Racist Heart of
                                  Empire.* Zed: London, 2018.

Chesterton, G.K.   *A Miscellany of Men.* Dodd, Mead
                                  and Company: New York, 1912.

Cloete, Stuart   *African Portraits: A Biography of
                                  Paul Kruger, Cecil Rhodes, and
                                  Lobengula.* Collins: London, 1946.

Colvin, Ian   *Cecil John Rhodes 1853-1902.* T.C.
                                  & E.C. Jack: London, 1913. *The
                                  Life of Jameson, Volumes I and II.*
                                  Edward Arnold and Co.: London,
                                  1922.

Conn, Charles et al., ed.   *Fighting the World's Fights:
                                  Rhodes Scholars in Oxford and
                                  Beyond.* Third Millennium
                                  Publishing: London, 2016.

Davidson, Apollon   *Cecil Rhodes and His Time.* Protea
                                  Book House: Pretoria, 2003.

Eddo-Lodge, Reni   *Why I'm No Longer Talking
                                  to White People About Race.*
                                  Bloomsbury: London, 2018.

Elton, Godfrey (Lord)   *The First Fifty Years of the
                                  Rhodes Trust and the Rhodes
                                  Scholarships, 1903-1953.* Basil
                                  Blackwell: Oxford, 1955.

Flint, John

Cecil Rhodes. Little, Brown and Company: Boston and Toronto, 1974.

Fuller, Thomas E.

The Right Honourable Cecil John Rhodes: A Monograph and a Reminiscence. Longman, Green & Co.: London, 1910.

Gardner, Brian

The Lion's Cage. Arthur Barker: London, 1969.

Gibbs, Peter

The True Book About Cecil Rhodes. Frederick Muller: London, 1956.

Gross, Felix

Rhodes of Africa. Cassell & Company: London, 1956.

Habib, Adam

Rebels and Rage: Reflecting on #FeesMustFall. Jonathan Ball: Johannesburg and Cape Town, 2019.

Hensman, Howard

Cecil Rhodes: A Study of a Career. William Blackwell: Edinburgh and London, 1901.

Holloway, Richard

On Forgiveness. Canongate: Edinburgh and London, 2015.

Hope, Christopher

The Café de Move-On Blues: In Search of the New South Africa. Atlantic Books: London, 2018.

Hutchison, Graham Seton   *Cecil Rhodes: The Man.* Oxford
                            University Press: London,
                            1944.

Jourdan, Philip   *Cecil Rhodes: His Private Life
                           by His Private Secretary.* Bodley
                           Head: London, 1911.

Kenny, Anthony, ed.   *The History of the Rhodes Trust.*
                           Oxford University Press: Oxford,
                           2001.

Kipling, Rudyard   *Something of Myself: For My
                           Friends, Known and Unknown—
                           The Complete Unfinished
                           Autobiography.* Pantianos
                           Classics. First published in
                           1937.

Le Sueur, Gordon   *Cecil Rhodes: The Man and His
                           Work.* John Murray: London,
                           1913.

Lockhart, J.G.   *Cecil Rhodes.* Duckworth:
                           London, 1933.

Lockhart, J.G. and   *Cecil Rhodes: The Colossus of
                           Southern Africa.* Woodhouse,
                           C.M. Macmillan: New York,
                           1963.

Lunestad, Geir   *"The World's Most Prestigious
                           Prize": The Inside Story of the
                           Nobel Peace Prize.* Oxford
                           University Press: Oxford, 2019.

Maguire, James R.

Cecil Rhodes: A Biography and Appreciation. With Personal Reminiscences by Dr. Jameson. Chapman & Hall: London, 1897.

Marlowe, John

Cecil Rhodes: The Anatomy of Empire. Paul Elek: London, 1972.

Maylam, Paul

A History of the African People of South Africa: From the Early Iron Age to the 1970s. St. Martin's Press: New York, 1986.

The Cult of Rhodes: Remembering an Imperialist in Africa. David Philip: Claremont, South Africa, 2005.

Maurois, André

Cecil Rhodes. Archon Books : Hamden, Connecticut, 1968.

Mencken, H. L.

Selected Prejudices. Jonathan Cape: London, 1927.

Menpes, Mortimer

War Impressions. Adam & Charles Black: London, 1901.

Meredith, Martin

Diamonds, Gold and War: The Making of South Africa. Simon & Schuster UK: London, 2007.

Michell, Lewis

The Life of the Rt. Hon. Cecil John Rhodes, 1853-1902 (two volumes). Edward Arnold: London, 1910.

Millin, Sarah Gertrude

Rhodes. Chatto & Windus : London, 1933.

Morris, Charles R.   *The Tycoons: How Andrew Carnegie, John D. Rockefeller, Jay Gould, and J.P. Morgan Invented the American Super-Economy.* Times Books/Henry Holt: New York, 2005.

Nyamnjoh, Francis B.   *#Rhodes Must Fall: Nibbling at Resilient Colonialism in South Africa.* Langaa Research and Publishing: Bamenda (Cameroon), 2016.

Oluo, Ijeoma   *So You Want to Talk About Race.* Seal Press: New York, 2018.

Parkin, George   *The Rhodes Scholarships.* Houghton Mifflin: Boston and New York, 1912.

Pellew, Jill, ed.   *Dethroning Historical Reputations: Universities, Museums, and the Commemoration of Benefactors.* Institute of Historical Research: London, 2018.

Plomer, William   *Cecil Rhodes.* Peter Davies: London, 1933. *At Home.* Jonathan Cape: London, 1958.

Radziwill, Catherine   *Cecil Rhodes: Man and Empire-Maker.* Cassell: London, 1918.

Rieff, David — *In Praise of Forgetting.* Yale University Press; New Haven and London, 2016.

Roberts, Brian — *Cecil Rhodes and the Princess.* J.B. Lippincott: Philadelphia and New York, 1969. *Cecil Rhodes: Flawed Colossus.* Hamish Hamilton: London, 1987.

Rotberg, Robert — *The Founder: Cecil Rhodes and the Pursuit of Power.* Oxford University Press: New York and London, 1988.

Samkange, Stanlake — *On Trial for My Country.* Heinemann: London, 1967.

Schaeper, Thomas et al. — *Cowboys Into Gentlemen: Rhodes Scholars, Oxford, and the Creation of an American Elite.* Berghahn Books: New York and Oxford, 1998.

Scott, Ann — *William Richard Gowers, 1845-1915: Exploring the Victorian Brain: A Biography.* Oxford University Press: Oxford, 2012.

Stead, W.T., ed. — *The Last Will and Testament of Cecil John Rhodes.* "Review of Reviews Office": London, 1902.

Stent, Vere   *A Personal Record of Some Incidents in the Life of Cecil Rhodes.* Maskew Miller: Cape Town, 1925.

Stewart, Jeffrey C.   *The New Negro: The Life of Alain Locke.* Oxford University Press: 2018.

Symonds, Richard   *Oxford and Empire: The Last Lost Cause?* Macmillan: London, 1986.

Tamarkin, Mordechai   *Cecil Rhodes and the Cape Afrikaners: The Imperial Colossus and the Colonial Parish Pump.* Frank Cass, London: 1996.

Thomas, Antony   *Rhodes: The Race for Africa.* St. Martin's Press: New York, 1997.

Thompson, Francis R.   *Matabele Thompson: An Autobiography.* Faber and Faber: London, 1936.

Verschoyle, John Stuart   *Cecil Rhodes: His Political Life and Speeches, 1881-1900.* Chapman and Hall: London, 1900.

Williams, Basil   *Cecil Rhodes.* Henry Holt & Company: New York, 1921.

Wilson, Monica, ed.   *The Oxford History of South Africa*, Volume II. Oxford University Press, New York and Oxford, 1971.

Ziegler, Philip	*Legacy: Cecil Rhodes, The Rhodes Trust and Rhodes Scholarships.* Yale University Press: New Haven and London, 2008.

Articles

Allen, Carleton Kemp	*Forty Years of the Rhodes Scholarships.* Oxford. University Press: Oxford, 1944.
Alley, Kelly D.	"Gandhiji on the Central Vista: A Post-Colonial Refiguring," *Modern Asian Studies,* Vol. 31, No. 4 (October 1997), pp. 967-994.
Anonymous British Officer	"The Responsibility of Cecil Rhodes," *The North American Review,* Vol. 170, No. 520 (March 1900), pp. 348-356.
Ater, Renée	"Communities in Conflict: Memorializing Martin Luther King Jr. in Rocky Mount, North Carolina," *Indiana Magazine of History,* Vol. 110 (March 2014), pp. 32-39.
Attwell, Melanie et al.	"Supplementary Report prepared for the University of Cape Town and Heritage West Cape", July 2016.

Baylen, Joseph O.   "W.T. Stead's History of the
                           Mystery and the Jameson Raid,"
                           Journal of British Studies, Vol. 4,
                           No. 1 (November 1964),
                           pp. 104-132.

Bouch, Richard   "Glen Grey before Cecil Rhodes:
                           How a Crisis of Local Colonial
                           Authority Led to the Glen Grey
                           Act of 1894" in the *Canadian
                           Journal of African Studies,* Vol.
                           27, No. 1 (1993), pp. 1-24.

Briggs, Madeline   "Misinformation in the Rhodes
                           Campaign," *The Poor Print* (Oriel
                           College Student Newspaper),
                           January 22, 2016.

Butler, Jeffrey   "Review of Cecil Rhodes by John
                           Flint et al." *The International
                           Journal of African Historical
                           Studies,* Vol. 10. No. 2 (1977), p.
                           272-275.

Chapman, S.D.   "Rhodes and the City of London:
                           Another View of Imperialism,"
                           The Historical Journal, Vol. 28,
                           No. 3 (September 1985), pp. 647-
                           666.

Cohen, William   "Statues in Nineteenth-Century
                           Provincial. France," *Comparative
                           Studies in Society and History,*
                           Vol. 31, No. 3 (July 1989), pp.
                           491-513.

Conn, Charles

"Thinking About Historical Legacies: Looking for Just Principles, Processes and Consequences", Working Paper, July 30 2017.

Dubow, Saul

"Review of Iain R. Smith, *The Origins of the South African War 1899-1902* (Longman, Harlow and New York, 1996)" in *The Journal of Southern African Studies*, Vol. 23, No. 1 (March 1997), pp. 156-157.

Foote, Kenneth E. et al.

"Hungary After 1989: Inscribing a New Past on Place," *Geographical Review*, Vol. 90, No. 3 (July 2000), pp. 301-334.

Gorra, Michael

"A Heritage of Evil", *The New York Review of Books*, November 7, 2019, pp. 11-13.

Graham, Lucy

"Olive Schreiner and Rhodes Must Fall," *Bulletin of the National Library of South Africa*, Vol. 70, No 2, December 2016, pp. 199-212.

Hoste, H. F.

"Rhodesia in 1890", in *Rhodesiana*, No. 12, September 1965.

JBHE Foundation

"Denigration and Disrespect: Black Colleges Are Mostly Ignored by the Rhodes Scholarship Committee," *The Journal of Blacks in Higher Education,* No. 34 (Winter 2001-2002), pp. 52-53.

Kammen, Michael

"Democratizing American Commemorative Monuments," *The Virginia Quarterly Review,* Vol. 77, No. 2 (Spring 2001), pp. 280-288.

Kerr-Ritchie, J.R.

"Reflections on the Bicentennial of the Abolition of the British Slave Trade," *The Journal of African-American History,* Vol. 93, No. 4 (Fall 2008, pp. 532-542.

Mangeu, Xolela

"Shattering the Myth of a Post-Racial Consensus in South African Higher Education: 'Rhodes Must Fall' and the Struggle for Transformation at the University of Cape Town," *Critical Philosophy of Race,* Vol. 5, No. 2 (Special Issue 2017), pp. 243-266.

McFarlane, Richard A.

"Historiography of Selected Works on Cecil John Rhodes (1853-1902)," *History in Africa,* Vol. 34 (2007), pp. 437-446.

Mortimer, Edward

"The Problem with Monuments: A View from All Souls", in *Serendipitous Adventures with Britannia: Personalities, Politics and Culture in Britain* (I.B. Tauris: London, 2019), edited by Wm Roger Louis.

Morrison, Alexander

"Oriel and the Wider World," in Jeremy Catto, ed., *Oriel College: A History.* Oxford University. Press: Oxford, 2013, pp. 444-475.

Murray, Andrew H.

"Generation Snowflake?", *RSA Journal,* Vol. 164, No. 4 (5576) (2018-2019), pp. 44-47.

Newbury, Colin

"Technology, Capital, and Consolidation: The Performance. Of De Beers Mining Company Limited, 1880-1889," *The Business History Review,* Vol. 61, No. 1 (Spring 1987), pp. 1-42.*istory ReviewHH*

Nicholson, Ernest

"Hawkins, Monro, and University Reform," in Jeremy Catto, ed., *Oriel College: A History.* Oxford University Press: Oxford, 2013, pp. 408-443.

Palonen, Emilia

"The City-Text in Post-Communist Budapest: Street Names, Memorials, and the

Politics of Commemoration,"
GeoJournal, Vol. 73, No. 3 (2008),
pp. 219-230.

Parry, Richard

"In a Sense Citizens, but Not
Altogether Citizens": Rhodes,
Race, and the Ideology of
Segregation at the Cape in the
Late Nineteenth Century",
*Canadian Journal of African
Studies,* Vol. 17, No. 3 (1983), pp.
377-391.

Philippon, Daniel J.

"Following the Equator" to Its
End: Mark Twain's South African
Conversion", *Mark Twain
Journal,* Vol. 40, No. 1 (Spring
2002), pp. 3-13.

Rohr, Gretchen

"An African-American Rhodes
Scholar Confronts the Ghost of
Cecil Rhodes," *The Journal for
Blacks in Higher Education,* No.
23 (Spring 1999), pp. 102-103.

Schaeper, Thomas

"The Black Trailblazers in the
Rhodes Scholarship Program,"
*The Journal of Blacks in Higher
Education,* No. 22 (Winter 1998-
1999).

Schuhmann, Antje

"Decolonization and
Denazification: Student Politics,
Cultural Revolution, and the

	Affective Labor of Remembering," *Critical Philosophy of Race,* Vol. 5, No. 2 (Special Issue 2017), pp. 296-319.
Strachey, Lytton	"Creighton," in *The Oxford Book of Essays,* edited by John Gross, Oxford University Press: Oxford, 1991, pp. 386-391.
Stroud, Scott R. et al.	"Memory, Reconstruction, and Ethics in Memorialization," *The Journal of Speculative Philosophy,* Vol. 33, No. 2 (2019), pp. 282-299.
Styron, William	"Almost a Rhodes Scholar: A Personal Reminiscence," *South Atlantic Bulletin,* Vol. 45, No. 2 (May 1980).
Walker, Eric A.	"The Jameson Raid," *The Cambridge Historical Journal,* Vol. 6, No. 3 (1940), pp. 283-306.
Warnes, Christopher	"The Making and Unmaking of History in Ivan Vladislavic's 'Propaganda by Monuments and Other Stories'," *Modern Fiction Studies,* Vol. 46, No. 1, South African Fiction After Apartheid Special Issue (Spring 2000), pp. 67-69.

Wright, Howell   "Address at Rhodes Memorial,
                              Cape Town on the occasion of
                              the 44th anniversary of Rhodes's
                              death," *South Africa* (London),
                              July 6, 1946.

About the Author

A former director of the World Bank, Robert Calderisi was a 1968 Quebec Rhodes Scholar. He studied history in Montreal, economics at Oxford, and African history at the University of Sussex. During his career in international development, he lived and worked in Africa for more than thirty years. He is the author of two critically acclaimed books: *The Trouble with Africa: Why Foreign Aid Isn't Working* (2006), which *The Economist* selected as one of the best books of the year, and *Earthly Mission: The Catholic Church and World Development* (2013). Reviewers have praised his gift for storytelling, his lively and unpretentious style, his combination of humanity and humour, and his challenging of received ideas.

Endnotes

Introduction

[1] https://www.thepatriot.co.zw/old_posts/godfrey-huggins-partnership-of-horse-and-rider-zimbabweans-must-be-vigilant/

[2] Hensman, p. x.

[3] Nyamnjoh, p. 38.

[4] https://www.asc.ox.ac.uk/sites/stage.allsouls.ox.ac.uk/files/Sermons/Sermon20161106-EdwardMortimer.pdf)

[5] Millin, p. 1.

[6] Quoted in Roberts, p. 298.

[7] Quoted in Millin, on back cover

[8] Walker, George, 'So Much to Do': Oxford and the Wills of Cecil Rhodes. Journal of Imperial & Commonwealth History, August 2016, Vol. 44, Issue 4.

Chapter One: "Rhodes Must Fall"

[1] Nyamnjoh, pp. 127-128, 143-149.

[2] Interview with Sandra Klopper in Cape Town, January 30th 2020.

[3] Nyamnjoh, pp. 38-39.

[4] Nyamnjoh, pp. 166-167.

[5] Xolela Mangcu, Back cover of Rhodes Must Fall (Zed, 2018).

[6] Rhodes Must Fall Oxford Founding Statement, May 28, 2015, in Rhodes Must Fall, pp. 4-5.

[7] Rhodes Must Fall, p. xix.

[8] Kealebogo Ramuru, "Black Feminist Reflections on the Rhodes Must Fall Movement at UCT", in Rhodes Must Fall, pp. 147-157.

[9] Brian Kobwa, "Decolonizing Whiteness," in Rhodes Must Fall, pp. 134-135.

[10] Tadiwa Madenga, "Skin Deep," in Rhodes Must Fall, pp. 31-32.

[11] Laura N.K. Van Broekhoven, "Calibrating relevance at the Pitt Rivers Museum," in Jill Pellew and Lawrence Goldman, eds., Dethroning historical reputations, pp. 65-79.

[12] https://www.oriel.ox.ac.uk/sites/default/files/statement_from_oriel_college_on_28th_january_2016_regarding_the_college.pdf

[13] Biggar, Nigel, "The Rhodes Affair", New Criterion, Jan 2017, Vol. 35 Issue 5, pp 45-48.

[14] Anthony Lemon, "Rhodes Must Fall: The Dangers of Re-Writing History", Round Table, April 2016, Vol. 105 Issue 2, pp. 217-219.

[15] Lowry, Donal, Round Table, June 2016, Vol. 105 Issue 3, pp. 329-333.

[16] https://www.breitbart.com/politics/2015/12/24/mud-huts-v-western-civilization-rhodesmustfall-must-fail/

[17] Brian Young, "'A dreary record of wickedness': moral judgement in history", in Pellew, pp. 117-123.

[18] https://www.timeshighereducation.com/news/lord-patten-speaks-out-rhodes-debate

[19] https://www.bbc.com/news/uk-england-london-52977088.

[20] https://www.bbc.com/news/uk-england-dorset-53004638.

[21] Flyer distributed by the "Rhodes Must Fall Oxford" campaign on June 9th 2020.

[22] https://www.bbc.com/news/world-europe-53017188.

[23] https://www.bbc.com/news/world-europe-53163714.

[24] https://www.washingtonpost.com/local/virginia-politics/richmond-lee-statue-removal/2020/06/18/492203ac-b106-11ea-856d-5054296735e5_story.html

[25] https://www.bbc.com/news/world-us-canada-53207649.

[26] https://www.oriel.ox.ac.uk/about-college/news-events/news/decisions-made-college-following-completion-independent-commission.

Chapter Two: A Vivacious Man

[1] Maguire, p. 272-273.

[2] Ibid., pp. 274-275.

[3] Millin, pp. 142-143.

[4] Maurois, pp. 99-100.

[5] Fuller, p. 254.

[6] Thompson, p. 93.

[7] Jourdan, p. 218.

[8] Michell, Vol. II, pp. 4-5.

[9] Lockhart, p. 87

[10] Williams, p. 293.

[11] Le Sueur, p. 15.

[12] Stent, pp. xiii-xiv.

[13] Ibid., pp. xiv-xv.

[14] Quoted in Jourdan, p. 285.

[15] Michell, Vol. II, p. 4.

[16] Baker, p. 81.

[17] Ibid., p. 80.

[18] Letter of January 11, 1939 in Rhodes Papers MSS Afr t.5 ffs. 188-190.

[19] Fuller, pp. 110-114.

[20] Jourdan, pp. 183-184.

[21] Michell, Vol. II, p. 14.

[22] Jourdan, pp. 186-187.

[23] Lockhart, p. 43.

[24] Michell, Vol. II, p. 6.

[25] Williams, p. 122.

[26] Thompson, pp. 67-68.

[27] Fuller, p. 224.

[28] Maguire, pp. 274-275.

[29] Jourdan, p. 164.

[30] Roberts, Cecil Rhodes and The Princess, pp. 53-54.

[31] Williams, p. 103

[32] Rhodes Papers MSS Afr s.1647, Box 1, Items 2-5.

[33] Plomer, p. 36.

[34] Tamarkin, p. 214.

[35] Letter of August 27, 1896, conveyed to the author by Pelly's granddaughter, Professor Ann Scott, of Tasmania, in an email dated February 19, 2020.

[36] Williams, p. 293.

[37] Rhodes Papers, Hildersham Hall Papers, Vol. I, f 79.

[38] Jourdan, pp. 97-98.

[39] Rhodes Papers, Hildersham Hall Papers, Vol. I, f 79.

[40] Michell, Vol. II, p. 2.

[41] Rhodes Papers MSS Afr t.5 f 272a

[42] Williams, p. 319.

[43] Fuller, p. 145.

[44] Ibid., p. 131.

[45] Ibid., p. 80.

[46] Cloete, p. 205.

[47] Ibid., p. 202.

[48] Jourdan, pp. 40-41.

Chapter Three: Stalked by Death

[1] Cloete, p. 206.

[2] Ibid.,, p. 202.

[3] Roberts, Cecil Rhodes and the Princess, pp. 169-170.

[4] Hensman, p. 322.

[5] Hutchison, pp. 11-12.

[6] Letter dated August 19th and September 3rd, 1891 in Stead, p. 68.

[7] Michell, Vol. II, pp. 104-105.

[8] Ibid., Vol. II, p. 13.

[9] Ibid., Vol. II, p. 13.

[10] Ibid., Vol. II, pp. 120-121.

[11] Lockhart, p. 90

[12] O.N. Ransford, Introduction to Cecil Rhodes: The Man and His Dream, Books of Rhodesia, Bulawayo, 1977 (unpaginated).

[13] Stent, p. ix.

[14] Roberts, Cecil Rhodes and the Princess, pp. 169-170.

[15] Le Sueur, p. 19.

[16] Rhodes Papers MSS Afr t.5 f 194.

[17] Maguire, pp. 401-402.

[18] Jourdan, pp. 171-172.

[19] Kipling, p. 73.

[20] Fuller, pp. 103-104.

[21] Roberts, Cecil Rhodes and the Princess, pp. 148-149.

[22] Jourdan, p. 25.

[23] Ibid., pp. 221-222.

[24] Menpes, pp. 103, 104, 109, 110.

[25] Meredith, p. 311.

[26] Williams, p. 9.

[27] Rotberg, p. 92.

[28] Quoted in Flint, p. 218.

[29] Jules Renard (1864-1910) in Chiflet, Jean-Louis, ed., L'Art d'exprimer ses sentiments (avec les mots de nos plus grands auteurs), Le Figaro littéraire : Paris, 2019, p. 20.

[30] Jourdan, pp. 164-165.

[31] Williams, p. 229.

[32] Jourdan, p. 162.

[33] Maguire, p. 275.

[34] Millin, pp. 138-139.

[35] Quoted in Cloete, p. 201.

[36] Email to the author from Robert Fry, July 3rd 2020.

[37] O.N. Ransford, Introduction to Cecil Rhodes: The Man and His Dream, Books of Rhodesia, Bulawayo, 1977 (unpaginated).

[38] Gibbs, p. 135.

[39] Michell, Vol. II, pp. 10, 13.

[40] Jourdan, pp. 7-8.

[41] Ibid., pp. 20, 25.

[42] Lockhart and Woodhouse, 1963, pp. 12-13.

[43] Roberts, Cecil Rhodes and The Princess, pp. 53-54.

[44] Plomer, pp. 39-40.

[45] Williams, p. 103.

[46] Lockhart, p. 88

[47] Plomer, p. 42.

[48] Flint, p. 80.

[49] Colville, The Life of Jameson, p. 38.

[50] Roberts, Cecil Rhodes and the Princess, pp. 100-101, 114.

[51] Le Sueur, p. 201.

[52] Jourdan, pp. 170-171.

[53] Plomer, pp. 46-48.

[54] https://www.kimberley.org.za/today-kimberleys-history-5-june/

[55] Jourdan, p. 243.

[56] Baker, p. 169.

[57] Stead, pp. 86-87.

[58] Colvin, pp. 89-90.

[59] Quoted in footnote of Stead, p. 86.

[60] Stead, p. 91.

[61] Ibid., p. 93 (footnote).

[62] Baker, p. 4.

[63] Marcus Aurelius, Meditations, translated by Martin Hammond, Penguin, 2014, Chapter VII, paragraph 69.

[64] Maurois, p. 140; Quoted in Strachey, p. 390.

Chapter Four: Achievement

[1] Lockhart, p. 14

[2] Caption at Rhodes Museum, Bishop's Stortford, June 2019 and Rhodesiana, Publication No. 12, Rhodesiana Society, Salisbury, Rhodesia, p.12.

[3] Nicholson, pp. 437-438.

[4] Michell, Vol. I, p. 69.

[5] Jourdan, pp. 149-150.

[6] Williams, p. 94.

[7] Thompson, p. 89.

[8] Plomer, p. 88.

[9] Chapman, p. 648.

[10] Ibid., p. 655.

[11] Ibid., p. 657.

[12] Williams, p. 71.

[13] Williams, p. 119.

[14] Ibid., p. 134.

[15] Ibid., p. 126.

[16] Baxter, p. 72.

[17] Thompson, p. 148.

[18] Ibid., p. 156.

[19] Baxter, p. 78.

[20] Ibid., p. 90.

[21] Rhodes Papers, MSS.Afr.s.8, ff3-5.

Chapter Five: Five Crucial Years

[1] H.F. Hoste, "Rhodesia in 1890", in Rhodesiana, Publication No.12, The Rhodesiana Society, Salisbury, September 1965, pp. 12-38.

[2] Ibid., pp. 4, 5, 7.

[3] Samkange, p. 11.

[4] Baxter, p. 120.

[5] Lockhart, pp. 59-60

[6] Michell, Vol. II, p. 81.

[7] Ibid., p. 86.

[8] Flint, pp. 150-154.

[9] Rotberg, p. 326.

[10] Ibid., p. 327.

[11] Flint, p. 137.

[12] Ibid., pp. 136-145.

[13] Rotberg, p. 333.

[14] Lockhart, p. 67.

[15] Williams, pp. 194-195.

[16] Tamarkin, p. 85.

[17] Ibid., p. 214.

[18] Ibid., p. 99.

[19] Fuller, p. 166.

[20] Parry, p. 384.

[21] Tamarkin, pp. 97-98.

[22] Quoted in Ibid., p. 1.

[23] Rotberg, p. 218.

[24] Tamarkin, pp. 204-205, 211-212.

[25] Parry, p. 382.

[26] Ibid., p. 383.

[27] Ibid., p. 385.

[28] Fuller, p. 176.

[29] Ibid., p. 175.

[30] Ibid., p. 177.

[31] Ibid., p. 178.

[32] Lockhart, p. 70.

[33] Fuller, p. 178.

[34] Williams, p. 214.

[35] Fuller, p. 177.

[36] Parry, p. 387.

[37] Bouch, p. 1.

[38] Parry, p. 388.

[39] Howell Wright, Address at Rhodes Memorial, March 24, 1946, p. 4.

[40] Baxter, pp. 117-118.

[41] Williams, p. 181.

[42] Rotberg, p. 338.

43 Roberts, p. 47.

44 Lockhouse and Woodhouse, p. 5.

45 Hope, p. 73.

Chapter Six: Disgrace

1 See Charles van Onselen, The Cowboy Capitalist: John Hays Hammond, the American West, and the Jameson Raid, Jonathan Ball, 2017.

2 Wilson, pp. 309-310.

3 Chapman, p. 660.

4 Quoted in Lockhart, p. 80.

5 Quoted in Hope, p. 16.

6 Plomer, p. 9.

7 Fuller, p. 187.

8 Rotberg, p. 531.

9 Maguire, p. 272-273.

10 Williams, p. 98

11 Rhodes Papers MSS Afr s.1647, Box 1, Items 2-5.

12 Radziwill, p. 46.

13 Fuller, p. 195.

14 Ibid., p. 192.

15 Rotberg, p. 518.

16 Ibid., pp. 523-524.

17 Ibid., pp. 535.

18 Flint, pp. 177-193.

19 Rotberg, pp. 543-545.

20 Fuller, p. 199.

21 Stent, p. viii.

22 Michell, Vol. II, p. 146-147.

[23] Le Sueur, p. 131.

[24] Rhodes Papers, Hildersham Hall Papers, Vol. I, f 79.

[25] Meredith, p. 337.

[26] Letter to the The Times by Sir William Gowers, July 30, 1896, quoted in Scott, p. 203.

[27] Fuller, p. 195.

[28] Parkin, p. 54.

[29] Michell, Vol. II, pp. 192-193.

[30] Fuller, p. 205.

[31] Ibid., pp. 211-212.

[32] Stead, pp. 106-107.

[33] Lockhart, p. 119

[34] Michell, Vol. II, p. 139.

[35] Williams, pp. 246-248.

[36] Fuller, p, 201.

[37] Rhodes Papers, Hildersham Hall Papers, Vol. I, ff 60-65.

Chapter Seven: War and Peace

[1] Rotberg, pp. 552-553, 568.

[2] Hensman, pp. 274-275.

[3] Stent, pp. 38-55.

[4] Rotberg, p. 569.

[5] Ibid., pp. 570, 573.

[6] Ibid., p. 577.

[7] Michell, Vol. II, p. 218.

[8] http://zimfieldguide.com/matabeleland-south/worlds-view-matobo.

[9] Flint, pp. 214-215.

[10] Michell, Vol. II, p. 261-262.

[11] Rhodes Papers MSS Afr s 8 f40

[12] Maylam, p. 71; Nicholson, p. 438.

[13] Williams, p. 313.

[14] Rhodes Papers MSS Afr s 8 f44

[15] Fuller, p. 217.

[16] Quoted in Hensman, p. 329.

[17] Hensman, p. 323.

[18] Michell, Vol. II, p. 264.

[19] Jourdan, pp. 94-95, 138.

[20] A British Officer, p. 352.

[21] Rotberg, p. 661.

[22] Jourdan, pp. 96-97.

[23] Chapman, p. 656.

[24] Jourdan, p. 256.

[25] Rotberg, p. 670.

[26] Jourdan, pp. 258-259.

[27] Ibid., p. 271.

[28] Quoted in Maylam, p. 87.

[29] Maylam, p. 100.

Chapter Eight: Judgement

[1] Cloete, p. 203.

[2] Nyamnjoh, p. 46.

[3] https://www.victoriafalls-guide.net/exhume-cecil-rhodess-bones.html

[4] https://mg.co.za/article/2015-03-24-statue-struggle-rekindles-bid-to-exhume-rhodes/

[5] Howell Wright, Address at Rhodes Memorial, March 24, 1946, p. 3.

[6] Williams, p. 5.

[7] Michell, Vol. I, (check exact page in Preface).

[8] Millin, p. 92.

[9] Plomer, p. 27.

[10] Rhodes Papers MSS Afr t.5 f 241.

[11] Ibid.

[12] Fuller, pp. 110-114.

[13] Williams, p. 98

[14] Fuller, p. 37.

[15] Flint, pp. xix-xx.

[16] Ibid., pp. xiv-xvii.

[17] Maylam, p. 10.

[18] Ibid., pp. 10-11.

[19] Cloete, p. 333.

[20] Plomer, pp. 44-45.

[21] Ibid., p. 336.

[22] Ibid., p. 192.

[23] Ibid., p. 274.

[24] Cloete, p. 286.

[25] Quoted in Maylam, p. 112.

[26] Maylam, p. 11.

[27] O.N. Ransford, Introduction to a 1977 reprinted version of W.T. Stead's The Last Will and Testament of Cecil John Rhodes, unpaginated.

[28] Maguire, p. 327.

[29] Jeffrey Butler, "Review of Cecil Rhodes by John Flint et al." The International Journal of African Historical Studies, Vol. 10. No. 2 (1977), pp. 274-275.

[30] Hope, p. 74.

[31] Mark Twain, Follow the Equator.

[32] Philippon, p. 8.

[33] Quoted in Davidson, pp. 304-305.

[34] Chesterton, p. 239.

[35] Cloete, p. 206.

[36] Maylam, last page.

[37] Radziwill, p. 230.

[38] Cloete, p. 325.

[39] Fuller, p. 63.

Chapter Nine: Imperialist

[1] Marlowe, pp. xii-xiii.

[2] Wilson, p. 246.

[3] Symonds, pp. 24, 27.

[4] Ibid., p. 33.

[5] Verschoyle, p. 623.

[6] Wilson, pp. 289-291.

[7] Plomer, At Home, p. 97.

[8] Ibid., p. 174.

[9] Jourdan, p. 284.

[10] Lockhart, pp. 61-62.

[11] Lockhart and Woodhouse, p.8.

[12] Mencken, p. 209.

[13] Quoted in Baxter, p. 124.

[14] Howell Wright, Address at Rhodes Memorial, March 24, 1946, p. 2.

[15] Williams, p. 41.

[16] Stead, p. 101.

[17] Stead, p. 97.

[18] Alexander, p. 100.

[19] Ibid., p. 103.

[20] Plomer, At Home, pp. 245-246.

[21] Philippon, p. 8.

[22] Rhodes Papers MSS Afr s.1647, Box 1, Item 6.

[23] Author's visit, January 22, 2020.

[24] Calderisi, p. 144.

[25] Plomer, pp. 81-82.

[26] Ibid.

[27] Maguire, p. 79.

[28] Clarke, p. 324.

[29] Millin, p. 206.

Chapter Ten: White Supremacist?

[1] Rhodes Papers MSS Afr s.1647, Box 1, Item 1, ff 1-103.

[2] Ibid.

[3] Ibid.

[4] Thomas, pp. 63, 80.

[5] Lockhart, p. 69

[6] Hensman, p. 226.

[7] Gibbs, pp. 14-15.

[8] Davidson, p. 234, citing Verschoyle, pp. 296-297.

[9] Stent, p. 26.

[10] Baker, pp. 92-93.

[11] Ibid., p. 66.

[12] Williams, p. 179.

[13] Michell, Vol. II, pp. 209-211.

[14] Maguire, pp. 402-405.

[15] Ibid., pp. 69-72.

[16] Ibid., pp. 402-405.

[17] https://www.whiteswritingwhiteness.ed.ac.uk/traces/thenword/

[18] Flint, pp. 204-205.

[19] Thomas, pp. 314-315.

[20] Madeline Briggs, "Misinformation in the Rhodes Campaign," The Poor Print (Oriel College Student Newspaper), January 22, 2016.

[21] Hensman, p. 226.

[22] Verschoyle, pp. 376-388.

[23] Ibid., pp. 152-153.

[24] Eddo-Lodge, pp. 10-11, 13-14, 22.

[25] Graham, p. 205.

Chapter Eleven: War and Apartheid

[1] Physicians for Social Responsibility, Body Count: Casualty Figures After Ten Years of the War on Terror, March 2015, p. 15. See https://www.psr.org/wp-content/uploads/2018/05/body-count.pdf).

[2] Maguire, pp. 313-314.

[3] Ibid., pp. 213-215.

[4] https://nationalpost.com/news/canada/here-is-what-sir-john-a-macdonald-did-to-indigenous-people.

[5] Thomas, p. 305.

[6] Dubow, pp. 156-157.

[7] Symonds, p. 42.

[8] Wilson, pp. 325-328.

[9] Stead, pp. 109-111.

[10] Hope, p. 123.

[11] Ibid., pp. 15-16.

[12] Tamarkin, p. 216.

[13] Ziegler, p. 42.

[14] https://www.chronicle.co.zw/de-klerk-attacks-plan-to-remove-rhodes-statue-from-oxford-college/

[15] Fuller, p. 219.

[16] Lundestad, p. 19.

[17] Maylam, p. 23.

[18] Wilson, pp. 357-358.

[19] Ibid., p. 358.

[20] Hope, pp. 71-72.

[21] Roberts, pp. 298-299.

[22] Ziegler, p. 10.

[23] Email to the author from Professor Rotberg, September 14th 2020.

[24] Ziegler, pp. 324-325.

Chapter Twelve: The Rhodes Scholarships

[1] Rhodes Papers, Hildersham Hall Papers, Vol. I, ff 60-65.

[2] Fuller, p. 35.

[3] Rotberg, p. 670.

[4] Ziegler, p. 82.

[5] Parkin, p. 85.

[6] Stead, p. 63.

[7] Ibid., pp. 113-114.

[8] Baker, pp. 153-154.

[9] Ibid., p. 134.

[10] Millin, p. 127.

[11] Baker, p. 71.

[12] Allen, p. 3.

[13] Jourdan, pp. 75-77.

[14] Quoted in Symonds, pp. 2-3.

[15] Symonds, p. 303.

[16] Allen, p. 4.

[17] Williams, p. 40-41.

[18] Ibid., p. 42.

[19] Lockhart and Woodhouse, p. 53.

[20] Fuller, p. 8.

[21] Ibid., p. 7.

[22] Williams, p. 43.

[23] Rotberg, pp. 677-678.

[24] Letter to Earl Grey from Rannoch Lodge, Scotland, August 25th 1901 in the Rhodes Papers MSS Afr t.5 f 506c.

[25] Aydelotte, pp. 24, 47.

[26] Parkin, pp. 100-101.

[27] Allen, p. 8.

[28] Aydelotte, p. 23.

[29] Flint, p. 239.

[30] Plomer, Cecil Rhodes, pp. 168-170.

[31] Styron, pp. 1, 3, 4-5.

[32] Ziegler, p. 58.

[33] Ibid., pp. 170-171.

[34] Flint, p. 217.

[35] Ziegler, p. 64.

[36] Francis Wylie, in Eldon, footnote on page 99.

[37] Ibid., p. 66.

[38] Ibid., p. 79.

Chapter Thirteen: Legacy in Practice

[1] Ziegler, pp. 64-66.

[2] Francis Wylie in Eldon, p. 99.

[3] Stewart, pp. 100-104, 121-126, 173-174.

[4] Ziegler, pp. 64-66.

[5] Schaeper, "The Black Trailblazers . . . ", p. 114.

[6] JBHE Foundation, p. 53.

[7] Schaeper, "The Black Trailblazers . . . ", p. 114.

[8] Ziegler, p. 138.

[9] Allen, p. 15.

[10] Data provided by Rhodes House, July 2020.

[11] Aydelotte, p. 100.

[12] Ibid.

[13] Symonds, p. 294.

[14] Parkin, pp. 102-103.

[15] Allen, p. 19.

[16] Ibid., pp. 19-20.

[17] Parkin, p. 224.

[18] Symonds, p. 297.

[19] Schaeper, Cowboys into Gentlemen, p. 46.

[20] Kenny, p. 87; Schaeper, p. 85.

[21] Elton, p. 70.

[22] Ibid., pp. 78-86.

[23] Kenny, p. 37.

[24] Lord Elton, p. vi.

[25] Parkin, p. 207.

[26] https://us.fulbrightonline.org/about/history

[27] Schaeper, p. 88; Eldon, p. 212.

[28] https://www.marshallscholarship.org;https://en.wikipedia.org/wiki/Marshall_Scholarship

[29] https://www.commonwealthfund.org/fellowships/harkness-fellowships-health-care-policy-and-practice

[30] https://www.thegatesscholarship.org/scholarship;   https://www.gatescambridge.org

[31] https://www.schwarzmanscholars.org/about/

[32] https://schmidtsciencefellows.org/overview/

[33] https://www.atlanticfellows.org/about

[34] https://www.rhodeshouse.ox.ac.uk/about/125th-anniversary-strategic-plan/

[35] Allen, p. 18.

[36] Rhodes House July 2020 ENewsletter, July 10th 2020.

[37] https://www.ft.com/content/336d57a8-fb234ec8333bb8e6bc36c98?shareType=nongift

[38] Ibid., p. 165.

[39] Schaeper, p. 295.

[40] Coon, et al., p. 177.

[41] Rhodes Scholar Magazine, #5, 2018, pp. 56-59.

Chapter Fourteen: Controversial Statues

[1] Hope, p. 105.

[2] Ibid., pp. 213-214.

[3] Ibid., pp. 260-263, 240-241.

[4] Atwell, Appendix One, p. 8.

[5] Atwell, p. 27.

[6] https://globalnews.ca/news/5379348/ecole-bilingue-cecil-rhodes/

[7] Rhodes Must Fall, pp. 103-135.

[8] Conn, p. 3.

[9] Ibid., p. 8.

[10] https://www.sundaynews.co.zw/put-rhodes-statue-in-public-for-all-to-see/

[11] https://www.thepatriot.co.zw/old_posts/of-colonial-statues-and-monuments/

[12] Hope, p. 300.

[13] Thandeka Khosa, "And after the statues fall?", The Sowetan, [April?] 2015.

[14] https://en.wikipedia.org/wiki/Godfrey_Huggins.

[15] Lawrence Goldman, "We have been here before: 'Rhodes Must Fall' in historical context", in Pellew, pp. 125-139.

[16] Anna Eavis and Howard Spencer, "Risk and Reputation; The London blue plaques scheme", in Pellew, pp. 107-115.

[17] "Addressing the Statue", Historical display and video at the American Museum of Natural History, New York City, September 2019.

[18] https://www.nytimes.com/2020/06/24/arts/design/theodore-roosevelt-statue.html

[19] "From objects of enlightenment to objects of apology: why you can't make amends for the past by plundering the present," in Pellew, pp. 81-91.

[20] Van Tunzelmann, Alex, History Today, March 2016, Vol. 66 Issue 3, pp 6-7.

[21] Hope, pp. 173-174.

[22] https://www.bbc.com/news/world-asia-india-34265882

[23] http://www.bbc.com/travel/story/20190325-the-birthplace-of-gandhis-peaceful-protest

[24] https://www.bbc.com/news/world-us-canada-48856994

[25] https://www.historians.org/news-and-advocacy/aha-advocacy/aha-statement-on-confederate-monuments

[26] Email to the author from Charles T. Joyce, specialist in the history of the Civil War and of Gettysburg in particular, February 16, 2020.

[27] Southern Poverty Law Center data, reported by Axios, April 25, 2021.

[28] Gorra, Michael, "A Heritage of Evil", in The New York Review of Books, November 7, 2019, pp. 11-13.

[29] https://www.washingtonpost.com/history/2020/02/10/charlottesville-slave-plaque-stolen/

[30] Edward Mortimer, "The Problem with Monuments: A View from Oxford", p. 214.

[31] https://www.ashmolean.org/article/a-nice-cup-of-tea.

[32] https://www.nytimes.com/2019/12/05/us/tufts-sackler-name-opioids.

[33] https://www.nytimes.com/2019/10/02/arts/design/whitney-art-museums-trustees.html.

Chapter Fifteen: What to Do with Them?

[1] Pellew, p. 12.

[2] Email from Edwin Cameron to the author, September 19th 2020.

[3] Ibid.

[4] New York Times, July 3rd 2020.

[5] https://www.nytimes.com/2020/06/24/arts/design/theodore-roosevelt-statue.html

[6] Rieff, pp. 122-123.

[7] https://www.nytimes.com/2019/03/29/opinion/women-statues.html

[8] Edward Mortimer, "The Problem with Monuments: A View from Oxford",

[9] https://www.nytimes.com/2019/10/25/arts/new-york-city-monuments.html

[10] Author's visit, January 30, 2020.

[11] https://www.nytimes.com/2019/07/26/arts/design/george-washington-san-francisco-murals.html

[12] Atwell, pp. 29-30.

[13] https://www.westerncape.gov.za/assets/departments/cultural-affairs-sport/resolutions_20_april_2015_national_department_of_arts_and_culture.pdf

[14] Atwell, p. 24.

Conclusions

[1] Williams, p. 6.

[2] Rotberg, pp. viii-ix.

[3] Plomer, p. 11.

[4] Hope, p. 177.

[5] Stead, pp. 113-114.

[6] Aydelotte, p. 122.

[7] Parkin, pp. 235-236.

[8] Roberts, pp. 298-299.

Manufactured by Amazon.ca
Bolton, ON